ROOKIE IN THE RAF

For my very dear friend Jim

Happy reading – and
Happy Christmas 2014.
Very best wishes.
Ken Stallard

by

Ken Stallard

Grosvenor House
Publishing Limited

The right of Ken Stallard to be identified as the author of this
work has been asserted by him in accordance with Section 78
of the Copyright, Designs and Patents Act 1988

The book cover picture is copyright to Ken Stallard

This book is published by
Grosvenor House Publishing Ltd
28-30 High Street, Guildford, Surrey, GU1 3EL.
www.grosvenorhousepublishing.co.uk

A CIP record for this book
is available from the British Library

ISBN 978-1-78148-664-1

*Dedicated to my lovely family and
all who have served and serve whoever
and wherever they may be.*

Also by this author

ROAD TO NOWHERE
GIVE US THIS DAY

CHAPTER 1

My aunt, a middle aged woman of ample proportions, stopped stacking wet cups on the draining board and looked at me in sheer disbelief.

"You have done what?" she asked.

"I have just been to the Recruitment Office and signed on for a three year engagement in the RAF" I replied.

"Well I don't know what your Mum and Dad are going to say", she went on, "it's bad enough being called up for National Service without volunteering but...." Her words just trailed away.

Similarly my Mum and Dad were speechless for some time. They had not known that I had gone to the Recruitment Office at Oxford, and, the fact that I had actually volunteered to go into the RAF came as a bit of a shock.

"He'll be sorry", my father muttered as he buried his head in a newspaper whilst Mum chided "What did you want to go and do a daft thing like that for?"

Too late, the die had been cast and I began to stammer out my explanations and hopes and aspirations.

The officer at the Recruitment Centre had made it all sound so simple and good.

First he reminded me that I would be called up for two years National Service anyway. Alternatively, if

I went for a minimum three year engagement I would have a wider choice of which branch of the Services I wanted to go in. Furthermore, I would get so much extra annual leave that all in all I would only be working approximately nine months in the last year. Now in retrospect, I realise it didn't quite work out like that.

I duly signed the document to apply for a written test for the Royal Air Force and was then whisked off for a top to toe medical examination.

A Sergeant escort very briskly walked me down a maze of corridors in the Government building complex. We rounded a corner and the sight which met my eyes caused me to stop in my tracks.

About half a dozen teenage lads like myself stood there in the draughty corridor, shivering, awkward and completely starkers. All waiting to be called in to the Medical Officer one by one.

"Take your clothes off and get on the end of the queue" said the sergeant none too kindly. "You can use that peg over there."

Sheepishly I took off my shoes and lingered over pulling off my socks. I never had undressed completely in front of anyone in all my young life and I felt that every eye was upon me.

The little line of men shuffled nervously but was completely silent. A couple had turned and were looking at the wall whilst most of the others just stood there shielding their privates with their hands. Moments later I joined the queue taking the same stance. I vaguely remember wanting to use my handkerchief but lacked the courage to walk naked to the peg. I just stood and sniffed and covered my modesty in a silence which could almost be felt.

After what seemed like an eternity, I was ushered into the presence of two elderly gentlemen who were most diligent in their examinations. Nothing was missed out on the inspection although I did seem to have a bit of trouble with the colour blind test. I never knew I had any trouble in that area, but, I seemed to get all muddled as far as knowing where different coloured patterns started and ended in the book. Eventually I was declared to be "A 1" which was the military term for being "fit to serve."

I was given six weeks to wind up my apprenticeship at a large grocers shop in Wantage, take a short holiday at Margate with my buxom aunt and her husband, and prepare for pastures new and the vigour of Service life.

CHAPTER 2

Although I had only just scraped through the written aptitude test for the RAF, it was enough to be called up as a serving airman.

Six weeks later it was with mixed emotions that Mum and I waited for the bus for Oxford. We lived in a small village about twelve miles to the west of the city. It was the furthest place I had travelled except for a couple of holidays with my aunt and, a single day trip to Head Office in London when I finished my apprenticeship with the grocery firm.

Mum had said she wanted to do some shopping in Oxford but I knew that she wanted to see me on my way. I wished she had stopped at home because I could see she was upset with the prospect of me leaving home for the next three years.

An old lady who knew us ambled by the bus stop and called to my mother. "Is he just going off then?" "Yes" I replied for her.

"It's not all a bed of roses" she retorted and went on her way shaking her head. Mum went very quiet and hardly spoke on the journey to Oxford. She gave two pieces of advice. "Make sure you get enough to eat" and "don't forget to write regularly" before she waved goodbye to me at the bottom of the High Street.

I returned to the Government buildings where it all began and found a coach already waiting to take a group of us to Oxford Railway Station bound for Bletchley in Buckinghamshire.

I sat next to a lad called Robin who looked the most unhappiest on the coach.

He soon made it clear to me that he was not going to like the new recruitment camp at RAF Cardington one little bit.

I told Robin that life was what you made it but I think I was trying to convince myself more than him.

After about twenty minutes on the train Robin began to sniff and look very agitated. Poking a finger at the grimy window pane he muttered, "I live just over there." He turned his head right around to watch his homestead disappear over the horizon. I decided I would try and take my mind off our circumstances by trying to cheer him up. I failed.

A Corporal and a three ton lorry were waiting to pick us up at Bletchley Station for the drive to RAF Cardington.

My first attempt at putting my foot in the little socket in the tail board and swinging my other leg over the top of the board ended in disaster. I swung too high and hit my forehead on the metal bar which held the canopy in place. It made me see stars.

My first recollection of Cardington and Service life was greeting it with a blinding headache and a big black bruise over my right eye.

We were herded like cattle into a large hall and ordered to sit at desks which were already covered with forms. One by one we filled them in as instructed by an officer and supervised by a large sergeant with an even larger voice.

"Right you lot, line up outside" he bellowed at the end of the form filling session. "I will take you over to the block and then we'll kit you out with the essentials."

The "block" turned out to be a row of huts and Robin and I were allocated to the second one along with another ten lads.

Inside it was bright and clean. Six beds were spaced out on either side of the room. A small locker and a tall wooden cupboard each side of the bed completed the area which henceforth would be known as the "bed space." Very original I thought. We all chose a bed and dumped our cases, carrier bags and whatever else we had brought our belongings in on the squeaky springs.

"Right you lot, line up outside." The Sergeant had reappeared from the adjacent huts and delivered his favourite line. Now he was trying to get us into some sort of marching order. "Left, right. Left, right. Left ... "he called whilst "us lot" shuffled and skipped in trying to keep up with him. Thus we approached the Equipment Store.

The store was large and the neat shelves were laden with just about every item of clothing and accoutrement that you could imagine. One storeman checked the items off a list whilst the other thumped the corresponding things into your arms.

"Blankets three, sheets two, pillows one, pillowcases one, bedcover one" he monotoned as the heap began to grow in my arms. And then I began to sneeze. It wasn't just an ordinary sneeze but a succession of sneezes which not only caused my eyes to stream, but, made the pile of bedding wobble in my arms.

"Stop sneezing" snapped the sergeant but his words were in vain so he poked me in the small of my back instead.

"I can't help it, Serge" I gasped and sneezed all the more. "It's the smell of camphor in these blankets."

"Serge?" he yelled. "Serge? Who do you think you are calling Serge? I would have you to know, laddie, that I am Sergeant and not Serge. Is that understood?" I could only nod as I sneezed again.

"What's camphor?" asked a dreamy looking kid standing beside me. Quick as a flash the Sergeant had an answer.

"Camphor" he said loud and low, "is a repellent for insects. We keep it in store for the likes of you! Now shut up and get into line!"

The storeman returned to his list at the counter.

"Knife one, fork one, spoon one" he went on as his colleague duly thumped these items on top of the bedding. His "Mug one" completed the lot.

As I turned to move away I sneezed again. The motion caused the china mug, which had been sitting precariously upside down on top of the bedding, to wobble and then crash to the floor. Almost before it hit the deck and shattered in a thousand pieces the storeman with the pencil said "One and thruppence" indicating that since I had just broken the mug, I would have to pay one shilling and three pence to replace it. I was required to sign to this effect.

The sergeant put the replacement mug on top of the blankets. With an exaggerated sickly smile he then thrust my arms into a position to steady the pile of kit that I was holding. I held my breath almost all the way back to the hut for fear of dropping the mug again.

The Sergeant was having a long day. It was after six in the evening and he still paced up and down outside the huts, waiting to take us over to the cookhouse for our belated evening meal.

The smell of the mess hall put me off as we approached. Pig swill just about summed it up but pangs of hunger spurred us on.

We all stood in an orderly queue clutching our mugs and irons. The first RAF slang I learnt was that you never referred to your knife, fork or spoon as such but lumped the lot together as your irons. We watched the chefs serving the lads in front of us sausages and chips. It looked good.

The meal tasted as good as it looked and for the first time that day we began to relax, introduce ourselves and joke about this new way of life. We were no longer under scrutiny and we could do as we wished as long as we stayed on Camp for the rest of the day and were in bed by ten thirty.

When the meal was over we all got up together and placed our plates on the rack for washing. Outside the hall stood a large metal trough just like the cattle troughs we have in the fields back home. The difference was that this trough was full of boiling water and a haze of steam shimmered above it.

I soon discovered that it was necessary to hold the irons by the tips of the handles and swish them in the boiling water for washing. I had to admit that little bits of vegetable floating on the top of the water was very off putting but decided that the boiling water would kill any germs.

As I swished my irons in the boiling murky water the fork slipped out of my grasp and floated to the bottom of the trough. I watched in horror as it clinked on the metal at the bottom. The water was about eighteen inches deep and since it was boiling there was nothing I could do to retrieve the thing. My new found mates just stood there doubled up with laughter at my misfortune.

Visions of a further payment for loss of equipment leapt to mind, or perhaps I could return when the water cooled? A voice broke into my thoughts.

"What's the matter, laddie?" It seemed that out of nowhere the sergeant had returned. I thought it was just my luck for him to appear when tragedy had struck again.

Feeling very uncomfortable I said, "I've dropped my fork in there and I can't get it out Sergeant", nodding in the general direction of the trough. "Is there any way I can get another one?"

I was unprepared for the sergeant's reply. "Do unto others as no doubt others will do unto you" he replied. "Nick one!" and with that parting shot he strode off.

Later as I lay in my bed I thought over what the sergeant had said. "as no doubt others will do unto you." Did this mean I had to take careful watch over all my possessions and live by my wits? Little did I know that the answer would be revealed the very next day.

CHAPTER 3

Was that bed hard! I twisted and turned, trying every position imaginable to find an angle that didn't make my body ache. The mattress was so thin that I might as well have laid on the springs. And as for the springs, they groaned and twanged like some redundant orchestra.

To make matters worse the bed had a loose iron head piece. It shook violently every time I moved and made such a noise that I was fearful of complaints, to say the least, from the rest of the lads. I resigned myself to lie as still as possible and hope sleep would overtake me soon.

I had never slept on a ground floor before and I tried to imagine that I was in some sumptuous bungalow. This was my Beverley Hills retreat and my Rolls Royce and swimming pool were just a stone's throw away. Any moment now my personal butler would call with my breakfast and turn up the air conditioning. Dream on.

Suddenly I experienced air conditioning of a different sort. Wilkie, the Scouse lad in the bed opposite blew off very noisily. "Cor blimey" muttered Pete in the bed next to him as I popped my head under the blankets accompanied with some more discord from the bed springs.

I smiled in the darkness. When I eventually emerged from the blankets, overcome with another bout of sneezing due to the camphor, I listened to some unfamiliar sounds. Some were snoring and others were breathing quite deeply. A couple of beds away from me a lad was moaning. On the right side of me I could hear a lot of sniffing. It was Robin and I knew instinctively that he was crying. I strained my ears, trying hard to hear what he was muttering to himself but his sniffing got louder.

I propped myself up on one elbow and tried to peer through the darkness at Robin's bed. I couldn't see a thing but I could hear his sniffing turn into stifled sobbing. I knew he was home sick but the only one, as far as I knew, who showed it. I decided I would have another go at cheering him up in the morning.

I must have drifted off into an uneasy sleep because when I awoke at 6am I felt stiff all over. I was soon to discover most of the other lads felt the same.

I watched a couple of lads get out of bed. One swore, the other stretched his arms above his head and then started twirling them like windmills. His expletive concerning the bed I well understood.

The two fellows draped a towel each around their necks, picked up their toilet bags in unison and made for the wash room. A third lad dragged himself from his bed, stuck a cigarette in his mouth and started fishing in his trouser pockets for his matches. He too wandered off to the wash room and I thought it was about time I followed suit.

Within about five minutes all the basins were occupied. We looked a sorry sight with our hair on end, our faces covered with shaving foam, and the mode of dress! We looked like a cross between down and outs, the Boy Scouts and the Home Guard.

Some were stripped to the waist and throwing water in every direction, some were in vests and pyjama bottoms or underpants, and we all looked very weedy. The chatter and humour was incessant.

"What are you shaving for Rusty?" chided one, "you have only got a bit of fluff'. "My, oh my" joked another to his mate, "Who's got the hairiest chest then?"

We all burst out laughing when one of the smallest lads, a real cockney, went up to the biggest lad in the hut and said, "Oh Mary, you do look lovely. Any chance of a kiss?" This prompted the rest of us to make lovey-dovey sounds or whistled as lofty proceeded to ignore him and splashed some vile smelling after shave on his cheeks, and to our greater amusement, in his arm pits.

We were not really prepared for what followed. Without so much as a word Lofty lifted up the little fellow by the back of his vest and dumped him unceremoniously face down in a basin of soapy water. It was then the big man's turn to emit a loud belly laugh, along with the rest of us, as his opponent coughed and spluttered in the sink.

The little chap might have drowned in that sink if it had not been for Pete who let out a loud exclamation. "Look out fella's!" he exclaimed, "make way for bleedin' Royalty."

We all stopped in our tracks and stared. Robin, clad in the most luxurious dressing gown of blue and gold with silk on the pockets and cuffs, entered the wash room with an air of grandeur. Unfortunately his very pale face and the dark circles under his eyes did little to compliment his attire.

Jolly John, so nick named because of his continual tendency for practical joking, started to skip and dance from side to side. "In the blue and gold corner weighing in at nine and a half stone we have Robust Robin", he said, "do we have any contenders please?"

Robin looked decidedly more miserable and muttered something inaudible as he elbowed his way into line at the sinks. Delicately he began to wipe his face with the flannel and let out a series of yawns. Finally he undid the belt of his splendid garment and with a flourish shrugged it off his shoulders.

He stood there looking helpless and since he couldn't find a nail on which to hang his dressing gown, he very slowly put it on again and started brushing his teeth.

It was about this point that somebody mentioned the time. With all the messing about we had lost sight of the fact that we had less than three quarters of an hour to get to the cookhouse, have breakfast, and muster outside the block before getting marched off for more interviews and to collect more kit.

I was one of the last at the sinks. I had been too pre-occupied by watching all the fun and, to be perfectly honest, reluctant to strip and wash and be on the receiving end of witty comments about my body. By now the hot water had run out as well.

When I got back into the billet I found it empty except for Robin. There was a mirror very low down on the inside of his cupboard door and I thought he was kneeling to pray, but no, he was simply kneeling down before the mirror to scrutinise the combing and brushing of his hair.

I sat on the edge of my bed once I had dressed and felt beneath it for my shoes but they were nowhere to be found. I started searching my bed space and other bed spaces to find out where they had gone but to no avail.

Robin eventually found them where someone had put them. On top of my cupboard no less.

"Oh no" I groaned. "Who's been messing about with my shoes?" They had not only played a practical joke by making me search for them but they had tightly knotted them together by the laces. I fumed as I fumbled to untie the mass of knots as Robin kept whining "We are going to be late."

Once I had got the shoes apart and on my feet I felt ready to face the day but I had great difficulty in being able to get Robin to sprint to the cookhouse with me.

The scrambled egg on toast looked and smelt good but I began to wonder how I was going to cope with it. I was still only in possession of a knife and spoon.

As we sat at the table to start our breakfast, the rest of our gang passed by grinning. They knew I had lost my fork in the boiling trough the night before. They thought it was hilarious when I lifted the toast to my mouth and the scrambled egg toppled down my front.

"I'll see you back at the billet" I called.

One lad paused long enough to give an impish grin. "Not if we see you first", he replied, "I have only one thing to say to you. Get knotted!" I thought it was a fair guess that he was responsible for doctoring my shoes judging by his comment. I decided there and then to make a mental note of his face.

CHAPTER 4

"Well chaps, you have already spent one night in the Royal Air Force and you will have some idea of the things we expect of you." The very young looking, pasty faced and lanky Pilot Officer shuffled about on the same spot as he addressed us in his plumy accent in one of the large classrooms.

"We do, of course, want men who are going to be a credit to the Service", he smiled weakly and droned on. "Men who are dedicated to any given task, prepared to uphold the high traditions of the RAF and can be relied upon to do their duty twenty fours a day." He paused and looked expectantly as thirty blank faces stared unsmiling back at him.

I was thankful that the long winded officer was winding up his lengthy discourse on our career and promotion prospects. He made it sound very easy but somehow I could not imagine myself obtaining the rank of Marshall of the Royal Air Force in three years.

"Well chaps", he concluded, "you have the whole weekend in front of you to decide what course of action you want to take. If you decide to go for a three year or longer engagement you will take the Oath on Monday. If, however, you decide Service life is not for you, and, you intend to opt for two years National Service instead, you will be sent home and recalled at a later date. Have a nice weekend."

We sat and relaxed as the Pilot Officer whispered in the ear of a Flight Sergeant hovering close to him. The Flight Sergeant saluted the officer as he moved away and then returned to address us.

It was Friday afternoon and the Flight Sergeant said we could spend the whole weekend as we wished. If we went off Camp we had to be on our best behaviour in the neighbourhood. It was for our good and the impeccable reputation of the RAF. With a stem warning of grave consequences if we were not back in the billet by 10pm, we were dismissed.

We went a bit wild when we got back to our billet and enjoyed our first taste of total freedom.

"Well chaps, what are you going to do?" mimicked Jolly John in the posh Pilot Officer's voice. "Will you stay with us for a three year holiday, or, disappoint us and stay for only two?"

A bit of banter and cursing from the lads and Jolly John disappeared under a barrage of pillows that we threw at him.

Only two lads from our intake decided not to go for the regular engagement and went home to be recalled at a later date for National Service. Sadly it was the two lads that I had got most friendly with. I understood their views about the discipline and restriction of freedom, but, they could not understand my determination to go for the three year stint. Jointly they tried unsuccessfully to get me to change my mind. I was sorry to see them leave.

I was at a bit of a loss to know how to fill in my free weekend. Two or three of the fellows invited me to go and watch a cricket match and join them on a pub crawl afterwards but I declined. I had very little money and hitherto I had been a bit of a loner so I felt quite happy to go into Bedford and mooch around on my own instead.

The Saturday turned out to be unbearably hot and wandering the streets of Bedford got quite uncomfortable. As the day wore on my spirits fell to zero. For the first time in my life I felt out of my depth, lonely, isolated and far from home. I began to wish that I had gone off with some of the other lads.

Suddenly the thoughts for the future seemed frightening. I had spent seventeen years of my life in quiet country villages. My days had been filled with long walks and cycle rides, roaming fields and enjoying the animals. I was not too sure how I would react to vigorous training and strict routine. Most of all I did not want to look like a local yokel or village idiot in front of the other chaps.

My mind was in a turmoil as I reflected upon my future. I had by this time found the river and walked along the dusty path at its edge.

"Straighten up number four! In, out! In, out!" a loud voice behind me interrupted my melancholy.

A young fellow riding a bicycle was calling through a megaphone to some lads who were rowing a boat in mid river.

"Step it up!" he called. "In, out. In out!" I stepped to one side of the path as he rode past me. His attention completely focused on the men in the boat.

I watched fascinated as the young rowers rowed as one. Their strokes looked very even and they were certainly moving at speed.

"In, out! In" and all of sudden the chap on the bike was! He had been so intent on calling out to the rowers that he failed to watch where he was going and went head first, bike and all, into the river. It was one of the funniest sights I had ever seen.

I doubled up with laughter as did the men in the boat. The tears ran down my cheeks when I saw the man bob up in the water with his straw hat floating several feet away from him. The look of sheer amazement on his face was a joy to behold as he pulled himself up the bank.

I was almost beside myself with laughter when he took his shoes off and emptied the water out of them. Then he put them on, and minus both bike and megaphone which were still at the bottom of the river, he started running again and called "Right chaps, Row!" He sounded just like our posh Pilot Officer all over again.

It must have been just the tonic I needed since the incident cheered me up no end, and later when I went to the cinema and saw Ann Blyth and Edmund Purdom in "The Student Prince" I thought life was worth living after all.

Mindful of not getting late back to Camp I left the pictures early enough to buy myself some fish and chips at a dingy cafe. It was my only meal of the day and, I am ashamed to say, I ended it by nicking the fork. At least my irons would be complete again.

The Sunday was a relatively short day since I enjoyed the luxury of a lie in until early afternoon. I also went to bed early in anticipation that all too soon Monday would hail the start of a new dramatic week.

I shall never forget that Monday when I took the Oath to serve in the Royal Air Force. I stood before a very large Union Jack Flag which was pinned on the wall beside a portrait of The Queen. As I held The Bible in my right hand, I promised to faithfully serve Her Majesty Queen Elizabeth the Second, Her heirs and successors and the Government of the day as duty bound.

My RAF Number 4171436 was hardly dry in my brand new Service Book before the Sergeant in charge of us bellowed at me to put it away and keep it safe.

Aircraftman Second Class (AC2) Stallard was now officially a Member of the Royal Air Force. Within the week he would be fully kitted out and sent up to Lancashire for square bashing and intensive training for three months.

So now I was a ranker. Second Class I might be but I was determined to show them that, do or die, I would go all out to become First Class.

I put on a brave face and thought "Look out Padgate, here I come!"

CHAPTER 5

The brilliant blinding sun shone mercilessly from a cloudless sky. The air felt thick making it almost impossible to breathe.

My body was wet with perspiration in contrast to my parched throat and lips.

Every muscle and sinew in my frame ached and I didn't think I could falter another step without collapsing.

No, I had not wandered in the Sahara desert or been let loose in some tropical forest, I was standing to attention in full Air Force kit on Crewe Railway Station on the first leg of travelling to RAF Padgate via Warrington.

A most helpful Warrant Officer at Cardington had told us to travel to Padgate in full uniform complete with greatcoat. One of the lads pointed out that it would be rather warm to travel on two trains thus attired but he disagreed.

"The more you wear the less you will have to carry" he said. "The Lord knows you will have enough to hump about before this day is through."

"With brains like that you can see how he became an officer" muttered Pete when our prophet of doom was out of ear shot. "I don't know why we have to travel on trains, you would think a flippin' Air Force would fly us up there."

My greatcoat was thicker and warmer than any blanket but my biggest problem was my collar. I had been at the end of the queue when collars had been handed out and I just missed out on the normal issue of flimsy detachable ones. I was handed four very stiffly starched collars with appropriate collar studs which I found difficult to marry up with any shirt.

The store man said I was lucky to have the stiff collars which were normally issued to officers only. Now as I stood perspiring on Crewe station with a sore neck, I felt anything but lucky.

If Crewe station was a rehearsal for heat torture we soon found out that there was worse to come at Warrington. About sixty of us wilted in the boiling afternoon sun whilst our feet burned in our boots on the station platform. Both of my heels were blistered which added to the agony as we waited for coaches to come from RAF Padgate to pick us up.

My kit bag and suitcase added to my discomfort especially as we had to keep moving from one end of the platform to another. Finally we were moved from the platform to the station precinct when at long last two coaches arrived.

Everybody was disgruntled but too nervous to complain when we bundled all the kitbags and cases on to the coach and started off on the short journey to Padgate.

The first sight of Padgate Camp was very impressive. Everywhere looked spick and span. Every window seemed to glisten. I recall several brass stands attached to white ropes roped off the area of the Guard Room just inside the Main Gate. The ropes were very white and the brass was very bright. I don't think it occurred to any of us that vigorous spring cleaning, commonly called "bull" would soon be the lot of all of us.

The coaches drove us to the edge of one of the large parade grounds and as we stepped off we experienced our first encounter of" The Three Musketeers." We called them this during our more benevolent moments but usually we called them something quite unprintable.

To say The Three Musketeers were drill corporals would be paying them a compliment. They said some very uncomplimentary things to us as they encircled us and observed us from every angle. We soon realised that they were not going to be our friends.

As we lined up on the parade ground one of the corporals informed us which billet we had been allocated to. The billets were very similar to Cardington.

One corporal was in charge of each billet. He was privileged to have his own private room which was called his "bunk" just inside the end of the billet. It was an occupational hazard to have to pass his room every time we entered the billet.

Twenty of us shared the billet, ten on each side. We each had the area known as our bed space which housed the single bed, tall single wardrobe and a fair size bedroom locker.

We were told the billet had to be bulled at all times. This meant that it did not have to be kept clean but it had to be spotless. The corporal wanted to see his face in the shine of the floor linoleum, in the shine of the lockers and in the toe caps of our boots. We couldn't think why because he had such a menacing and ugly face anyway.

The corporal emphasised that we would all arise at 6.30am and be in bed with all lights out at 10.30pm. We were warned that the Orderly Sergeant would make spot checks on the billets to ensure these orders were strictly observed. Anyone found guilty of breaking the rules would suffer the consequences.

The corporal went on to explain that every week each billet would be competing against each other to obtain a shield for the best spring clean. Anything less than spotless baths, showers, sinks and toilets would result in a loss or restriction of privileges.

Each airman was responsible for high maintenance of cleanliness for his own bed space. No way was he to encroach on a neighbouring bed space and make it untidy.

Alan, who unfortunately had very large ears like bat wings, was heard to complain. "Geezers in prison get it easier than we do." This brought an immediate response from our corporal who gripped one of Alan's ears and jerked his face within inches of his own.

"Listen to me laddie" he hissed, "any further comment from you and you will be running the perimeter of the parade ground but your feet will not touch the ground. Understand?"

Alan mumbled that he understood as he gingerly rubbed his ear.

Then came the bomb shell. The corporals in charge of each billet appeared to hate each other. Each one was determined his group of recruits would be best drilled, best trained and finally turned out immaculately at the Pass Out parade. Winning the coveted shield for excellence was the aim of each of the corporals who were all out for promotion and wanting to impress the Station

Commander. They also enjoyed the power and authority they yielded over us rookies.

The language that was poured out to us was filthy. We were seldom spoken to and soon got use to all the screaming and abuse. I guess there wasn't one in the entire company who didn't quake in his boots. The corporals instilled terror from the word go and we soon learnt to do exactly as we were told even if the command was stupid or degrading.

The rules and regulations would have been further explained but for the fact that Billy fainted. The heat and all the standing in full kit had taken its toll. We had now been wearing all the gear for hours. Then, just as the corporal was about to dismiss us and send us to the allocated billet, I did something unforgivable. I ran my fingers around the inside of my collar to ease the rubbing on my sore neck. That was a grave mistake. Whilst the entire company was ordered to take their kit into the billets, I was told to stay on the spot.

I felt sick, not only from the excessive heat and all the standing but because of the look on the corporal's face. He twisted his mouth, narrowed his eyes and gripped the lapels of my great coat.

"Who gave you permission to shuffle about?" he spat, his face about three inches from my own. "Did you listen to a word I said?"

"Yes sir", I answered nervously but quickly.

"I am not Sir, I am Corporal" he yelled in my ear, "and what's your name?" "Stallard" I blurted out.

"Stallard" he repeated it sarcastically, "Stallard! I will be looking out for you Stallard. Now get to your billet. Move it. Fast!" I ran as quick as my heavy kit bag and suitcase would allow to the first billet.

The door was open and I staggered inside. The sight that met my gaze was almost unbelievable. No-one appeared to be walking but rather dancing around the floor and my eyes fell to the feet of my comrades.

Every lad had his feet on two little square pieces of felt, and, a further pile of felt pads were stacked just inside the door. The previous occupants had left the pads behind so that we would not have to walk on the brilliant lino and get it dirty. As we shuffled across the billet on the felt pads they helped to maintain the brilliance of the floor covering. It looked silly dragging our feet in that manner but it was very effective. We must have looked like a lot of skaters on ice.

My delay with the corporal meant I was the last to enter the billet and so I had no choice of a bed space. I looked around for the only one which remained empty and it happened to be in the very centre of the room.

"I have saved you a bed next to mine" whined the ever faithful Robin.

I groaned. This just wasn't going to be my day. I was lumbered with a bed in the middle of the room right adjacent to the one and only electric socket. This would mean that the ironing board would of necessity be erected on my bed space. Consequently all and sundry would be trampling over it to use the iron. Uniform pressing was a daily ritual for some.

There was nothing I could do about the situation because the lads had no other alternative. With a sigh I put extra felt pads near the bottom of my bed.

To cap it all I had Robin as a neighbour again. I didn't mind so much at Cardington because I thought his immediate presence would only be for a week but now

I was stuck with him for three months. If he had cried nightly at Cardington, he would break his heart here.

The arrival of the Corporal took all further thoughts from my mind as he demonstrated how the beds had to be made up. One blanket covered the mattress and three were folded of equal size. The two sheets were similarly folded to the same size and placed between the blankets like cream in a biscuit. The squared off pack was placed next to the pillow at the head of the bed.

A new very white towel was to be spread over the centre of the bed. During the day we had to place our clean mug upside down in the centre of the towel when not in use. The knife, fork and spoon had to be arrayed in a certain position around the mug. We were told that all the handles on the mugs had to be lined up, bed by bed, and pointing to the right. There was so much to remember.

It was a very miserable looking bunch of fellows that later on sat in the cookhouse for tea. The salad had wilted as much as the men and the prospect of square bashing on the morrow, which marching was so called, did little to brighten our spirits.

The heat of the day turned into a massive thunder storm as we sat and ate our tea. The lightening flashed every few seconds and the thunder crashed around us. The heavens opened and we lingered over the meal in the hope that the storm would stop before we went back to the billet.

We had no choice but to dash through the downpour because the chief cook turfed us out of the mess. On arrival at the billet the felt pads began to squelch underfoot from our wet boots and the lino dulled.

Amazingly none of us had the sense to remove our wet boots before donning the pads.

I noticed that the window above my bed was wide open and rain was coming in on the bed. I hastily positioned my mug in the centre of the towel and placed fork and spoon in their appointed place by it. No sooner had I placed the knife on the towel when there was a blinding flash of lightening which danced the length of it and scorched the towel. Only a second earlier I had been holding it.

I stared wide eyed at the mass pattern on the knife. It was all colours of the rainbow, similar to the appearance of oil when spilt on a wet road. The colours seemed ingrained in the metal and they never disappeared right up to the day I had it stolen.

Our corporal had entered the billet quietly and as I turned I saw him for the first time. His face was ashen and quite kindly he placed a hand on my shoulder.

"Blimey, you were lucky there, mate" he said. "A second earlier and you would have been a gonner. The lightening would have electrocuted you." Shaking his head and without further comment he returned to his room at the end of the billet.

Later as I lay in bed I reviewed my position. My most immediate concern was the corporal. Earlier he had warned that he would be looking out for me. Was that a threat? Then he seemed to have a grain of human kindness when he was concerned about the lightening and actually called me "mate."

I turned over in the darkness, thankful that the bed was more comfortable than the one at Cardington. Sleep however did not come easy. Somehow I just had the feeling that I wasn't going to be a mate in the morning.

CHAPTER 6

"Are you completely stupid, laddie?" Corporal Brown shouted so loudly in my ear that I cringed. "I said are you completely stupid?" When he yelled the question the second time, I simply shook my head vigorously and lamely replied "No sergeant!" "Sergeant?" he bawled his face now contorted in rage. "Sergeant? Have you not learnt the ranks of the RAF yet?"

I nervously bit my lip and thought it best to remain silent. At Cardington we had been shepherded about mainly by a sergeant and the rank had somehow implanted itself upon my brain. It was now very apparent that Corporal Brown did not appreciate the promotion I had so unwittingly given him.

My crime was that I didn't seem to know how tall I was. The Corporal had told us to get into line, tallest on the left and shortest on the right. I thought I had sorted it all out for the best and shuffled next to a lad who appeared to be the same height as me. Unfortunately when the line was complete and I glanced each side of me, I found to my dismay that there was a taller lad on both sides. I stuck out like the middle part of the letter V.

"Airman, don't you dare move" Corporal Brown threatened as I tried to reposition myself in the line. "One more step and I will have you running around this square so much that you will only be four feet six at the end of it!" He would have said more since he considered his comment very amusing but some of the lads started to snigger at that point and so he threw abuse at all of us instead.

To my untrained mind "Dressing from the right" caused me to wonder if you put your right leg in your underpants first or possibly your right arm in your vest. I soon discovered that it was nothing to do with dressing but meant positioning oneself in a long line of men in height order.

Corporal Brown went to great lengths to show us that we had to put the fingertips of our right hand on the left shoulder of the man standing immediately on our right. I thought it would have been much easier if he had said, "Be one arm's length away from the chap beside you." But no matter how he meant it, it didn't stop him making us practice it at least a dozen times. And all in the gruelling sun of another sweltering day.

All the morning we had gone through basic drill movements. The corporal exaggerated every move as he demonstrated how to stand to attention, stand at ease and stand easy. I was quietly congratulating myself that I was picking up all the moves quite well.

Several of the lads had their ears yanked or a poke in the chest from the corporal's baton. A high percentage also fell afoul of his angry outbursts but mercifully I missed all these. My turn was about to come.

"When I say stand at ease I mean be slightly relaxed" he shouted directly into my face. "Not lounge there like a pregnant fairy." I dared to smile until he snapped, "And get that stupid grin off your face. Straighten that back and pull that stomach in."

Over lunch our squadron was in complete agreement that a morning had never seemed so long. Although the afternoon training session was shorter than that of the morning, it seemed twice as long. The marching was relentless. "Left, right. Left, right. Left right, halt and about turn."

By 4 o'clock the intensive heat made Corporal Brown as irritable as the rest of us. His orders were punctuated with increasing swear words and obscenities. Occasionally we were allowed a short period of rest but it didn't usually last more than five or ten minutes at a time. We threw ourselves down on the grass verge beside the parade ground, pulled off our thick leather boots and inspected our blisters. This was a mistake because it was more painful to put the boots back on again. Not only were my heels raw but a red rash had developed around the bottoms of my legs where the boots had rubbed them raw.

The first day of training didn't go very well at all. Before the corporal dismissed us for the day he called us a "shower" and intimated that we were to be back on parade the following morning at 8.30am wearing greatcoats again. Greatcoats in mid-July. His parting shot was, "First thing in the morning, when you are on parade, I'll start by inspecting your dress. I want to see well pressed trousers and gleaming tunic buttons and woe betide anyone who lets me down."

That entire evening was taken up with the bulling of our kit. The ritual of bulling the toe caps of our boots was most time consuming. The process involved spitting on the toe caps. Black boot polish was melted in the tin lid by means of holding a match under it and then the polish was applied to the spit and rubbed in by a series of small circles with a piece of rag.

Everybody trampled over my bed space to use the iron and ironing board for pressing tunics and trousers. I constantly moaned about having a bed right next to the electric socket. The situation wasn't helped when one of the chaps carried a fire bucket full of water and dumped it unceremoniously in the middle of my bed space. This was needed for damping the pressing rag before applying it to the creases in the trousers. Every time a drop of water spilt on my area, I dabbed at it with one of the felt pads. I didn't want to keep polishing my space for room inspections.

The job I hated most of all was blancoing the webbing. Blanco was a kind of dark blue paste in a tin very similar to boot polish.

The webbing consisted of a wide body belt which held a bayonet frog or aperture for holding a bayonet; cross straps to hold a large canvas pack on your back and a smaller pack to be positioned at your side, also a water bottle.

Each piece of webbing had brass pieces attached for fastening purposes and holding all the gear together. I never did master the art of not getting blanco on the brass bits, or, Brasso cleaning fluid on the blanco bits. I was constantly being picked up for one or the other misdemeanours.

Robin wandered up to my bed and glanced morosely at the kit I had laid out in readiness for wearing in the morning. He gently picked up one of my officer type starched collars and enquired "How do you get them nice and stiff and shiny like that? Mine are thin and flimsy."

Without a moment's hesitation I quipped, "You have to use plenty of blanco on 'em, Robin." "Oh, I didn't know we had to blanco our collars" he mumbled and went off to dig out his tin of the stuff.

I smiled as I watched Robin spread all his collars out on the top of his locker.

He took a brush and dabbed at the tin and transferred liberal amounts to each collar in turn. "Don't forget to let them dry" I chortled.

Half an hour later Robin looked across at my bed. "I've brushed my collars", he said, "they don't look shiny and stiff like yours though." "Never mind", I replied, "it's pretty obvious that you have put some thought and effort into it."

Most of us missed breakfast the following morning because we were too eager to appease the corporal. All our time was taken up washing, shaving and grooming and undertaking last minute titivation of our uniform and boots. It was quite a posh looking bunch that marched right around the parade square before we were lined up for Corporal Brown's personal inspection.

Not one of us escaped a reprimand for one reason or another. I was ordered to get a haircut and it was the same for the lad standing to attention beside me. When he got to the centre line of men he stopped in front of one of our most senior men.

"Pomeroy, did you use a mirror when you shaved this morning?" he asked.

"Yes Corporal" was the sharp reply but it brought a more sharper reply from the corporal. "Next time use a razor!" Then Corporal Brown arrived in front of Robin. His eyes almost bulged out of their sockets and the veins stuck out in his neck as he took a deep intake of breath. F or a few seconds he opened and shut his mouth again, like a fish out of water, but nothing came out. For once he was rendered speechless. When he did find his voice he asked Robin a direct question with a hiss.

"What is that blue mark all around your neck, airman?"

"It's blanco" said Robin mournfully. "I've got hot with the marching and the blanco is melting."

"What on earth are you doing blancoing your collars?" the corporal exploded.

"I could put you on a charge for this, you lunatic. Don't you know this is a misuse of Government property?"

"Ken Stallard told me to do it. He has blanco'd his collars" Robin said defensively. Upon which the corporal took him by the ear and dragged him over to where I was standing. He demanded to know what it was all about.

Robin looked decidedly dejected and on the brink of tears when I explained it was all a joke. I thought the corporal was going to explode. I had never seen him so furious.

"You will return to your billet immediately" he said. "I can't stand the sight of either of you a minute longer." He then told Robin to go and wash his collars and ensure that he was wearing one at 6 o'clock that evening. At that time both Robin and I would be required to report to him at his bunk.

I tried to explain that I had not blanco'd my collars but this fell on deaf ears.

"Both of you report to my bunk at 6 o'clock sharp" he bellowed. "I will teach you not to get up to stupid tricks and make a fool out of me."

When we were out of earshot and on our way to the billet Robin broke down completely. He said I had let him down and that he would never play such a nasty trick on me. He had considered me to be his friend and it was now my fault that we were both in a lot of trouble.

Although I apologised profusely I was feeling extremely guilty. I tried to console him by giving him one of my collars since his were now ruined. I didn't think he would be able to wash the offending collar and get it dry and in a fit state to wear so quickly.

We took our time sorting out and washing the collars. We were in no hurry to get back to the square bashing. The longer we stayed at the billet meant less time at drill practice. Obviously we were learning fast.

Later we emerged from our hut and made our way back to where the squadron was being marched up and down, still in sweltering greatcoats. "Left, right. Left, right!" It was endless.

"What another day this is going to be" moaned Robin. "I wonder what Brown has got lined up for us at 6 o'clock tonight." I wondered too. We were not going on a picnic and that was for sure.

CHAPTER 7

Earlier on at Cardington it had been impressed upon us all the necessity of reading the Daily Orders, which were published and pinned on the Unit Notice Boards. The orders gave details of parade venues and times, kit inspections, accommodation checks, medical examinations and so on.

A separate sheet of orders gave more details of the Airmen, listing promotions, demotions, charges, courses, et cetera. We were required to read the orders on a daily basis. Excuses for not reading the orders would not be accepted. They were as important as verbal military commands and must be obeyed at all times.

I read "AWOL" next to one of the names on the list. A couple of mean looking corporals stood reading the orders and I enquired what this meant.

"AWOL" means" A Wet Outlook Likely" said one nonchalantly. "No it doesn't" piped in his friend "It stands for A Waste Of Life."

Seeing the puzzled look which crossed my face as I was trying to fathom out what the weather, or, a potential suicide had to do with an airman, the more aggressive corporal broke into my thoughts. "It means Absent With Out Leave" he said, "in short, Airman, it means a guy who cannot take the pace has decided to run away so becomes absent without leave." Then he grimly added "just until he very quickly gets caught and is brought back and put in the glasshouse!" All of us knew that the glasshouse was a term used for a military detention centre, the military equivalent of a prison.

I was weighing up the pros and cons of going AWOL as I prepared for the rendezvous with our corporal at 6 o'clock. Robin and I were in for some kind of punishment following the saga of the blanco'd collars earlier in the day.

At a couple of minutes to 6, Robin and I duly reported to the Corporal's bunk. At my first timid knock there was no reply. I grimaced at Robin as I knocked a bit louder and then louder still. There was no response whatsoever. Perhaps the corporal was asleep so I knocked again very loudly.

At this point we heard a roar from outside the billet. "Stallard and Hill, where are you? Get out here. Now!" We immediately recognised the voice of Corporal Adams who was in charge of the recruits in our neighbouring billet. Robin and I hastily responded to the summons and came to attention in front of him outside the door of our hut.

"Brown has been put on Guard Duty tonight" Adams explained. "I am standing in for him here. He tells me you two are on extra discipline. Fair enough. Get back inside, pick up your rifles and be back here in two minutes flat." He tapped his watch to emphasise his words.

Somewhat stunned, Robin and I paused long enough to look at each other. "Go on then", bellowed the corporal. "I said be back here in two minutes."

Neck and neck Robin and I raced back inside our billet. We ran to our bed spaces, forgetting to use the felt pads, grabbed our rifles and ran back to the corporal still standing outside.

"Right" he commanded, "lift your rifles at arm's length above your heads."

Obediently we both endeavoured to lift the rifles above our heads single handed.

"Use both hands" he growled, "balance it!" We obeyed.

"Now maintaining that position you keep running around the square until I tell you to stop" he ordered. "Move it!" Side by side Robin and I jogged once around the square. The rifle seemed incredibly heavy after just a few paces and I felt the muscles in my arms and back beginning to ache.

One lap of the square was enough for me. I didn't run very fast and Robin, quite breathless, was some way behind me. As my rifle lowered in my weary arms I allowed it to sag until it rested across my shoulders. The temporary rest made all the difference until I got to the place where Adams was watching. He was enjoying the opportunity of disciplining us because we were not from his billet. In his eyes we were on opposite sides. He wanted to prove that he was just as hard and loathsome as our Corporal Brown.

"Get those arms up Stallard, and move it. Faster!" he called. I tried to oblige but I was already stumbling rather than running. I could hear similar orders were being bellowed at Robin behind me.

At the end of the second lap I was conscious of running alone. I could no longer hear the panting and grunting of Robin behind me. Glancing back over my shoulder I saw him hunched over on the grass verge at the side of the square.

The corporal kept bellowing at Robin who didn't appear to be taking any notice. When I drew nearer to him I could see he was being violently sick. I stopped at Robin's side as the corporal ran across to us.

"What is the matter with you, Airman?" he asked but Robin shrugged his shoulders and vomited again on the grass.

"Take his rifle, Stallard."

I took hold of the rifle and stood there looking like the Lone Ranger as I tried to balance both rifles.one under each arm.

"Get those rifles back to the billet" he implied and I got away as fast as I could before he changed his mind.

When Robin came into the billet a quarter of an hour later he looked like death warmed up. "I was too hot" he gasped to no-one in particular. "I was too hot." With that he just keeled over on his bed and very soon he was asleep whilst Pomeroy and some of the others intimated that Corporal Adams was illegitimate.

For once in my life I was delighted to see it pouring with rain the following morning. The air was much cooler and we were all ordered to assemble ourselves in the drill shed. We were back under the orders of our own Corporal Brown, who surprisingly, didn't make any mention about the punishment of the previous night.

Another blessing was that we were not required to wear the greatcoats but No.2 dress instead which consisted of short tunic, trousers and beret. It was the order of the day to wear the blanco'd webbing belt and the bayonet frog attached to it.

The drill shed was very large and had a tin roof. It was difficult to hear the corporal's words of command for the sound of the torrential rain hitting the tin. Worse still, it caused the shed to have a weird echoing effect so that one appeared to hear a command coming from the front and behind at the same time.

I was in the middle row of three rows of men lined up in front of the corporal.

He was teaching us to salute.

"Salute to the right" he barked, and our right hand with extended fingers flicked up to the side of our head. "Salute to the left" he went on and we did a similar manoeuvre except we had to turn our heads to the left as we saluted. So it dragged on time after time.

As the rain fell heavier on to the tin roof, the corporal's yelling echoed more so from the tin at the back of the drill shed. I felt it increasingly difficult to hear the commands because of the echo. I started to anticipate the order. If he said "Salute to the left" last time, I reasoned that it would be "Salute to the right" the next time. I was wrong. Just to confuse things he used the same order twice and consequently I saluted in the wrong direction.

Corporal Brown descended upon me like some demented animal. He swore and even blasphemed, then walked round the back of me and grabbed me tightly around the neck and shook me like a rabbit. I could not breathe and I thought I was going to choke. Then he suddenly released me and proceeded to humiliate me in front of the entire squadron.

"Right Stallard, I can see you require some personal training" he said very sarcastically. "Gather round men, you might learn something." I was then singled out to do a series of salutes at all angles. "To the left, to the right" and so he went on, faster and faster, until my arm was flashing like a windmill. Satisfied that he had made a fool of me enough, he finally decided to dismiss us and send us for lunch.

During the afternoon we had to report to a store to collect our bayonets. They were old, not too sharp and some were incredibly rusty. Mine was so bad that it was difficult to get it to fit in the frog on my belt. Once it was in after a struggle, it was difficult to pull it out again.

Because of the continuing rain we were ordered back to the drill shed to be taught how to fix the bayonets on the end of our rifles.

The corporal gave each command by a number. When he yelled "Bayonets fix- one" we had to slap the bayonet which was hanging in its frog on the right side of our belt. When he ordered "Two" we had to swiftly withdraw the bayonet from the frog and position it on the end of the rifle, the butt of which was firmly standing on the toe cap of our left boot.

At the command "Three! Bayonets fix!" we had to click the bayonet into the fixed position on the end of the rifle.

A series of clicking noises were heard as we struggled to fix the bayonets on the ends of our rifles. He made us practice it several times.

Every now and then the corporal approached one of the squaddies and tried to deafen him regarding some mistake he had unwittingly made. One could not get the bayonet free from the frog, another made the mistake of dropping it on the floor. The most common problem was that we could not get the bayonets to fix on the ends of the rifles, metal to metal. For once I had got the hang of the procedure and any little mistakes I made went un-noticed.

After another dozen attempts to fix bayonets we had got the right idea. The corporal was not, however, happy to hear a series of clicking noises as bayonets were being fixed to the end of the rifles. "I want us to do it all together" he said. "I want to hear only one loud click as you fix the bayonets together." He explained it fully whilst emphasising that it had to be a universal click rather than a series of clicks.

So we had to go through the drill one more time. Quietly for a change the corporal demanded "Fix bayonets" and we went through the procedure by numbers one, two and three. He tilted his head slightly and listened for the one universal click but he was disappointed. A series of clicking noises could still be heard as a lot of us struggled to marry up the bayonets to the rifles.

"Did I not say one click only?" roared Corporal Brown, now almost beside himself with rage, "I say again, one click only, and if anyone dares to muck it up, I will have his guts for garters."

The order was given and amazingly there was one simultaneous clicking sound. This put a smile on the corporal's face. "Very good", he complimented and then it was "Bayonets off" in readiness for one last excellent performance.

It is one thing putting a bayonet on a rifle whilst the rifle is resting on your toe cap, but, quite another when the bayonet is on the rifle and you are ordered to slope arms.

Throwing a rifle with a bayonet attached up the left side of the body is no easy feat. This was an extension to the original order for fixing bayonets. The order for one universal click now being paramount.

It was then that I noticed Wills standing in the row directly in front of me had not got his bayonet tightly fixed on the end of his rifle. It was obviously loose, due to the fact that the bloke was too scared to make a loud click after everybody else had got theirs fixed. He had decided not to fix it rather than invoke the corporal's wrath.

I watched fascinated but somewhat nervously as Wills encountered every drill move. The bayonet wobbled at each move but thankfully did not come adrift from the weapon. I began to wonder what would happen if the command was given to slope arms. I decided I would have to keep an eye on that bayonet in case it decided to go off on a course of its own. I didn't have to wait very long.

The corporal ordered the dreaded "Slope arms!" and like a flash all the rifles flew up the left side of the bodies.

As Wills rifle was thrown on to his shoulder the loose bayonet flew off the end of it at speed, and I ducked as it whistled past my ear and clattered on the floor behind me.

For about fifteen seconds the corporal was speechless. He narrowed his eyes and brought his lips into a menacing straight line. When we noticed how his nose characteristically wriggled we knew he was about to blow a gasket.

Brown positioned himself directly in front of Wills but pointed directly at me.

"I hate that specimen behind you" he spat "but that gives you no excuse to try and kill him!" Wills looked like he was going to cry as he turned and mumbled "Sorry" in my direction.

"Very soon we shall be going out on enemy bayonet practice" the corporal explained. "We shall have bags of straw suspended from a beam for that purpose, but, today I am very tempted to go for the real thing." And this, punctuated by further swear words, was said like it was meant.

When we were dismissed for the day I wasn't sure who was most relieved, him or us.

Once we were back in the billet collecting our mugs and iron for tea one of our chaps sidled up to me. "What's the matter with your neck, Ken?" he asked.

I had no idea what he was talking about and took a quick glance in a mirror. I was horrified to see four dark bruises on both sides of my neck. I bruise easily and I remembered how our corporal had grabbed me around the neck only that morning.

Lee stepped forward and said, "If you reported that to the Commanding Officer, Brown would be in a lot of trouble. He has assaulted you. That's grievous bodily harm." I knew this chap was a bit of a trouble maker and nothing would make him happier than to see our corporal get into trouble. I knew what he had said was not out of genuine concern for me.

Without exception all the lads in the billet gathered around me to see what the corporal had done. They wanted revenge and in me they saw an opportunity for hitting back at our tyrant. They tried their hardest to persuade me to report Brown to the Commanding Officer but I did not want to cause a fuss. I could only envisage it leading to further trouble or reprisal.

As I sat in the mess hall having my tea that evening Corporal Adams, the NCO (Non Commissioned Officer) from the next hut made his way to my table. I expected

him to make some comment about forcing Robin and
I to run around the square but he didn't.

"I want to see your neck" he said. "Lift your head
up." I did as I was told.

"I've just been told about that" Adams went on.
"You've got mates you know!"

They are concerned about you. Looking at those
bruises I think you should show them to the Commanding
Officer and say how you got them."

I felt very uneasy at his comments. I knew the thing
was being blown up out of all proportion. Here was
another guy grabbing at a chance to devalue a colleague.

I tried to make light of it and said I had always bruised
very easily and it looked much worse than it was.

The pressure mounted when Adams pointed out
that I could be in serious trouble for not reporting the
incident. Brown could go too far with someone in the
future and do some very real harm. It was my duty to
get it stopped whilst I had the bruising evidence so that
no-one else was made to suffer in a similar fashion in the
future.

I felt more miserable by the minute. I just wanted to
get on with each day and keep out of trouble. I needed
help but I didn't know where to find it. I decided to go
for a walk around the Camp and try desperately to sort
out my thoughts and decide what to do.

A lot later in the evening I returned to our hut. I was
greeted by Alex who wanted to know where I had been.
He promptly asked the question that all the others
wanted to hear. "Have you reported Brown, mate? What
did Adams have to say?"

I tried to quieten everybody down. All went very
silent when I announced "I have not done anything

about it and I don't intend to. I reckon it's best left alone because it will only cause repercussions."

Ben pushed his way to the front of the circle of fellows flicking a towel as he did so. "I think you should know something has already been done" he said. "We saw Adams talking to Brown outside the 'phone box just now. They were there for ages. Since then Brown has been in here three times looking for you. He said you have got to report to him as soon as you come in."

I took a deep intake of breath as I felt my stomach lurch. What now? So it was with some misgiving that I made my way towards the privacy of his bunk.

CHAPTER 8

I kept trying to convince myself that I was worrying needlessly. I could see no way how Corporal Brown could possibly know about the controversy which had arisen in the billet because of the bruises he had inflicted on my neck. I decided that he must want to see me on a different matter. Even so, it didn't stop me rehearsing words in my mind just in case he challenged me about it. My mind was in turmoil as I approached his bunk.

I took a deep breath and knocked sharply on his door. For a full thirty seconds there was no reply and I began to wonder if he had gone out but left his light on.

As I stood outside the door nervously contemplating whether I should go looking for him, or call back later, I heard a cup clatter on a saucer from within. I waited.

It seemed like an eternity before Corporal Brown opened the door and then I was taken off guard completely by his mild manner. He actually smiled when he said, "Come in, Stallard. I have been expecting you."

I stepped into the neat little room. It wasn't very big and not very well lit. "Are you interested in stamp collecting?" he asked as he moved to the table which was covered with hundreds of stamps and catalogues and albums.

"Not very" I ventured as he picked up a very large brightly coloured stamp in one hand and a magnifying glass in the other. The corporal was silent for some time as he studied the stamp through the glass.

"You can sit there" he indicated with a nod of the head towards his bed. I hesitated.

"Go on, sit down" he went on, "I'll be with you in a minute."

I sat gingerly on the bed which was already made, anxious not to crease the cover or step out of line.

"You should have a hobby, Stallard" he advised. "It's a diversion. It helps you to relax. Do you good!" He looked at me expecting some kind of answer but nothing came and so an embarrassing silence followed.

"I expect you are wondering why I have asked you to come" he said at last.

"The truth is, I want to be completely frank and honest with you and I want you to be the same with me. Is that understood?"

"That's fine by me" I replied and looked him straight in the eye waiting for his next move.

"One of my colleagues told me that I bruised you rather badly today" he began, "Will you show me what I've done please."

PLEASE! I could hardly believe my ears. I never imagined this man, who was constantly sarcastic and barked every order, could ever stoop to say PLEASE, I didn't answer but merely pulled the top of my collar less shirt open and lifted my chin up.

"Good gracious you do bruise easy, don't you" he admonished. "Did I really do that?"

A weak "Mmm" was all I could manage as he continued to question me whether my neck was sore or was I in any pain. I wasn't but I lied and said I was because I wanted him to have a conscience for what he had done to me.

"I would like to apologise for that" he continued and offered his hand for me to shake. I did so lamely feeling just a little bit embarrassed.

"I guess you know you could go to the C.O. and report me for that" he said softly. "And I couldn't blame you if you did. However, before you do anything drastic I want to tell you something in the strictest of confidence."

For the next ten minutes or so I sat and listened to all he said without one single interruption on my part.

I heard he was no friend of the Commanding Officer who had already carpeted him several times for not training his flight well enough before the final Pass Out parades. In short, the C.O. had given him his last chance to produce a first class turn out with us.

He concluded by saying "The next time the old man takes the salute at the Pass Out parade, he will be looking out for you lot and me especially."

"Where do I fit in to all this?" I enquired sounding more brave than I felt. The corporal sighed and continued.

"I am not asking you not to report me to the C.O." he said, "but I would appreciate it a lot if you didn't. That would finish my chances as a flight instructor for good. I would just like to ask you to understand my position please." There it was - that word "please" again. "I am asking you to consider helping me to keep my job."

He was almost pleading now.

Brown obviously wanted to get me on his side and was desperately searching for words. I began to feel sorry for him when he said "It's important for you, the men, the reputation of this Station and me personally to train a good flight. I am sorry if I'm overzealous sometimes but everything depends on this intake."

He looked downcast and quite pathetic.

I knew it had taken a lot of guts to confess all that he had. I was particularly touched when he said "I know I can trust you to keep what I have said to yourself. Do not mention a word of it to the others in the billet. I am sure we will get on just fine during the rest of your time here but I'm asking you not to let me down."

I promised the corporal I wouldn't go to the C.O. and also assured him that I had not intended to from the start. I said I would do my best because I was keen not to make a fool of myself on the prestigious Pass Out parade.

I made some flimsy excuse for the reason the corporal wanted to see me when I got back to the lads in the billet. More pressure was put on me to report Brown for the bruising but I flatly refused. A couple of the fellows refused to speak to me for a week. Such is life.

No sooner had I congratulated myself on winning a victory over the corporal when I had a run in with a new sergeant instructor who was posted in.

He was a short tubby man with a very round and rather red face, He sported a large grey to white moustache and he had the most sinister and piercing steel blue eyes. He never missed a thing that you didn't want him to see. From the first day we saw him we nick-named him Tubbs because of his tubby size.

Tubbs strutted around like a large fat pea-cock. He had a deep loud voice which would do justice to a combined mixture of thunder and sand paper. Whenever he reprimanded an airman he always finished by saying "I hate you!" We hated him too.

On the first day he arrived I received some very obscene talk from him as he observed my fly was undone as we lined up for him to hand out our mail. I explained that was the fruit of dressing in a hurry for a parade that we had not been warned about. He said I was insolent and later on I had to ask Robin what that meant.

On his second day, Tubbs took me to task for running across a patch of grass which had a notice on it saying "Keep off the Grass." That time he had some very uncomplimentary things to say about my eyes and my brain.

I recall saying "Third day never like the rest" but I was to be proved wrong. It wasn't Tubbs' third day but the third night that his luck ran out.

Tubbs was a stickler for time. He prowled between the huts at exactly 10.30pm to ensure all hut lights were out. Woe betide anyone discovered talking after lights out. If he caught some unsuspecting airman cleaning his boots by the light of a candle, he made him do press up's until he dropped from exhaustion.

One of the lads had brought an old electric radio with him and it stood proud on the shelf above my bed. It had to go there because the one and only electric socket was by my bed. This meant one of my extra chores was to stand up on my bed, nearly always in the dark, to switch the thing on and off.

The only luxury we allowed ourselves in the billet was to listen to the radio after lights out. We could only have it on very low so that it couldn't be heard outside. We didn't want Tubbs to confiscate it.

I enjoyed the radio most of all because I was directly beneath it and I could hear it. Sometimes one of the fellows would whisper loudly in the darkness, "Ken, turn it up" and I would have to stand up on my bed and twiddle with the knobs.

It was nearly midnight and most of us were still awake listening to "Top Ten."

It was a popular programme which broadcast the best ten bands, groups and songs of that week. We would lie in the darkness and sing quietly or judge and criticise everything that was played.

Suddenly we heard a roar at the next hut and saw all their electric lights go on.

"Tubbs is on the rampage" muttered one of the lads, "he is sorting them out next door."

"Be quiet" whispered Ben, "he'll be in here in a minute. Pretend to be asleep!" Everyone fell silent and here and there one could hear an exaggerated snore or a little giggle. Then a lad a couple of beds away from me called across.

"Ken" he whispered urgently, "switch the radio off. I can hear Tubbs coming." "Oh, I'm afraid" I admitted it openly and shivered under the bedclothes.

"I'll do it" called Ged in the bed directly opposite me. Like a flash he was out of bed, crossed the room, jumped on to my bed and switched the radio off.

Then everything happened at once.

Tubbs burst in and caught all the light switches with one movement of the hand.

The billet was flooded with light.

Ged leapt off my bed and caught his foot on the edge of the fire bucket standing by the erect ironing board on my bed space.

With a resounding crash the ironing board toppled sideways as the fire bucket rolled in a circle on my bed space, spilling water everywhere. Ged was in tears, gripping his foot and saying "ouch" at every few seconds.

"Out of bed and stand at the bottom of your beds" Tubbs thundered. It was with a lot of moans and groans the fellows began to throw off the bedclothes and do as they were ordered.

We looked an awesome sight standing to attention at the bottom of our beds.

Some were completely naked, some wore pyjamas, some with tops and no bottoms or vice versa, and here and there some were clad in underpants. An inspection straight from bed at midnight is not a pretty sight.

The strange thing was that everybody automatically reached for their little felt pads and stood on them at the end of the bed.

Tubbs made a bee line for me, of course.

His arm tightened on his cane and his moustache fair bristled.

He looked up at the radio above my bed and then at the ironing board lying on its side. His gaze fell on the upturned fire bucket which had been used earlier on for damping the cloth for trouser pressing. He took in the abundance of water which lapped over my toes causing my little felt pads to become very cold and uncomfortable under foot.

When he looked right into my face I could see evil. He looked me up and down and I felt embarrassed because my pyjamas didn't fit very well.

The water was quickly spreading from my bed space to the next one, helped on its way by the sergeant's boot. "You'll pay for this" he warned and then yelled very loudly, "What do you think this is? Bleedin' Noah's Ark?"

Somebody at that point made the grave mistake of laughing out loud which infuriated Tubbs all the more.

He strode over to Pomeroy and barked, "Since you find it all so amusing, you can get yourself over there and dry that mess up."

"I didn't laugh" Pomeroy began to stammer. "It wasn't me" but his comment fell on deaf ears.

Pomeroy came across to my bed space carrying a couple of felt pads which he tried, not very successfully, to dry up the water with. In the end he had a go at it with a face flannel whilst I did my best to soak up the water with a couple of old comics.

Ten minutes later, when most of us were blue with the cold, having dabbed at the floor with a variety of objects, Tubbs strutted majestically to where the light switches were. His face was a study as he surveyed us all.

"You will be on restricted privileges for the rest of the week" he announced.

"You will also have an extra bull night to get this billet up to standard ....." Anything further he might have said was interrupted by Ged. "Excuse me, Sergeant" he began.

"No I will not excuse you. I hate you" retorted Tubbs. "I want this whole floor re-polished tomorrow. Not just where the flood is. I shall expect .... ""Excuse me, Sergeant" Ged tried again and by the look of him I thought Tubbs was going to have a heart attack.

"I have already told you to be quiet" Tubbs snapped. "Right. I am going to put these lights out in fifteen seconds so everybody back in bed. At the double!" "But Sergeant ....." Ged looked desperate and quite unhappy now as he tried to get a word in with our late night intruder.

"For goodness sake, boy, will you go to bed or do you want me to charge you?"

Ged wavered but didn't move.

Tubbs now almost beside himself with rage marched into the middle of the room and tried to spin Ged round to face him. "What is wrong with you boy" he demanded, "What are you trying to say?"

"I'm sorry, Sergeant", Ged apologised, "I only wanted to say I think I have broken my toe!" Every eye gazed at poor old Ged's swollen and useless toe as with a groan he hopped a couple of paces nearer his bed.

"Why didn't you say so in the first place?" Tubbs wanted to know. "Stay here and I will go and contact the Orderly Officer and have you taken in." As he said these final words he distinguished all our lights in one go.

We all stumbled about the room to locate our beds and to avoid the ironing table and the fire bucket in the confusion. We knew it was more than our life's worth to put those lights back on again.

Then suddenly a piercing scream in the darkness.

"Ouch, Oh no! Oh no!" It was Ged. Someone had trodden on his toe in the darkness and he fainted.

CHAPTER 9

We had a saying at Padgate. "There's a right way to do something, a wrong way to do something and Padgate's way of doing something." In short if anything could be thrown into chaos or confusion, we had a knack of doing it. Getting Ged to the Sick Bay was no exception.

First the Orderly Officer called to see Ged and ask a hundred and one questions then disappeared. He was closely followed by a corporal who prodded the toe, asked further questions and actually committed the answers to paper. He left as promptly as the officer.

Tubbs returned to see if the Orderly Officer had called and we affirmed that he had. He complained that he wasn't going to get any sleep at all that night and left, but not before he bowled out one of the lads for allowing his cigarette to smoulder in an ash tray on top of his bed cover.

The sound of a car approaching gave us hope that Ged would be transported to the Sick Bay - but no. It was merely the Medical Officer who had been summoned to inspect the toe.

We all stood about looking helpless as the M.O. twisted and squeezed Ged's injured digit. The latter giving very loud groans at regular intervals.

The corporal who had entered the billet earlier returned from destination unknown. He gave the

M.O. a smart salute and said "Transport is on its way, Sir" The sound of another motor approaching gave us renewed hope that it might be an ambulance. Again we were to be disappointed. This time it was a couple of the military police with yet two more corporals that appeared on the scene.

Apparently the police had been told someone in our billet had been injured in a fight. They took a lot of convincing to see that was not the case. Jumping on a fire bucket seemed just too incredible. The four-some made various threats and promised to be looking out for us in the future before they left.

Almost another half an hour slipped by before the ambulance eventually arrived and two medics wandered in with a stretcher. Ged argued that he didn't want to go on a stretcher and started to hop on his good foot towards the door. He was swiftly intercepted by the medical orderlies who swiftly changed his vertical position to a horizontal one on the stretcher.

He waved with one weak arm as he disappeared in that position through the door to the awaiting ambulance.

The M.O. and corporal then left our hut to follow the ambulance in the M.O's car.

"What a bleedin' fiasco" observed our cockney inmate. "It has taken more than an hour and eight geezers to get old Ged into doc with a busted toe. Good fing he weren't bleedin' or he would have bled to death." He had summed up our thoughts beautifully.

We didn't see much of Ged after that night. He spent a few days in Casualty hobbling about in plaster, and he couldn't wear his boot so he was excused drill and parades. I know he spent a lot of time reading comics and was eventually sent home with a promise of recall to resume training at a later date.

A lot of us thought about damaging our feet to be excused marching but no one was brave enough, or daft enough, to put such a plan into effect.

One of our lads was of Flemish origin and we nick named him "Flemish Joe" from the first day he joined us. He went into graphic detail to tell us how his grandfather shot himself in the foot to be invalided out of some war.

"Did it get him out of the Army?" I foolishly enquired. "No" was the emphatic reply. "it only got him into the nick!" At that point we all decided it was best to go on marching.

After a whole week of foot slogging it was a great relief to sit at desks in a classroom.

The officer who addressed us looked a right twit. He was getting on for seven feet tall and thin like a bean pole. His beret stuck out flat on his head like a mushroom and he peered at us through very thick glasses. I wondered what he was doing in the RAF with such poor eye sight.

"Well chaps ..." he smiled sickly at us.

Oh no, I thought, do all officers have a plum in their mouths and get trained to address men with "Well Chaps".

"Well chaps" he repeated. "I am here to talk to you about R and I. Briefly that means Reliability and Initiative. I will give you the theory today and send you off on practice tomorrow."

"Goody, goody" murmured Jolly John sarcastically but rather too loudly. "Stand up that Airman" bleated the officer, craning his neck forward and trying hard to get our friend into focus. "What do you have to say for yourself?"

KEN STALLARD

"I am glad we are going on R and I, Sir" replied John with a facial expression which didn't entirely agree with his statement.

"Then I will tell you about it" the officer went on.

It soon became apparent that about a dozen of us were to be taken out into the wilds of Lancashire and left to find our way back to Camp without compass or asking anyone the way. That, in short, was to be the test of our reliability and initiative.

At first I was speechless when he went on to say that we would be sent out without any money or food. Even more so when he put me in charge of the operation.

I tried to explain that I was not very good at leadership but the officer would not listen. He was adamant that he had made his decision and I had to stay behind for a briefing whilst all the others got dismissed.

He repeated the no money and no food policy. We had to look for our first clue in some church yard and that would direct us to our next venue and the next clue.

It was an essential part of the exercise to return to the Camp with all the clues to prove we had completed the course. It was a case of covering nearly forty miles in a set time.

"Just imagine you have been parachuted behind enemy lines" he concluded.

"You cannot approach the enemy for food or information. It is imperative for you to be relied upon to return to base by using your initiative."

I didn't sleep a wink that night for worrying about the trek next day. I decided to ask all the others to help me so that we would work as a team. It had to be a joint effort rather than me being in charge. I was extremely grateful and relieved when all agreed to this strategy when the lorry dropped us off in some obscure village miles from anywhere the following day.

"There's a main road over there" observed Flemish Joe pointing across two or three fields. "If we make a bee line for that we should find a signpost which will give us some good idea where we are." This made sense and we all agreed as we clambered over a five barred gate into the first field.

An instant mooing stopped us all in our tracks. "I'm not going this way" uttered one. "Nor me" added another. "There's a bull over there!" "That's not a bull" I chided. "Those are cows. And they are harmless. Come on, let's get going."

When we were in mid field the cows began running toward us. I didn't mind because I was brought up the son of a farm labourer and spent most of my life on farms. Some of the town lads, however, took to their heels and ran beside the hedgerow which bordered the field. Unfortunately most of the group fled in opposite directions which slowed down progress considerably.

I picked up a large stick just in case a cow decided to get nasty. I thought some form of defence might be necessary but there was nothing to worry about. I went straight across the field to a gate on the far side and waited for the lads, who had made a wider detour, to catch up.

It was another scorching day and soon everybody was complaining about the heat. One lad started sneezing and said he was affected by pollen.

There was a lot of joking going on and quite a lot of larking about. One held a buttercup under his mate's chin and said "Hold on, Porky. Let me see if you like butter." Everybody laughed whilst another suggested making a daisy chain.

It was great to feel so free. It was a lovely day and just marvellous to be away from the all-seeing eyes of the military.

We crossed the next field and the next but by this time we had lost sight of the road. We stood in a cluster in the middle of the field and argued amongst ourselves regarding the direction that we should take. We decided to go straight ahead.

Two fields later one fellow slipped up on a cow pat and swore quite a bit. His mate took the micky out of him until he reacted by pulling a lump of the muck off his boot and threw it directly in his friend's face.

"You dirty devil" uttered the mate and chased his pal to the far side of the field, caught him up and forcefully rubbed his face in the grass.

By the time the rest of us had ambled across they had got up but met us with a sad pronouncement.

"We need to go straight on but we can't because there is a river and no-where to get across." Everybody stopped and looked at me for wisdom since I was supposed to be in charge.

"That's not a river" I said, "it's only a wide brook and if it's not too deep we can paddle across."

"Let's walk along the bank and see if there is a narrower part" and we shuffled along in a single line. "We are in luck" shouted a lad who had taken up the lead, "there's a bridge up here."

It wasn't actually a bridge but a kind of a wooden fence which forded the stream to give the cows a watering place. At that point the stream was quite wide and deep but at least if we stepped on to the fence, one at a time, we should be able to cross to the field on the other side. It looked quite sturdy.

Our leading lad stepped on to the fence and gingerly made his way across. "It is not very strong in the middle where the water is deepest" he called across "but you will be O.K. if you take it steady." One or two had a bit of trouble balancing and swaying on the bridge but they made it to the other side.

Six or seven of us, including myself, got across the stream with no trouble at all, but, you can always guarantee there will be one awkward soul in a pack.

Our heaviest lad, Ronnie, swung just a bit too heavy on the thin batons and he hollered as the entire thing fell forward. With a huge splash the fence and he with it went face down in the water. He came out gasping and coughing and swearing, complaining that the water had got into his watch and it would be ruined.

A cry of despair went up from the three lads who were now stranded on the wrong side of the brook. "How are we going to get across" one asked.

I suggested they walk further along the bank in the hope of finding another crossing place. A couple of them got fed up and eventually slipped off their boots, socks and trousers and waded across in their underpants. The other lad refused and ran further along the bank.

"Hey fellows, there is a bridge up here" he called and disappeared from view behind some trees. The next thing we knew he was running, red faced, to meet us on our side of the stream. Everybody groaned since he was the only one who had crossed with absolutely no bother at all.

We found the main road and trudged along it for miles. The good humoured banter had long disappeared as everyone got very hot, thirsty and hungry.

I was overwhelmed with all the complaints and threats about thirst until I decided to call at a house and ask for some water.

A very homely woman smiled when I told her about our plight. She filled a bucket with cold water and offered it to me with a milk jug. I took mouthfuls of the liquid refreshment and carried both jug and bucket out to the others.

"We are not supposed to talk to anyone" said Phil who was the most serious and quietest man among us. "We wouldn't go asking for water if we were behind enemy lines". "Oh, shut up!" this from Pomeroy. "We are just using our initiative for today."

We all drank deeply from the bucket and I resisted all the urging from the group to ask for some food as well.

Robin, who had said little so far, came out with a classic statement. "They told us on Camp that we mustn't drink water unless it has been boiled first. You can catch polio from drinking un-boiled water!" We ignored him and trudged on.

Like so many of those hot summer days, this one turned dark and then the thunder storm came. As the first drops of rain fell we all ran to shelter under some trees; ignoring the possibility of being struck by lightning. We stayed under those trees for ages but the rain just got worse.

Some time later a couple of the lads started walking off into the rain without so much as a word, The rest of us followed like sheep.

Now utterly miserable, tired and hungry, we hoped for some form of transport. Somebody suggested splitting up into pairs and to try hitch hiking back to Camp. We reasoned that some driver might be going to Warrington and from there we knew the way to Padgate.

Robin tried to tell us that we were still in enemy territory and would be in trouble for hitching a lift. He was soon told that initiative was the order of the day and if he wanted to walk all the way to Padgate alone then he was most welcome.

"Quick, here's a bus coming" yelled Ron and started to run towards it with the rest of us in hot pursuit.

I cried out that we had no money for fares but no one seemed to listen or care.

Ron flagged down the driver and jumped on the open end of the double deck bus as it stopped. "Hang on, mate" he said to the somewhat surprised conductor, "there's a few more coming."

There were only about half a dozen passengers on the bus and they stared at us.

None of them smiled or made any comment. Just sat and stared. "Don't get sitting on the seats with those soaking clothes" said the conductor, "you can stand in the aisle."

Where's the bus going?" Ron went on as the conductor looked puzzled. He gave a single word reply. "WIGAN."

We groaned in unison knowing that Wigan was in the opposite direction to our destination. The conductor adjusted his ticket machine and looked expectantly for us to state our intentions.

"Stop the bus" mumbled Ron, "we want to get off."

With a huge sigh the conductor pressed the bell and the bus stopped to allow a dozen very wet dishevelled airmen to leave the vehicle. At this point the rest of the passengers began to smile.

The rain had turned to drizzle as we left the bus and started walking again. We were very discouraged to find ourselves walking back along the route we had just rode over. Tempers got short and we began to bicker and grumble at each other.

Then for me came the final straw. Robin sidled up to me and said "Have you seen Bunce? Where is he?"

I looked around and counted up our number. Bunce was missing! "Oh, no", I groaned. "Has anyone seen Bunce?"

"He was one of the first on the bus and dashed upstairs" said Ron. "Come to think of it, I didn't see him get off I reckon he is still on the bus and don't realise we are gone."

I looked back only to find that the bus was now out of sight and there was no sign of Bunce anywhere.

Reliability and initiative! I could not be relied upon. Not to actually lose an airman! I felt as though I was in a living nightmare that never had an ending.

CHAPTER 10

"When we get back to Camp without Bunce, how are we going to account for his absence?" I had called the group to a standstill at the side of the road and decided it was about time for us to pool our ideas.

"How are YOU going to explain, not us!" said Phil rather pointedly. "It was a stupid idea to get on the bus in the first place."

"Alright, big head!" remonstrated Ron who had been responsible for the bus stopping to pick us up. "Have you got any better ideas?"

"I think we would do better to split up in pairs and hitch hike" said Pomeroy.

"Yes. I agree" chipped in Robin. "The first lot to get back could get someone to come out and pick up the rest of us."

"Oh yeah" Pomeroy continued assuming a very falsetto voice, "that shows great initiative. What do we do? Wait for Daddy's yacht?"

"Let's start thumbing" went on Flemish Joe and broke up the group by striding off alone.

It was a full ten minutes before the first car came along. We stopped and stared and most of us stuck our thumbs up. The driver drove by as though we were invisible. Several vehicles that followed ignored us too. We were too intimidating, too many and too soaking wet for anyone to want us on board.

A signpost indicated that we were drawing near to a village. Somebody suggested we find a telephone kiosk and make a reverse charge to the Camp. It sounded a good idea except no-one wanted to take on the responsibility for making the call.

Here we were in hands breadth of communication with the outside world.

Surely there must be someone we could share our plight with.

One of our lads was called Dennis and he smiled as he thought he had a brain wave. Drastic situations calls for drastic solutions and he outlined a cunning plan.

Den explained. "Why don't one of us lie down in the road and we can dial 999 and say he is ill. Somebody will have to come out in an emergency and pick us up."

A ray of hope appeared on one or two faces whilst some groaned. Robin summed up the thoughts of us all by declaring, "They would send an ambulance and only pick up the one who is lying in the road. Then when they discover he is not really ill, he will be in a lot of trouble and so will the rest of us".

"At least it would show initiative" butted in Ron, "they couldn't accuse us of not trying".

Finally we decided the whole charade could get too complicated and just ambled away from the 'phone box, grumbling as we went.

"I can see a shop down there" called Phil who had climbed a steep bank to get a better view of what lie ahead. "Shall we call there and see if we can get something to eat for free?"

"You'll be lucky" I murmured as he, taking on a sudden spurt of energy, ran down the bank and made off for the shop. He went in alone.

The rest of us pressed our noses up against the shop window and peered inside.

Phil appeared to be pressing our case for nourishment but we could see the old chap behind the counter shaking his head.

We watched as Phil continued talking but it was impossible to hear a word.

Then I spotted the man go to an inner door and open it. At this point my heart missed a beat. I was just hoping the old chap wasn't going out of the shop just in case Phil decided to help himself to some free stock.

Almost in answer to my thoughts the shop keeper stopped in the doorway and called to someone outside. A woman appeared in the shop but we couldn't see what she was doing because her back was toward us. The next thing we knew Phil was accepting something from her.

It was a jubilant Phil that emerged from the shop with four over ripe bananas and a packet of biscuits.

"The old man wouldn't give us anything" he began, "then he remembered he had some bananas which he thought he couldn't sell and he called to his missus to bring them in. I gave her a sob story and chatted her up for a packet of biscuits".

Phil was most thoughtful and generous. He opened the biscuits and solemnly handed us one and a half biscuit each. "You can share out those bananas between you" he said, thrusting three that were most over ripe into my hands. "I deserve a whole one for using my initiative."

We stopped just long enough to share out the frugal meal. Willie volunteered to break up the bananas into pieces for handing out until stopped by Phil.

"Not with those filthy hands" he chided, "you ain't washed your hands since you got that cow pat off your boots."

Half an hour later found us still in a group chatting merrily away as we trudged downhill. The village was now behind us and we had given up all hope of getting a lift. The rain had stopped and our clothes were drying on our bodies.

The sudden appearance of a large old coal lorry took us by surprise since it bore down upon us with the wheezing of its horn. A young curly headed fellow leaned out of the cab window and called to us as he drew alongside and stopped.

"You haven't got very far" he laughed, "can't you get a lift?"

"Where are you going mate?" asked Ron, "any chance of giving us a lift?"

The young driver explained that his parents kept the shop in the village. It was his mother who had given Phil the biscuits. "If you all want to get on the back of the lorry" he said, "I can give you a lift for about five miles." Thankfully we all hurried to the back of the lorry and leapt on to the long flat surface which supported nine or ten bags of coal. Some of us sat on the side of the vehicle and let our legs dangle over the edge, others like me chose to stand and lean against the bags of coal for support. The air ripped through our clothes and helped them to dry.

It wasn't the most comfortable of rides but at least we were covering ground at a pace. Every mile done was a mile less to do.

Our driver dropped us off at a coal yard adjacent to a small country railway station, whereupon, we weighed up the pros and cons of continuing our trek to Warrington by train.

The station was deserted but finally we found a railway man in a small goods shed. He had an up turned bicycle in front of him and was mending a puncture in the tyre. He told us that trains from that station were few and far between but he gave us the best news of the day.

We were directed to a lonely house some way from this second village. It appeared to be one of the largest dwelling places in those parts and on one side of it was a large paddock with several horses in it. On the other side of the house was a big concrete yard with several large open fronted barns. Two single deck buses occupied a couple of the barns and a third bus stood by a small green painted gate that led to the front garden.

The owner of the house ran a small taxi business and contract buses to convey children to and fro local schools. One of the schools was on the outskirts of Warrington.

Our friendly railway man had advised us to call at this house. It might be possible, he led us to believe, to cadge a lift on a school bus on its inward journey to pick up the school children.

At the side of the house we found a man pouring a quantity of diesel from a large drum into a metal can. He looked far from happy as I led our little group to where he was standing.

I explained that we were on a military exercise and were anxious to return to Padgate. He listened but never said a word. I went on to say how exhausted we were and we would very much appreciate his help with our test. He still said nothing and I was beginning to wonder if he was deaf and dumb.

At the third attempt I appealed for a lift for us on his bus. It was only then that he spoke. "It's not my bus" he said, "I'm only the driver. You will have to go and see the gaffer".

I decided it would probably be better for me to go and see the boss alone as a representative of a group of airmen. I reasoned that it would not be so off putting as to be presented with a bunch of wet coal streaked and dirty lot of individuals. We looked a sorry sight. I sought out the Goodman of the house but it was the lady wife who responded to my knock.

I explained our circumstances and the extremely pleasant lady invited me to step inside the hall way. I heard her call her husband from some room at the back.

When the bus owner arrived he gave me a long hard look. His eyes opened wide when I repeated all that I had said to his driver. At first he shook his head and put forth objections. It was true that the bus was going near Warrington but there were rules. "It's a matter of insurance" he said, "there would be trouble and no compensation if any of you got injured in an accident".

What happened next was nothing but an act of God. I merely said "I am a Christian and I'll pray that we don't get an accident".

The silence for a minute was electric. Then the attitude of the man standing before me changed completely. He smiled, grabbed my hand and called me "Brother". This was followed by a lot of questions about my Christian persuasion. He liked what he heard and promptly agreed that we should travel on the bus. He now considered he was doing both God and us a service which I readily agreed.

Any further conversation was cut short by Phil coming to seek us out. He had plucked up courage to ask if he could use the toilet. One by one we all used the loo as the owner of the bus went to speak to the driver. It was very touching to see each of the group being polite and on their best behaviour. There wasn't a single swear word to be heard as we said our goodbyes to these Christian folk.

We spread out on the bus, glad at last to be able to rest our weary feet. We were going in the right direction and, hopefully, it shouldn't be too long before we get back to Camp.

I closed my eyes and leaned back in the seat and reflected on our position. We had not found one single clue. Furthermore we had broken every rule regarding the reliability and initiative test. Not only that, but I had lost an airman into the bargain. I thought back to the day I first joined the RAF and waited for the bus in my own village to take me to Oxford. My Mum's friend had wandered by and said, "It's not all a bed of roses" and I was finding her prophecy had come true.

I decided to make the most of the luxury which the school bus offered. There was plenty of time to get back to Camp where no doubt I would pay dearly for the misdeeds of the day.

CHAPTER 11

The driver of the school bus did not take us right into Warrington as we had hoped but dropped us off at a large mixed school some way outside of town.

We shuffled off the bus looking more like a bunch of geriatrics than a fine body of young fit airmen.

The road into town was very busy but by now we had abandoned all hope of getting a lift and trudged on in single file.

All were silent except Ron who persisted in whistling "You are my sunshine" over and over again. The more Robin moaned about it, the more Ron did it to annoy. Like a group of small children we all started to whistle, each of us trying to outdo the other in volume. This brought a lot of stares from folk that passed by. We must have looked a grim sight as we walked in a line, looking decidedly the worse for wear, coal streaked but whistling.

Ron, who started the whistling epidemic, suddenly went silent and looked serious. I took little notice until he approached me, presumably because I was in charge, and announced that he wanted to go to a toilet. No sooner had he put his thoughts into words then most of the others wanted a toilet as well.

After another couple of miles further on we still couldn't find a toilet. We were in a residential area now with large private houses and gardens on each side of the road. We passed a couple of surgeries and churches but still no sign of a public convenience.

Ron kept grimacing and by now was getting quite agitated. He started to get very cross and not appreciating the wise cracks that most of the lads were giving him. He made his feelings very plain and said that he was going to use one of the private gardens as a toilet and started looking for a garden that had a wall in front of it rather than a hedge. When he said "has anyone got any paper?" I felt quite alarmed especially as we didn't have any paper between the lot of us.

All of a sudden Ron announced "O.K. fellas, that's it. I can't wait any longer" and promptly disappeared through two large gates which were situated in the middle of a six foot wall. Appearing above the wall but otherwise obscured were several very tall trees.

The property adjacent had a very long low wall and we all sat on it waiting for Ron to re-appear.

Within a couple of minutes we heard two loud voices from within the walled property. First a woman's shrill voice followed by a roar from a man. It was obvious that this couple had found they had an unwelcome visitor.

We all got off the wall in unison, our eyes riveted on the gates of next door.

Ron dashed through them like some Olympic sprinter, tugging his trousers up his thighs as he did so.

"Beat it" he called as he hopped and skipped past us, still pulling at his trousers, and we were quick to do as we were told. We chased him down the street for about a quarter of a mile. At least the escapade seemed to take our minds off the immediate need to find a loo.

Our attempt to equal the four minute mile seemed to restore our sense of humour. It was either that or the fact that we were coming into the town.

Warrington and the sight of a cake shop never looked so inviting but, sadly, we could only look at the cakes in the window because we didn't have money between us to be able to buy any.

Phil, still fresh from his success at the village shop decided to try his luck at obtaining some free cakes. He entered the shop with a beaming smile but emerged with a scowl. The young girl assistant had giggled at his request for free samples, but, the ticking off he received from the Manageress meant a very final "No! We scolded Phil for his lack of success. Not because we thought he had failed but to draw the attention of two pretty young ladies who were standing at the bus stop. It worked and very soon they opened a conversation with us.

In most groups of men you find one who is considered to be the super stud and in our group it just had to be Keith. He was tall, tanned and certainly good looking. His short blond hair was for ever in contact with his comb.

Keith was super fit with great muscles, the envy of us all, and he sported the bluest of blue eyes. Nice teeth and a dimple in his chin went along with his charm and self-confidence. He made the most of the situation and chatted up the girls by asking their names.

Within five minutes he had found their names were Cathy and Carol, where they worked, where they lived, what music they liked and that both of them were fond of dancing. He introduced the rest of us with a wave of the hand simply as "this lot are my mates from the RAF at Padgate." The girls just stared and giggled.

Keith didn't waste much time in getting to the point. With his usual charm he quipped, "Which of you good ladies are going to buy me a cream bun then?" After some more giggling from Carol she produced some coins and stared at them in the palm of her hand. "Yes, I will buy you a cake" she offered, but before Keith could get his hand on her money, Cathy broke in. "Hang on a minute" she said as we all looked on expectantly.

Fishing in a little green handbag she produced another handful of coins and made a quick calculation. Turning to Carol she said, "If we put our money together we could buy a couple of boxes of cheap jam tarts. They come six to a box and they could all have one." I thought that was very good reasoning and we nodded in approval.

As we munched on our jam tart our faith in human nature was restored even though our hunger was just as acute.

The arrival of the girl's bus brought any further conversation to an end but not before Keith had got the telephone number of the shop where Carol said she worked. On the long walk back to Padgate he spoke of nothing else but his fascination to women and boasted of his conquests with them.

The charmer made out that he had joined the RAF to escape the responsibility of caring for a pregnant girlfriend back home. He had a good imagination and was always contradicting his colourful stories. It was obvious that he thought he was God's gift to women and Romeo and Casanova all rolled into one.

Keith's fantasies were alright but the charm that he switched on to the opposite sex was irritating to most of us. We were not going to admit it but deep down we were just plain jealous about his technique.

An hour later we were still trying to put the world right as we made our leisurely walk to Padgate. When the lights of the Camp came into view we sighed and some cheered.

How happy and relieved we were to see the guard standing at the main gate. He grinned as we sauntered by.

The lights at our billet had never seemed so welcoming but by now we were starving and not able to get any food. Breakfast seemed such a long way off. We all needed a shower but the first thought was to crash out on the pit - the common term for bed and get some shut eye.

"I don't believe it!" this from Pomeroy who was first in the billet. He stood staring as we came in behind him. There propped up in his bed, looking clean and pristine in his pyjamas was Bunce! Everybody gathered round Bunce's bed and started talking at once. "When did you get back? How did you manage to get home before us? We were very eager to hear his story but I was personally very relieved to see him there. He obviously had come to no harm and was none the worse for getting lost.

The conductor had allowed Bunce to stay on the bus when he explained the reason why he had no money. "I have got a lad like you in the Navy" he said, "I would like to think someone would give him a helping hand in a desperate situation."

Bunce left the bus at Wigan and headed for a petrol station where he asked several drivers, who stopped for petrol, if they could give him a lift en route for Warrington. An elderly couple did take him as far as a roundabout and advised him to stand there and thumb a lift until someone else came along to pick him up.

Two young fellows in a small van soon stopped to give him a lift. When they opened the back door of the van he noticed there was a lot of wood and implements inside. One of the fellows very kindly pushed the bits and pieces to one side explaining they were carpenters returning from a job.

The ride was not very comfortable and Bunce was covered in sawdust when he was dropped off a few miles further on. Almost immediately a lorry driver picked him up and took him right into Warrington.

It must have been Bunce's lucky day because the lorry driver gave him two cheese sandwiches and a very generous swig from his large flask of tea. Bunce had used his initiative to explain his circumstances and the fact he was very hungry and thirsty.

For the last leg of the journey Bunce had got a lift from Warrington right to Padgate by one of the RAF officers and his wife. The officer said he would not have picked him up if he had known he was on a reliability and initiative test earlier. Bunce only let that slip out when they arrived at the main gate of the Camp.

Buncie just couldn't stop laughing when we told him all about our adventures of the day. In comparison he had done very little walking since we last saw him boarding the bus. He had got back five hours before us in time to get his tea.

I was quaking in my boots when the goofy officer and a training sergeant came in to the classroom the following morning. As leader on the R and I test it was up to me to produce the clues, evidence of where we had been and a full report of the day's activities.

We were flabbergasted when the officer and sergeant burst out laughing. We were not in trouble at all. What happened to us was nothing more than was expected. They told us some extremely funny stories about former airmen and how they had fared much worse than us on previous tests. We had a mild telling off just for not finding the very first venue and clue. The clue would have put us on the right track for a far shorter journey and took us through an orchard where we could have picked as much fruit as we wanted.

"If you had adopted your methods and strategy behind real enemy lines you would not be with us today" the officer remarked, "think on that! Never mind, tomorrow we leave for Frodsham Moor and a few days living under canvas. There will be much harder and stricter tests for you there. If you work exceptionally hard you may pick up on points you lost yesterday".

We were encouraged to pack our kit bags with all the necessities required on the full military exercise and to get to bed early. Goofy officer said we would need all our energy and stamina for the forthcoming vigours of Frodsham Moor. Having said this he instructed the sergeant to dismiss the class.

Conscious of the fact that we had to make up some points for our miserable performance on the R and I test, I decided to ask the sergeant how many points we had been awarded on it.

"None whatsoever" he replied quite briskly. "If you don't shine, and I mean shine very brightly on the Frodsham Exercise, I can see you training and re-training at Padgate for the next twelve months".

I made up my mind there and then that was never going to happen. Whatever the cost I just had to make Frodsham a success.

CHAPTER 12

My first impression of Frodsham Moor was that it was much bigger that I had imagined.

We arrived in a convoy of three ton lorries which conveyed the men, tents and all the gear required for a few days exercise.

I had never put up a tent in my life and I was detailed along with Robin and another dozy lad to strike our first canvas home. Not one of us had a clue so we copied our neighbours in laying out canvas, poles, pegs and what seemed like miles of rope. There were ground sheets and bases for beds and some dirty looking sleeping bags.

Stacked beside the layers of canvas were piles of tin plates and mugs and some strange square metal things with a handle called mess tins. I was horrified at first because I thought they were to be used for toilet purposes. How relieved I was to discover that in fact these were simply a dual purpose plate and bowl to use when the food was dished out.

The very first time I used my mess tin was for stew. I did think I might have been allowed to wash it out before the cook spooned out dollops of semolina in the same tin. No wonder they were called mess tins. I was told there was a shortage of water on Camp and one would get use to main course and desert in the same tin and sometimes at the same time. After all, we were told, these were war conditions.

Robin made a start on erecting our tent. He stood in the middle of the field holding a pole in the vertical position. From a distance it would have been difficult to tell which was the pole and which was Robin.

Our third lad, Alan, lifted a heavy piece of canvas which looked like the main part of the tent and threw it over Robin and the pole simultaneously. All we could see was a flurry of arms and hear a lot of muffled shouting from the depths of the canvas. Robin threw it aside and emerged very red faced and breathless.

I suggested erecting two poles a short distance apart and have another go at throwing the large piece of canvas over both of them. I reasoned that it would give us more room underneath. Unfortunately when I threw the heavy canvas over the poles they both collapsed under the weight of it. Alan scolded Robin for not putting the poles deep enough into the ground and we had another go.

At the second attempt of getting the canvas over the two poles one fell down so we delegated Robin to get underneath to help support the weight.

"What time is the unveiling?" asked Corporal Brown with great sarcasm as he came across to where we were, and then punctuated it with, "Oh no!. It just had to be you!" as Robin disentangled himself from the folds.

"What's that supposed to be?" he went on. "A wigwam in a typhoon or part of the Siegfried Line?" We all smiled but said nothing.

Then with a roar that made our ears ring the corporal called to Pomeroy. "Pomeroy, Pomeroy, come and show these three wise men how to put a tent up".

With a lot of muttered complaint Pomeroy inspected our tent which was all out of shape and spread eagled over the two poles. "I've seen better scarecrows" he said and yanked the poles out of the ground.

The three of us watched as Pomeroy erected our tent single handed in a very short space of time. He was very cocky about it. "That is the way it should be done" he said with a very superior air and a wave of his hand. I was generous with my thanks, appreciation and admiration at his skill. I said all the things I knew he wanted to hear because I thought it was very likely that we might need his assistance again before the course was through.

Tubbs wandered by with a corporal I had not seen before and smiled as he watched us putting our sleeping bags and kit inside the tent. It was just big enough to sleep three of us with very little space for anything else. I was just a little bit mystified why Tubbs and the corporal still stood some distance away but were watching us very intently.

At last our little home was complete. Three bed bases with our sleeping bags on them lined up side by side with our kitbags placed as pillows. Beside each bed we placed our mess tin, mug and irons for easy access. We knew we had to keep the tent tidy to conserve space.

A large shadow fell across our tent flap as Tubbs peered inside. "Is there anyone at home?" he asked sweetly and I replied lamely "Yes, Sergeant".

We were instructed to step outside and Alan, Robin and I emerged like Winking, Blinking and Nod! "Right fellows, are you happy with the tent now that it is up?" enquired Tubbs and I spoke for all of us when I said we were. "Good" he continued, "then you can take it down again right away".

The three of us looked at the sergeant in a kind of a daze. "Go on", he urged, "dismantle it". We could see he meant it.

Several of the lads drew near to watch with amusement as Robin, Alan and I brought our possessions out of the tent. We had difficulty in fathoming out how to erect it, now we were having more trouble in dismantling the thing. The pegs wouldn't come out of the ground for a start.

Little by little and with words of advice from our onlookers, under the careful scrutiny of Tubbs and the corporal, our tent ended up flat on the floor.

"Now let me see you erect it again" the sergeant addressed us not unkindly. After three false starts and with a little help from Tubbs himself we did manage to get the tent upright and pegged. It appeared to lean more to the east than the west but he said it would do. Thankfully we arranged the interior again although we didn't seem to have so much room this time. By this time I was feeling very tired and I was looking forward to sleeping in it but I soon discovered that it wasn't going to be that night.

Just before it got dark, the corporal we had seen earlier with Tubbs and whose name we discovered was Phillips, introduced another new officer, Flying Officer Taffy Jones from South Wales.

Jones called us all together and then split us up into two groups for an all-night exercise. There was the red team and the yellow team. I was with the red group and was handed a red sash to wear like the Order of the Garter. It had to go over my left shoulder, across my chest and ended up on my right hip. Corporal Phillips duly handed out yellow sashes to the other team.

Four lads were detailed to erect a platform in the middle of the moor. It had a wooden post at each corner and was roped off. It looked exactly like a boxing ring. I thought we would have to go sparring but it was not to be.

"That which looks like a boxing ring" explained Jones as though in answer to my thoughts, "is a Concentration Camp! You get in there at your peril". We all stared and waited for further information.

"Reds are the enemy of the yellows" he went on. "Reds will line up on that side of the moor ..." he pointed north, "... and yellows will line up on that side", he pointed south. "We shall be doing that at midnight exactly. Corporal Phillips will now outline the object of the exercise".

"You will all lay flat on your stomachs" the corporal began, "then quietly you will wriggle through the long grass until you meet someone in the middle of the moor who is wriggling towards you from the opposite direction. That will be the enemy. Someone from the other side who has a different coloured sash than you. Is that clear so far? Nobody said anything so he continued.

"Now the object is for you to take at least one prisoner from the enemy. You do that by seeing him before he sees you. When you spot him, you jump on his back, put your arm up in the air and shout MY PRISONER! You will then take the prisoner you have captured and put him in the Concentration Camp, namely the boxing ring and you stay with him there. Any questions?"

"Yes" volunteered Pomeroy. "Why are we wearing sashes? No-one is going to see them in the dark."

The officer sounded exasperated now and answered on the corporal's behalf.

"The different colours will determine which side took most prisoners by morning light" he said. "Remember take prisoners only but make sure you yourselves are not taken prisoner". At this point Tubbs waddled up and told us to get some rest and ordered us to be back at the boxing ring to play the silly game at a quarter to midnight.

At the appointed time reds and yellows inter-mingled until we were declared "enemies" and delegated to take up our positions on the opposite sides of the moor. It was extremely dark and ideal for the purpose it was supposed to serve.

I lay on my stomach at my end of the moor and then had what I thought was a good idea. I would only wriggle a little way forward. I would then lie completely still on the same spot and not move. I was not going to be brave and worry about catching the enemy. I was just going to concentrate on not letting the enemy catch me. I put my plan into effect.

I felt very nervous as I lay for some time on the same bit of ground. It felt hard and a bit damp and I could hear insects buzzing in the grass. There was an eerie silence and my nerves tingled as I knew men were out there somewhere in the darkness. I yawned and wanted to sneeze but resisted the urge. To make myself more comfortable I wriggled forward about another six feet and decided to stay there. I lay like that motionless for well over an hour.

I felt more tense by the minute as I waited for something to happen. It didn't. I gently moved each limb to stop getting numb as I began to feel cold. Then it happened! I heard the breathing first and then very slight movement not more than three feet away from me. My heart started to pound and I felt myself shaking all over. My eyes tried to pierce the darkness and the area from whence the sound came. I held my breath and listened but all was silent.

Then I heard a sudden intake of breath and distinct movement directly in front of my head. If I didn't move quick he would crawl right on top of me. As I just saw the form of the man within arm's reach, I made a snap decision and sprang on his back with full force.

"MY PRISONER!" I yelled at the top of my voice and threw one arm in the air.

I just vaguely heard the hoarse shout "MY PRISONER! MY PRISONER!" twice as a ton weight seemed to descend on my back. All the wind was forced out of my body as I was sandwiched between the fellow I had pounced on and the guy who had pounced on top of me.

I struggled to my knees and with some difficulty stood upright as my prisoner, cursing wildly, got to his feet. I just wanted the ground to open and swallow me up when I discovered my prisoner was the officer in charge of my side.

The big chap who had just jumped on us was one of the enemy. He very unceremoniously dragged the officer and myself to the Concentration Camp as his prisoners.

I wasn't quite sure whether my officer was going to kill me or have a stroke. He kept shouting and swearing and protesting.

There we stood like a couple of lemons in the middle of the boxing ring. It was extremely embarrassing because we were the only two prisoners of the entire night. A fact neither of us ever lived down during our days at Padgate.

"I'll get even with you" the officer threatened time and time again. Little did he know then that things were going to get very much worse for both of us.

CHAPTER 13

The second day at Frodsham Moor promised to be more entertaining than the first. We were awakened from our slumbers by someone shouting "Wakey, wakey!" at the top of their voice. The shouting was accompanied by a continuous banging on a saucepan with a spoon or some similar object.

Figures began to stumble their way out of canvas folds. The sight of forty or fifty men clad only in their underpants is not the ideal sight to greet a new day.

There were a lot of oaths and swear words uttered everywhere as the lads tried to shave with cold water and blunt razor blades. Many a tender cheek or chin got nicked and the spots got covered with little pieces of toilet paper.

Breakfast was a choice of burnt sausages or burnt porridge. Lying prostrate in the bottom of the mess tin one couldn't tell which was the porridge or the sausage.

Hygiene was not at its best at Frodsham Moor either. We wiped our mess tins clean with grass and wore the same sweaty shirt and trousers day after day.

After breakfast the squadron was split up into different flights of men, approximately eight to ten men in each flight. A senior NCO was put in charge of each flight and we were ordered to assemble for roll call and to be given our exercise details for the day.

Each flight had to do yet another Reliability and Initiative test. I knew I had to do well since my track record hitherto wasn't very good.

I found myself put in a group which had to make a derrick seat for conveying men from one high vantage point to another. I couldn't fathom out what the Warrant Officer was trying to explain. I just hoped that all would be revealed when we reached the venue and assembled the thing.

The entire squadron was taken to a very high field. Its banks were very steep, almost vertical, and dropped to a narrow roadway about thirty feet below. A similar field with deep banks could be seen on the other side of the road.

A row of trees lined the top of the banks and overshadowed the road which ran beneath.

One group of our men was ordered to make a bridge merely consisting of three ropes. The bridge had to be secured to a tree on our bank, stretched tightly across the road and anchored firmly in one of the trees on the opposite side.

I watched, fascinated, as three airmen shinned up a tree, each carrying a rope.

These were very securely tied to the branches and the ends left to dangle down into the road.

Airman on the bank on the other side came to retrieve the dangling ends of the rope. They threw them up to their comrades to secure them on the trees on their side. After a very long time, and several adjustments, the ropes were ready for use.

My stomach somersaulted what I saw what was required of that bunch of lads.

One rope spanned the drop as a kind of a tight rope and the other two ropes were positioned as hand rails.

Arguments broke out between the men as each one refused to be the first to walk the rope. It had all the appearance of being a tight rope over a ravine. It looked very high indeed. I could see that if one lost his balance, or missed his footing, he would fall a very long way to that hard road beneath.

As in answer to my thoughts a very young Pilot Officer appeared on the scene.

He ordered several men to take up positions in the road beneath the suspended ropes. They held a large catch sheet in their hands similar to those used by firemen. Whoever walked the tightrope had the small consolation of knowing that he might, just might, be caught in the sheet if he fell.

The young Pilot Officer started shouting orders in his posh university voice commencing with the inevitable "Right chaps!". "I want one airman at a time to step on to the bottom rope. Place your hands on the other two guide ropes, and in your own time, walk across to the other side".

"Who does he think he's kidding?" muttered one of the lads at my elbow. "If he ain't careful it looks like the whole lot will come down and smack him in the kisser!" Nobody moved. "Did I make myself clear?" the officer enquired impatiently.

More arguing broke out amongst the group huddling beneath the tree. Clearly there was no volunteer for the first walk.

The Pilot Officer cupped his hands to his mouth to give his order more impetus.

"Bunce, get on that rope", he hollered. More arguing broke out but Bunce was pushed up against the trunk of the tree.

A scapegoat had been found and the other lads were determined that Bunce was going to make the first walk.

Taking plenty of time, Bunce gingerly climbed the tree. When he reached the ropes he looked terrified and hesitated to put his foot on the lower one. "It looks a long way down from here" he moaned.

"Yeah" bellowed Pomeroy from my side, "but don't worry old son; the worse you can do is break your bleedin' neck".

"Shut up, Pomeroy" snapped the officer, and then turning to Bunce who was still dithering up the tree, he called a single word - "Proceed!" Bunce did not proceed. He wavered, swayed a bit from side to side, then very carefully put one foot on the lower rope and quickly withdrew it again when it sagged a little.

"Go on Buncie, shut your eyes and step out" called the unquenchable Pomeroy only to evoke the wrath of the Pilot Officer.

"One more word out of you, Pomeroy" he fumed, "and you will replace Bunce on the rope!" That did the trick and Pomeroy was rendered speechless.

We all stood looking up at Bunce in silence, thankful it wasn't us who had to make that maiden crossing.

Nothing happened for some time and the officer got impatient. "For goodness sake, Bunce" he called, "we haven't got all day. Get a move on!" More advice and instructions followed from the onlookers.

Bunce placed his foot gingerly on the lower rope and gripped the top two for all he was worth. The bottom rope sagged again beneath his weight but Bunce managed to leave his foot in place. It was some minutes before he ventured to take his second step and then his third.

The Pilot Officer is now appearing to be pleased with Bunce's efforts and his orders are replaced by encouragement.

"That's right lad", he shouted, "guide yourself along with your hands and don't keep looking down. Fix your eyes on the tree on the other side".

We noticed that Bunce had decided not to take steps as in walking but chose to slide his right foot first along the rope. His left foot slid along just about eighteen inches behind.

We all held our breath as we watched Bunce suspended high above the road.

Those holding the catch sheet below were moving along underneath him.

A few more minutes and Bunce managed to reach the safety of the tree on the other side of the road. A great cheer went up and he beamed from ear to ear. "It was great" he had the audacity to yell, "who is coming over next?"

The rest of the morning was spent in watching several reluctant airmen crossing the abyss. One took fright and froze mid-way across. All the coaxing in the world could not convince him to make a move and in the end he dropped into the catch sheet and amazingly was caught.

A second lad got rope burns on his hands and one missed his footing and plummeted into the waiting sheet.

Over dinner I remarked that I was glad I wasn't in that particular flight. I didn't have a head for heights and tightrope walking was not for me.

Wilkins promptly filled me with more than a little concern. Our task was to make a derrick seat he said. It would be a similar exercise with ropes suspended between the trees. The only difference would be that a seat would be used to lower us over the ravine instead of walking over it. It was just as dangerous because the seat could slip or even disintegrate.

After lunch our flight was duly kitted out with a mass of ropes, a peculiar shaped piece of a wooden log and some metal hoisting wheels, pulleys, nails and other gadgets.

A couple of sergeants showed us how to fix the ropes to the pulley wheels and to anchor the hoist wheels to the trees. The ropes ran over little wheels contained within a bigger wheel.

I still couldn't see where the derrick seat fitted into all of this.

The wooden log was securely lashed in the centre by two ropes; the ends of which ran through another pulley wheel which was attached to a rope that crossed the ravine.

I soon discovered that the log which dangled served as the seat. I never did discover what the word derrick meant. I could see the funny side because all the ropes lashed together with a log dangling from them was an amazing replica of some gallows. I imagined "Derrick" might have been the man they hanged.

Each airman was expected to be lowered and rolled across the ravine whilst sitting astride the log. He was expected to hold tight to the rope that was attached to his seat to the overhanging rope above him. Unlike the tightrope he had nothing to do but sit on the log and be winched across that awesome drop. Each airman would be completely dependent on his mate who operated the pulley and lowered the seat.

I volunteered to operate the pulley which looked
simple enough. In that way I would keep two feet firmly
on the ground and not go aloft on a man-made chair lift.

The rest of my flight was thrust into a disorderly
queue awaiting their turn to be winched out and across
the road. The Pilot Officer assured us that all would be
well as long as we didn't look down.

The log was tested for durability and the pulley wheel
for rope clearance. I was instructed to go steady with the
feed of the rope so that the seat wouldn't bounce,
become entangled with the down rope, or, take the
airman across with too much speed so that he crashed
into the opposite tree.

I listened intently to all the officer said. I thought this
was my opportunity to do a good job and compensate
for my earlier failures.

Just as the first airman was about to sit on the log and
I held the rope steady, a very fat Squadron Leader
waddled up. He looked very hot and was mopping his
brow with a handkerchief.

He scrutinised the log, peered at the pulley wheel and
grunted. The rope was then taken out of my hand and,
for one awful moment, I thought he was going to offer
to lower me over the edge and winch me across the
ravine.

"Very good" he cooed, "you can winch me across!"
Our sergeant looked horrified and made a quick check
on all the working parts that came into operation. "Be
careful" he hissed in my ear as I took up the strain on the
rope as the Squadron Leader sat astride the log.

Very slowly and carefully I released my end of the
winch rope. The log bobbed forward. The officer in
charge of our flight found it necessary to call out

instructions for me to follow. "Right hand up, left hand down a bit".

The fat perspiring Squadron Leader looked a bit foolish astride the log and clinging to his rope. He looked far too big and heavy on such a small piece of wood but he appeared quite at ease and didn't stop smiling.

"Give him stick, Ken" whispered one of my mates with an impish grin which I chose to ignore. I was now engaged on some serious stuff.

I eased off more rope and winched the Squadron Leader clear of the branches of our trees as he headed for the open road.

I was getting a little concerned because the rope wasn't running through the wheel as easy as it should. It had run through with no problems during the rehearsal. I reasoned this was because of the Squadron Leaders weight. I could see that the log was starting to spin as well but the old chap didn't seem to mind and kept on grinning.

Being careful not to let the officer's weight tug the steadying rope out of my hand, I hung on as tightly as I could. I dug my heels into the ground and hung on like I was at tug 0' war. Then I saw the rope stop travelling over its wheel and the log with the Squadron Leader attached dangled precariously over the middle of the road, still spinning.

"Lower away" he called, but I couldn't. "Lower away" he called a bit louder, but alas, the rope had got itself well and truly jammed in the hoist wheel.

I tried shaking the rope but nothing happened. I tried to make the rope sway a bit and although it released the wheel in part, it only succeeded in jamming again.

This last procedure caused the derrick seat and the Squadron Leader to jerk forward and then stop; jerk forward some more and stop again.

By this time the Squadron Leader was looking very scared and was calling orders that I couldn't hear. Pomeroy was at my elbow and kept singing in low tones. "He flew through the air with the greatest of ease, the daring young man on the flying trapeze."

"Cut the rope and let him go" giggled a callow youth standing near, whilst another chipped in with "you will have to tell the old boy to let go and jump into the catch sheet below". That was the last thing I wanted to do. I considered that with his size it would either cause him to have a seizure or a heart attack. There was every possibility that he would go right through the catch sheet the poor lads would have to bear below.

As the minutes ticked by the Squadron Leader looked very worried, especially as his down rope and log started to spin at an alarming rate.

"Get me across or winch me back" he kept shouting but I had to admit the pulley wheel was tightly jammed and I couldn't do either.

Like a genie out of a lamp the flight officer from my team appeared. It was the first time I had seen him since we had been taken prisoners the night before. He swore and hissed, "Stallard, is there anything you can do right?"

Shouting encouraging words to the Squadron Leader, my officer took the rope out of my hand and tried to loosen it at the wheel. He only succeeded in getting it more jammed. Now the Squadron Leader started spinning furiously and his cap fell off into the road below.

A lot of giggling went on both sides of the road and several cryptic comments were made. One started singing "A life on the ocean wave" and another mimicked "You put your right foot in, you put your right foot out - you do the hokey cokey and you turn about ...." "By now I couldn't even raise a smile. I felt the whole thing was getting more out of hand by the minute. I envisaged a catastrophe was about to take place and that the Squadron Leader's career was about to come to an abrupt end.

"No wonder the wheel is jammed" our flight officer muttered, "can you see how rusty it is?"

The next twenty minutes or so seemed like an eternity as chaos broke out and everyone seemed to be shouting orders at once. The Squadron Leader continued to dangle on high whilst a gang of chaps stood below with the ever ready catch sheet.

No matter what technique my officer or the non-commissioned officers used, they just could not get the rope to budge. The Squadron Leader had gone strangely silent and looked very grey as he twirled aloft.

Finally it was dear old Sergeant Tubbs who came to the rescue. He decided to get another rope and throw it to the Squadron Leader which was easier said than done. It is no easy feat to throw a rope to a man suspended in mid-air who is now holding tight with both of his hands on a rope that he is already dangling from.

Tubbs, in the sweetest of voice, kept calling "I am throwing it now, Sir" whilst Sir, hanging on with all his might cautiously tried to catch the rope that was being tossed in his direction.

Pomeroy couldn't stop making jokes about this. "Cor blimey!" he exclaimed, "they are trying to lasso the old chap now. Talk about the Indian rope trick. If he ain't careful he will get hung up there!" Nobody dared to laugh.

Tubbs tried to be accurate with the rope throwing but it kept falling short of the Squadron Leader's reach. Twice it hit him in the face but amazingly he kept silent until finally he managed to grab hold of it. A sigh of relief went around all of us.

As he listened carefully to wise old Tubbs' instructions, the Squadron Leader tied the new rope to the one above his derrick seat log. The other end of the new rope was thrown across to the airmen on the other side of the ravine and they had the job of manually pulling the old man across. At first it didn't look as though it was going to work because the rope was hardly long enough. Little by little and very slowly the Squadron Leader was hauled across by a series of jerking movements and a great deal of spinning and swaying.

It was with some difficulty that the Squadron Leader descended the far tree and snatched at his cap which was politely proffered. For a long time he stood glaring but silent as he struggled to regain his breath and his composure. Then with face twitching and eyes bulging he gave full vent to his lungs.

"Right you lot" he yelled, "get yourselves fell in immediately". This loosely interpreted meant he wanted us to get in a straight line before him as soon as possible. He was very angry and snorted like a bull.

"Today's performance is a disgrace" he began. "I will not tolerate such a performance. Why wasn't the equipment inspected? Has no-one heard of oil? Did you learn anything in the classroom? Alright If you cannot perform with equipment, tomorrow you shall be put on an exercise without equipment and see how you manage". With further mutterings which included the words "shower" and "imbeciles" we were duly dismissed.

With the departure of the Squadron Leader the rest of us gathered around our flight officer and the instructors. We wanted to know what an exercise without equipment entailed.

"I have no idea" said the officer wearily "but tomorrow will come soon enough and we will find out then".

All the ropes and other paraphernalia had to be gathered up before we were allowed to get our evening meal. As we waited for the lorry to arrive for picking up the gear we chatted amongst ourselves. Each one put forward a thought or theory about a non-equipment exercise but most seemed too daft to even contemplate.

I kept thinking on the Squadron Leader's words "an exercise without equipment". What could that possibly mean? I had the sudden feeling that the morrow was going to be just about as bad as today.

CHAPTER 14

Weasel Green looked mournfully into the empty marmalade dish at breakfast. "Just my flippin' luck" he complained, "I come a bit late and you lot have scoffed all the marmalade".

Half a dozen of us sat at breakfast in the mess hall. We had been sitting in silence for some time. It was very unusual for us to be so quiet and we had hardly noticed the late arrival of Weasel.

The fact that we had eaten most of the bread and all the marmalade available was put down to comfort eating. After the dismal performance with the derrick seat the previous day, we were still wondering what fate had in store for us today.

None of us could imagine what the threatened exercise without equipment could mean. Everybody was still making wild guesses which did very little to raise our hopes. One thing was certain, within the hour all would be revealed.

"Hey! Don't take the last bit of bread as well" Weasel moaned as Scouse reached for the last slice.

"I'll share it with you" Scouse offered and proceeded to cut the last slice in half.

"Thank you very much for your generosity" said Weasel sarcastically, "with friends like you, I don't need enemies. Remind me not to do you any favours in future". We all lapsed into silence again as Weasel and Scouse polished off the remains of the bread.

When we left the mess hall is began to rain which dampened our enthusiasm for the day even further. When it began to pour we ran fast to the billet to collect our wet weather ponchos. They were slipped over the shoulders and came down to a point at the front and the back, making us look like a pack of walking diamonds in a deck of cards. They were supposed to be waterproof but were far from it. Minutes later we were lined up on the parade ground under the watchful eye of our billet corporal.

"Rabble!" our corporal said it with meaning. "Rabble!" If you lot don't shine, and I mean shine very brightly today, I will personally have your guts for garters". Every syllable was punctuated.

Just at that moment I made the mistake of moving my head ever so slightly and smiled at Ron who was next to me in the line.

"What do you think is so funny, eh?" I found myself eye-balling the corporal as his face came very close to mine.

"Nothing" I murmured and looked away.

"Nothing?" he replied very loudly. "Quite right, sonny, you are nothing! You will always remain nothing unless you look, listen and learn! It's the three L's - Look, Listen and Learn".

"Three hells and we are in all of 'em" I heard Flemish Joe whisper behind me.

I smiled again. A fact which did not go un-noticed.

"You do think this is all a joke don't you, Airman?" I could hardly believe my ears. It seemed that Corporal

Brown had promptly promoted me from "nothing" to "Airman". So I really did exist after all.

"Well, we shall certainly take that stupid grin off your face today" he went on menacingly.

The narrative may well have continued but for the timely arrival of the Squadron Leader in his car. There was certainly no smile on his face but he didn't look any the worse for wear for his high adventure on the derrick seat. We went through the rigmarole of saluting to the right and were all duly counted and accounted for.

The Squadron Leader held a whispered conversation with Corporal Brown but for once he ignored us completely. He then got into his car and drove very slowly around the parade ground in second gear. The corporal brought us to attention and then ordered us to run along beside the officer's car. It took us on a route that we had never been on before. We ended up outside a square red bricked building that had one door but no windows.

Adjacent to the building was a three ton lorry with its tail board in the dropped position. Clearly we could see a mountain of gas masks in the lorry, some in boxes but the majority were unboxed and piled in a heap.

The Squadron Leader eased himself out of his car and addressed us in usual fashion.

"Well chaps, we will do our best to gas you today". A sickly smile appeared on his very round face.

"You will each be issued with a gas mask before entering this building". He jerked his thumb in the general direction. "You will run around the inside of that building wearing your gas mask. When Corporal Brown gives you the signal, by a down motion with his hand, you are to remove your gas mask but continue running. As you run you will sing! Sing - "She'll be coming round the mountain" or something" His voice trailed away as he watched very closely for our reaction.

I heard Alex whisper to Ben "I don't believe it! Sing? Why do we have to sing?" but before Ben had chance to reply the corporal cut in. "Fall out and collect gas masks" he snapped.

Within seconds we were all huddled up against the tailboard at the back of the lorry. Two lads inside the lorry proceeded to dole out the gas masks that looked like they were left- overs from the First World War.

Some of the lads gingerly turned the masks from one angle to another, inspecting them like they were some contraption from out of space. Others started to pull the masks over their faces.

The Squadron Leader clapped his hands to attract our attention. He looked somewhat embarrassed as Corporal Brown handed him his mask.

"Right chaps" the Squadron Leader began, "you put your gas masks on like this."

We all watched in amusement as the officer tried to pull the straps over his head. He had clearly forgotten to remove his cap and he had failed to adjust the straps on the gas mask. The corporal tactfully whispered in sir's ear and dutifully held the mask whilst the cap was removed.

At the second attempt, and with a great deal of struggling effort, the Squadron Leader's mask was in place. Unfortunately we could not hear a word he was saying through the thing. Hopefully he didn't hear Alex say "That's an improvement on his ugly dial".

It was Corporal Brown who finally gave us the gas mask donning demonstration and there we stood looking like a lot of aliens from out of space.

My mask had a peculiar musty smell. The visor was so badly smeared and scratched that I could hardly see out of it. When we were called into line I had to feel my way since of necessity it had to be by feel rather than sight.

The corporal explained that this was a very special and important exercise without any equipment. It was a very simple matter of running in a single file around the inside of the gas chamber. After a short time of running with the gas mask in place, he would give a signal by a sudden down movement with his arm. When the signal was given we had to pull off the gas mask, continue running whilst singing "She'll be coming round the mountain." I couldn't see the man in front of me through the visor of my gas mask so I couldn't think how I would see the arm dropping signal. Then light dawned. I could hear even if I couldn't see. I would simply listen for the singing and when it started I would know it was time for the mask to come off.

Corporal Brown headed up the line as the Squadron Leader opened the door to the gas chamber. That was very considerate since that was all he did except for closing it again when we were on the inside and him still on the outside. On the word of command we all started running behind the corporal.

There was a very dim light in the centre of the floor and it was as though we were running through dense steam or fog. This, I figured, was the gas and the reason we were wearing the masks.

I wasn't the only airman stumbling around that building rather than running.

With no vision I was constantly running into the back of the chap in front of me, and got his elbow in my stomach as a reward.

Round and round that little room we ran like a gerbil on a treadmill. Now I am running with my arms stretched out in front of me to give arm's length from the chap in front of me. I was getting fed up with being elbowed in the stomach.

Then it started. Singing or something that resembled it! So I snatched off my gas mask.

The effect was electrifying. Instantly my eyes poured with tears and felt like they were being stung. I felt a tightness in my chest and it was almost impossible to breathe. I didn't get out more than four words of "She'll be coming round". Then my throat felt as though it was on fire and I started coughing. Consciously I was staggering now and I tried desperately hard to hold my breath.

All of a sudden daylight appeared as the door was opened and we all staggered outside.

We all breathed in large lungful's of air. The taste of the gas made me feel sick and I had a blinding headache.

I noticed that Corporal Brown was looking very pale and sickly but then our attention was diverted to Gareth who suddenly doubled up and collapsed on the ground. He was from Merthyr Tydfil. A very serious young man who constantly objected to being called Taffy. It was a pity he objected because that made most of the lads more persistent in calling him by that name.

It was obvious that Gareth was unwell. He was making very strange noises and his Adam's apple was bobbing up and down at an alarming rate.

Corporal Brown gently rolled Gareth on to his side. The Squadron Leader, looking very anxious, began to fan him very swiftly with his clipboard, and urged us all to stand well back to allow him more air.

It wasn't long before Gareth opened his eyes and then started coughing and retching. He struggled to sit up because he was lying on very wet grass. He was unable to speak and looked deathly pale. Clearly he was very unwell.

The Squadron Leader held Gareth upright and fired a succession of questions at him. Each question was met with a shake of Gareth's head which didn't seem to make any sense at all.

Corporal Brown ordered the rest of us to return our gas masks to the lorry and we just stood around looking at Gareth and willing him to recover. But Gareth didn't recover. Instead he seemed to get very sleepy and when the Squadron Leader and the corporal tried to get him on his feet, he just slumped forward.

At this point the Squadron Leader and our corporal came to a joint decision.

The corporal was to take the Squadron Leader's car and go to the nearest telephone and call for the Medical Officer. Silently I hoped the procedure would not take as long as the performance we had when Ged broke his toe.

Fortunately within a few minutes a small ambulance arrived and a very groggy Gareth was hauled inside. As we watched it speed away we all fell very silent. We fervently hoped that Gareth would live to see another day.

CHAPTER 15

Gareth spent two whole days in the Medical Centre. He was given all sorts of tests for asthma and other lung problems but was none the worse for the gas chamber ordeal.

We were spending most of our days now sitting behind a desk in a class room or doing marching drill on the parade ground. It was now a case of rehearsal after rehearsal in preparation for the final pass out parade. Listening to commands, turning this way and that, getting into line, saluting, and doing arms drill went on relentlessly, I had to admit that I was feeling the fittest I had ever been. I could run very fast and enjoyed cross country runs. It was like being back home in the fields again. Swimming was my favourite past time and I was one of the best in the flight. A fact I always brought out when it was suggested I was hopeless at just about everything else. Even the weakest of us have some strengths.

Although generally very physically fit I had to admit that my throat was still sore days after the stint in the gas chamber. I found it difficult to understand why because everybody else was fine. I preferred being out of doors rather than being in a classroom. Classroom was a must, however, because we had to learn all the theory work in connection with a 303 rifle.

In class I sat next to a lad from Surrey called Davie and we became the best of pals. Although we were a bunch of lads thrown together for a common purpose, we seemed to naturally sort ourselves out into closer relationships. It was the same for all of us. If a couple of lads discovered they supported a particular football club they teamed up on a shared interest basis. Another two or three would hang out together because they shared an interest in some sport or hobby. Davie and I enjoyed films and went to the cinema whenever we could afford it and had the time. We also shared the joy of long walks which meant we chatted a lot together. Davie and I helped each other to fathom out some of the technical stuff in the manuals and tested each other with questions from the text books. Sometimes we cribbed off each other and got into trouble when it was discovered that we got identical answers and the same mistakes. By and large Davie and I decided that united we would stand and divided we would fall.

This was all very well to a point but often led to one leading the other into trouble, as we found to our cost when we combined our efforts to master the workings of the 303 rifle.

We had a good instructor. His name was Sergeant Wheeler. A kindly fellow from the Isle of Wight who somehow got stuck with the nickname "Wight Wheeler" although his Christian name was George.

George was good in the classroom. He gave us a thorough grilling on the 303 rifle emphasising the safety of the weapon at all times. I had very serious doubts that a pea shooter would be safe with us lot.

Davie voiced his fears during the NAAFI break. NAFFI, so abbreviated for the Navy And Army Forces

Institute, was an organization where one could go and buy refreshments, toiletries, sweets and cigarettes and so forth. Sometimes the NAAFI van would drive around a Camp and stop at vantage points where you would queue up to get served with whatever goodies you needed at the time.

Neither Davie nor I had ever handled a gun. I had already had a near miss when Wills bayonet had not been fixed properly on his rifle and it had whistled past my head during bayonet practice. Dodging a flying bayonet was one thing but if a gun went off in your direction, how do you miss a bullet? Davie reminded us in solemn tone "George said when we aim and pull the trigger we shall feel a kick in the shoulder? Will it hurt?"

"I don't know" I confessed. "I have never fired a rifle in my life" Davie was a very troubled man and wandered from man to man asking further questions. He cheered up considerably when he discovered most of us had never fired a rifle either.

Later that night Pomeroy tried to give us all a demonstration with a broom. He looked very impressive as he stood to attention in the middle of the billet clad in his pyjamas.

The broom head was pulled well into his right armpit whilst the handle pressed against his side. Suddenly without any warning he shouted "Shoulder arms" to himself. Gripping the handle with both hands, he flicked it across his chest until it came to rest on his left shoulder with the butt in his left hand. There was a pause then as it seemed Pomeroy wasn't quite sure what came next. None of us had any idea so we just gathered around him looking gormless whilst he returned to the first position.

With the broom head firmly back under Pomeroy's right armpit, he now points the other end of the handle at hapless Robin who stuck out like a sore thumb in his very regal and luxurious blue and gold silk dressing gown.

"You have got to shut your left eye and look down the rifle barrel with your right eye" explained Pomeroy. "You have to be accurate to get him properly into sight". As he said this he obligingly shut his left eye and gazed along the extended broom handle with his right. This was all done very precisely. "You have got to get your enemy lined up where you want to shoot him" Pomeroy explained.

"Well, how can you line him up" asks Keith. "It might be dark and you don't know where he is. You wouldn't know where he is coming from, how can you line him up?"

Pomeroy swore. "When I say you line him up, you idiot, I mean you line the end of the gun towards the position where you want to shoot him in his body". He demonstrated by pointing the end of the broom first at Robin's head and then lowered it to a point in the middle of his chest. Then, very majestically, Pomeroy held his breath, and stretching to his full height shouted "Bang!" at the top of his voice and then fell, laughing hysterically on the nearest bed.

Although Pomeroy thought it was all very funny the rest of us took it all very seriously. One by one we all had a go with the broom, listening intently as Pomeroy suggested lifting the handle higher or lower as necessary. None of us, Pomeroy included, seemed to know just whereabouts on the handle the trigger would be. We fathomed that it would be obvious when it came to the real thing.

My spirits rose the next morning. There wasn't a cloud in the sky as we were marched to the armoury to collect the rifles. Davie sticking by me was very thoughtful and came out with a gem of a statement. "It's only practice" he said, "good job it's not the real thing. Not a lot can go wrong." I think he was trying to convince himself more than me.

As we approached the rifle range we were just in time to see a red flag being hoisted on the flag pole. We laughed when someone started singing "We'll keep the red flag flying here." Davie marching beside me began to giggle which did not go down very well with Wight Wheeler our sergeant instructor.

The sergeant seemed irritated and showed a harder side that we had not seen before. He gritted his teeth and almost spat out his words. "That red flag is flown to let all and sundry know this is a danger area. You lot are going to be let loose with live ammunition but goodness only knows why. They do not come any more dangerous than you lot".

As we approached the shooting area I heard a sudden intake of breath from Davie. "Oh no", he groaned, "look who is waiting for us".

Standing on the concrete platform before the firing range was the large Squadron Leader I had let dangle from the derrick seat. He did not look very pleased to see us.

Sergeant Wheeler brought us to a halt and saluted the officer who asked one direct question. "How many airmen are here?"

"Sixteen" the sergeant replied and recounted us to make sure.

The Squadron Leader opened a very large metal ammunition box and took out a hand full of bullets or so I thought.

"How many bullets do each of us get?" asked Pete and got one of the Squadron Leader's glares that could kill an ox from thirty yards.

"Five" he answered very abruptly, "and they are not bullets, they are called rounds. You get five rounds each."

I looked very warily at the five rounds lying in the palm of my hand and tried hard to remember how you put them, one at a time, into the rifle breech. I remembered how our instructor in class had emphasised over and over "the breech is the part of the firearm behind the barrel". I need not have worried because the sergeant called us to form a circle around him whilst he gave us a demonstration. It all looked fairly easy.

At the further end of the range was a very large brick wall and before it a mountain of sand. Stuck in the sand were wooden poles about fifteen feet apart, and upon these were pinned red, white and blue targets. The red bull's eye in the very centre of the target was what we had to aim for. That, we were told, would be the area of the body we would be aiming at if called to do the real thing. A very sobering thought.

It didn't take long for the Squadron Leader to remember me. I noticed the way he glared and his upper lip trembled as he addressed me personally for the benefit of all the others.

"Any silly mistakes this time can have very serious consequences" he remonstrated. "Let us think very carefully before we act. Aim carefully at the target by letting your sight travel down the barrel of the rifle. Pick out the bulls eye in your sight, aim, keep perfectly still, pull the trigger firmly and fire!" Sergeant Wheeler took over at this point. "Right you have five rounds each" he said, "the Squadron Leader wants to see five nice holes in those targets in, or as near as possible to, that red bulls eye. I will personally deal with anyone who brings me a target with less than five holes in it".

Buncie pulled a face and complained that the targets were placed too far away but there was no response. I offered up a silent prayer that I wouldn't get less than five holes in my target as I fed the rifle with my first round.

I went through the procedure we had been taught slowly but with caution.

Taking aim, I held my breath as I pulled the trigger. The expected kick in the shoulder with the butt was nowhere as harsh as I expected. When the rounds had been used I felt a sense of achievement and felt fairly confident that I had done well.

When the noise of firing had stopped and we all stood there looking pleased with ourselves, the officer ordered us to collect our targets, get in a line and show him the results. We had to tell him how many holes were in the target as we handed it in as though he couldn't count for himself.

My face must have been a study as I removed my target and got into line. I had already had a few embarrassing moments in my short time with the RAF but this exceeded them all.

The airmen in the queue in front of me handed the Squadron Leader their targets as they confirmed their hit scores.

"Five sir. Five sir. Four sir. Five sir. Five sir. Then it was my turn. "Nine sir!" I said it very quietly.

"Nine? Nine?" the officer looked at me in sheer disbelief, with his eyes bulging and his face getting redder by the second. Even the sergeant peered over his shoulder to see the evidence with some surprise.

Moments later the penny dropped. It became apparent that Davie and I had been shooting at the same target and one of us must have missed a round altogether. When Davie handed in his blank target it was obvious that he had been shooting at mine. For once it was not that I had in any way failed. It was all Davie's mistake and God had answered my prayer after all. There wasn't less than five holes in my target!" There was a mountain of dead rounds that had been fired on the edge of the platform. We were also required to deposit ours there at the end of the firing. When I collected mine I discovered I only had four rounds and to my horror I realised there was still one unused in my rifle. This accounted for the missing hole in our target. I quickly took the unused round out of the rifle and threw it into the pile of dead ones.

No sooner had I disposed of my one live round when the Squadron Leader made a statement which shook me to the core.

"I take it that no-one has any live rounds left?" he enquired. "The dead ones are melted down. If any live rounds were amongst the dead ones they would explode and could kill or seriously injure someone".

I was terrified at the prospect of someone being hurt because of what I had done so I went to the Squadron Leader to confess. Strangely he didn't make any fuss as I expected, he was quite calm and actually thanked me for owning up.

"You shall go through the dead ones until you find it", he said, "and when you have found it, guard it with your life, and I will collect it from you when we return this afternoon".

The entire class was marched off whilst I knelt beside a mountain of dead rounds looking for the live one. Actually I found several live rounds so it wasn't a wasted exercise. The Squadron Leader was very impressed and said "Well done!" Those two words from him more than made up for missing the lunch and, I felt went some way to redeeming me for all my other misdemeanours.

The afternoon was without incident on my part although Davie got into trouble several times. We all laughed because he tended to close his eyes each time he pulled the trigger. Our sergeant, was on hand to give him extra personal instruction but exploded once when Davie forgot himself and called him George.

George was quite friendly and patient and it was possible to have reasonable conversations with him. He was a good instructor and went to great lengths to assure us or warn us about things we needed to know.

"All in all you handled the 303 rifle very well today and I was impressed" he said. A few words like that work wonders to build confidence and it did make us feel good. Then he had to go and spoil it.

"Tomorrow in class we shall start learning about the Bren Gun, now that is a different kettle of fish. There is a lot more to learn about that weapon which is very much more complicated than the 303 rifle. It is more sophisticated, effective and deadly".

I didn't say anything but began thinking on the progression of our training.

KEN STALLARD

Looking back the marching wasn't too bad once you got use to the boot blisters. It was fairly straightforward to fit and use a bayonet. Graduation to a rifle was more brain taxing and dangerous but the Bren Gun seemed a giant step into the unknown. The progression of things wasn't getting any easier. In many ways I felt as though I was swimming against the tide. I just hoped that the Bren Gun wouldn't let me sink altogether.

CHAPTER 16

It was too hot to be in a classroom. I knew I had got a temperature and I was feeling sick and dizzy. A very sore throat and a head-ache did little to alleviate my feelings.

A new Flight Sergeant was pointing out the various parts of a Bren Gun on a colourful chart on the wall.

Feeling so unwell made it extremely difficult for me to concentrate. I was feeling very tired and I found it hard to understand the Flight Sergeant's Scottish accent.

The morning dragged on and by lunch time it was apparent that I was now suffering. The Flight Sergeant ordered me to report to the Medical Centre.

"You have got a very bad bout of tonsillitis" the Medical Officer confirmed.

"We will keep you in for a bit."

I had plenty of time to think as I lay in the hospital bed. Hitherto my time in the RAF had not been very inspiring. I pondered on what my Dad had said earlier on. "He'll be sorry he volunteered" and now I was beginning to think he was right.

Perhaps it would have been more sensible to be called up for National Service. The extra year to serve a three year short service regular engagement didn't seem to be a good idea. It was no good crying over spilt milk, however, I had made my decision and now I had to abide by it.

The next couple of days seemed so long. My sore throat was getting worse and it was almost impossible to swallow. My spirits sank to zero and I thought I was dying of boredom until something very interesting happened. Davie was admitted to the same ward.

Davie had got tonsillitis too or so he said. His impish grin didn't really impress me that he was suffering like I was. He had convinced the Medical Officer that he was poorly and he ended up in a bed right opposite me.

Although I felt Davie was malingering to begin with, it soon became evident that he was becoming unwell. He started to refuse the food that he had been complaining about and he certainly did not look very well. My guess was that he had caught his sickness from me. He insisted it had something to do with the stint in the gas chamber but I knew that was ridiculous.

Davie and I spent a week in that immaculate ward, passing most of the time doing a thousand piece jig saw puzzle; only to find that about a dozen pieces were missing when we completed it. As the days passed and we both knew we were well on the mend, we actually looked forward to getting back to the billet and the banter of the other lads.

We returned to a billet where the conversation was non-stop all about the Bren Gun. The lads had received a thorough grounding on the use of the weapon and had been instructed how to assemble and dismantle it. It sounded a very macho weapon which was capable of doing a lot of damage. I was beginning to wonder if there were plans afoot to transfer us to the Army. No mention of all this weapon training had been mentioned at the Recruitment Centre.

All the lads were getting excited and very enthusiastic with the prospect of going out to actually fire the Bren Gun after the weekend. The time had come to move on from theory to practice. The only problem was that Davie and I had not received any theory because of the time spent in the sick bay.

Davie looked at me in horror which wasn't anything unusual. "We can't go out and fire a Bren Gun, Ken" he protested, "we have not had any lessons."

"They will take that into consideration" I replied more confident than I felt but the thought did keep me awake most of Sunday evening.

Monday morning came too soon for me. I was still feeling weak after the time spent in the sick bay, and, I remembered the fiasco Davie and I caused the last time we went to the shooting range. The only compensating thought this time was that we had a genuine excuse because of lack of tuition.

We assembled at the classroom in the normal way after breakfast and then got marched off to the armoury to collect the Bren Guns. The Flight Sergeant collected the now familiar metal boxes of ammunition whilst the rest of us were entrusted to the care and watchful eye of the senior man from our billet. A Senior Man was a bit like a school prefect, a go between authority and the rest of us. He only landed the job because he had spent a week or two with some air cadets prior to joining the RAF. His name was Bill.

Bill had wheedled all the information we sought from the Flight Sergeant in charge of us. The airmen, two at a time, would fire the Bren Gun at a wooden target of a man. The man targets would be approximately fifteen feet apart at the wooden pillars which had been used for the 303 rifle shoot.

Each airman was required to lie flat on mattresses positioned fifteen feet apart on the concrete platform in front of the targets. At the command "Detail Load!" two airman had to dive literally on to the mattresses and assemble the guns which were lying at the right side of them.

When the guns were assembled, the airmen had to wait for the order "Fire!" before bringing the butt of the gun up into the right shoulder and pulling the trigger.

All this information didn't make much sense to Davie and me because we had missed the lessons. Bill assured us that we would soon get the hang of the gun if we carefully watched how the others fired the weapon. At that moment I had a brilliant idea which I was swift to share with Davie.

"If only two airmen fire the gun at a time" I explained, ""we need to be the last two in the line. We can watch what all the others are doing and learn, and, just copy what they are doing." Davie thought that was a brilliant idea.

The Flight Sergeant duly arrived to give us a final briefing about the shoot as the red flag was hoisted up the flag pole. When he ordered us into line to be marched on to the range, I whispered in Davies' ear. "Let us get to the back of the line" I said, "we need to be the last in to watch how the others shoot." I felt very pleased with myself that I was learning some initiative.

"Left, right. Left, right. Left, right." The Flight Sergeant marched us on in step with Davie and I bringing up the rear. "Left, right. Left, right. Halt! About turn!" Davie and I looked at each other in dismay and disbelief.

We had been marched right past the wall of sand and we were approaching it from a different direction. On the command "About turn" we were now the first two at the front instead of being the last two at the back.

We knew the Flight Sergeant had done this deliberately by the smile on his face.

It was Davie that got addressed by him for the benefit of us both. "Don't think I don't know what your little game is, laddie", he began. "You have to get up very early in the morning to get one over on me."

Davie opened his mouth as though he was going to say something but changed his mind. I thought he was going to reveal that it was me who had the idea but thought better of it.

"You will be my guinea pigs" the Flight Sergeant went on. "I will take you through each procedure slowly and precisely so listen carefully. If there is anything you do not understand, say so." Then, turning, to the rest of the grinning bunch of fellows he said, "It will not do you any harm to have a refresher course."

Davie and I were shown how to put nineteen rounds into the Bren Gun magazine and how to fix the magazine to the gun itself. There was a simple clicking and connecting device which married the gun and magazine together but it proved too difficult for me. The boss was very patient and kept me practicing the art until I got it perfected.

A very complicated instruction came next. At the command "Detail Load" we were required to dive on to the mattresses. The magazine had to be fixed to the Bren Gun with speed and then the weapon aimed at the wooden man target standing in front of the mountain of sand. On the command "Fire" we simply had to pull the trigger and shoot the wooden man.

I listened very carefully to the instructions. Although I asked questions about the firing method, I was still confused about the difference between single and repetition shots. So it was with some trepidation that I stood behind my mattress waiting for the command "Detail Load!" When the order came I got down on my knees on the mattress. "Up! Up! Up!" postulated the Flight Sergeant flapping his hand in an upward motion. "You are supposed to be war trained airmen, not old ladies with arthritis in their knees. You do not kneel on the mattress as though they are prayer mats, you dive on them! You must be quick. You must act fast and get down and shoot the enemy before he shoots you."

Davie looked across at me and grinned whilst I wished the boss would take more notice of him than me. "Right we shall start again" he began. "Detail Load."

At the word of command I dived with all force on to the mattress and nearly knocked myself out. The concrete beneath the flimsy mattress was very hard as my body discovered when I hit it.

Breathless I looked expectantly at the boss who just shook his head sadly.

"Right then, if you are now comfortable" he began sarcastically, "assemble the weapon, take aim and wait for my command to fire."

I reached for the magazine containing the nineteen bullets and with incredible ease fixed it to the gun. I then pulled the butt of the gun into my right shoulder and aimed it at the target.

"Sights" said the Flight Sergeant wearily "Sights!" I didn't know what he meant and I looked at him expectantly.

"Sights!" he said it again and then bent down to pull up a little gadget on the gun barrel. It was like a little window had appeared with a black cross in the middle of it. I was wisely informed that the centre of the cross had to be lined up with the chest of the wooden man before I shot him. The 'sights' were there to help me find a more accurate spot to shoot. I thought this was ingenious.

The Flight Sergeant repeated his comments on single shot and repetitive firing and careful use of the safety measures of the trigger. The trigger had to be pushed in one direction in order to fire a single shot, and, into a different position to fire a volley of shots. Sadly I did not know the difference between the two.

"Aim." The boss watched very closely as I tried to make myself more comfortable on the mattress and aimed the weapon at the target before me. I let my sight travel along the barrel of the gun as I used the sights to get the chest of the little wooden man into view. "Safety catch off."

With some fumbling I yanked the safety catch off, causing the gun to wobble dangerously. "Steady" the boss advised. "Take aim." For the second time I squared up to my target as I listened for the next instruction.

"Finger on the trigger. Single Shot. Fire!" I pulled the trigger and then it all happened. There was a blast and a series of rat a tat tat fire as the butt kept pounding my shoulder and a spray of bullets hit the target. The little wooden man disintegrated.

The Flight Sergeant was jumping up and down in rage and exploded with a mouthful of swearing and cursing. I had learned a very valuable lesson concerning the difference between single shots and repetitive firing.

The lads watching were holding each other up in laughter. Davie, now lying on his back on his mattress, was hysterical.

I received the full vengeance of the boss's wrath. "You have just put nineteen bullets into one enemy man" he exploded, "how are you going to cope with the other eighteen men who are coming for you."

"Run." I said it most positively but that only brought another tirade from the boss.

My shoulder was hurting like I had been kicked by a mule but the Flight Sergeant insisted that I went through the entire procedure again. The method of firing was explained to us all in great detail. Thankfully I got the single and repetitive shots figured out and was able to relax and laugh as Davie was singled out for extra tuition.

I reasoned that I had not missed out too much by missing the week in the classroom.

Davie never mastered the Bren Gun totally and the boss thought it wise to transfer him to a class for the Sten Gun instead. I was glad that I wasn't recommended for that course although perhaps it would have been better if I had.

Thankfully the August Bank Holiday weekend was coming up and we were due for a long weekend to do as we please. Within reason, of course. We were reminded continually that we were at all times to uphold the great reputation of the Royal Air Force.

I don't think that long weekend did very much for the RAF reputation or mine but we planned to enjoy it.

CHAPTER 17

The weeks of recruit training were passing quickly. The heat of that summer continued and I had lost two stones in weight. I think most of this was due to all the square bashing in full battle kit and sometimes in great coats as well. It was a welcome relief when the Commanding Officer gave us a three day rest period over the August Bank Holiday weekend. We had Saturday, Sunday and Monday all to ourselves.

At this time in my service Keith and I were getting on well although he couldn't stand my pal Davie. He said Davie was neurotic and a worrier when life was for living. Davie said he was too good looking and athletic and full of himself for his own good. It was the first time I had ever heard the saying "He thinks he is God's gift to women." I insisted on remaining neutral because I found Davie and I had a lot in common, especially for getting into trouble.

On the other hand I found Keith very useful. Although he was Padgate's answer to Adonis with his good looks and charm, he was very worldly wise and very keen on girls, drinking and gambling in that order.

I hated ironing shirts and pressing trousers and Keith sometimes offered to do it for me for a shilling. To me it seemed cheap for the price, for Keith it meant a shilling bet on a horse at the bookies. Apart from the financial side of our agreement, I had to admit that Keith did a first class job. He was an asset.

Although we didn't get much spare time in the evenings after blancoing our webbing, polishing our boots and tunic buttons, and keeping our uniforms pressed; Keith used what spare time he had in writing endless letters to girlfriends and studying horse racing form in the newspapers.

Sometimes on a Saturday evening and, or a Sunday afternoon, Keith went missing and more often than not arrived back at the billet after lights out at 10.30pm. Consequently he was forever getting into trouble and punished with extra duties. Whenever we asked him where he had been he refused to answer. He would just grin and say, "Mind your own business. I've got a nice little thing going and I'm not going to let you lot in on it."

My shillings were obviously most welcome so Keith shared more conversation with me than most. When he found I could be trusted he began to take me into his confidence more and more.

Just before the Bank Holiday, Keith took me aside for a private chat. I had never seen him look so serious.

"I don't trust any of the others" he said, "but I want to ask you a very special favour. I am asking you because I know you will not laugh and you will take it seriously. I know I can trust you to keep it to yourself'. He was most earnest and curiosity was getting the better of me.

"Do you remember Carol and that other bird we met in Warrington?" he asked.

"You know those girls who bought us the jam tarts when we were coming back from the exercise."

"Yeah, I remember Carol and Cathy" I replied. "They must have been keen or mad to cough up the dough to buy us cakes."

Keith was looking deadly serious now. "I phoned Carol at the shop like I said I would and we met up. Now we have got it going together. That is where I have been some of those Saturdays and Sundays."

So that was it. Keith's secret was out but why was I the privileged one to hear this little gem? I didn't have to wait long for the answer.

"Carol spends a lot of time with her mate" he went on. "Cathy I presume? I replied. Keith shook his head.

"No Ken" he continued, looking over his shoulder as though the world was listening to his every word. "She has got a female friend that she usually goes out with on a Saturday night. Not Cathy. The friend is getting a bit fed up because she feels she is getting pushed out. To put it to you straight, mate, Carol will only agree to go out with me this Saturday if I can get her mate fixed up. She wants us to go out as a foursome. Will you do me a very big favour and make up the foursome?"

I am not sure what made me agree. I cannot remember if it was because I was getting bored with all male company, or, that I didn't want to offend Keith and jeopardise my chances of getting my ironing done. I had got absolutely nothing lined up for the weekend so I impetuously agreed to accompany him for his Saturday afternoon date.

Any further conversation was cut abruptly short by the unexpected arrival of the Padre no less accompanied by a Flight Lieutenant we had never seen before.

We all sprang to our feet as was customary when an officer was present and on this occasion we had two in the billet.

The Padre was a very nice homely sort of chap and always insisted that a cup of tea or coffee and a biscuit was on hand after his compulsory Sunday Services. "Which one of you is Ronald Smith?" enquired the Flight Lieutenant and every eye fell on Ron as Corporal Brown, in charge of our billet, came up behind the officers.

"I am Smith", ventured Ron looking decidedly nervous. He had gone as white as a sheet and looked as though something devastating was about to happen. Sadly it was.

"You can use my bunk room" Brown said very quietly and the Padre, the Flight Lieutenant, Brown and Ron disappeared into the corporal's room at the end of the billet.

The rest of us got together in a cluster and all began talking at once. It looked like something serious was afoot. Flemish Joe seemed to think Ron had been caught pinching something but Robin was quick to point out that the RAF would have sent the police, not a Padre.

A long time went by and then we heard voices in the corridor outside the corporal's room. When the voices stopped the door to the billet was opened and Ron came in looking awful. Without a word he threw himself face down on his bed and broke into uncontrollable sobbing.

We all clustered around his bed. "What's up mate?" somebody asked, whilst a couple of lads sat either side of him on the bed and tried to hold him.

Ron was inconsolable and shaking from head to toe. He struggled to sit up and with tears pouring down his face announced "My brother and a couple of his mates have been killed in a car crash back home in Huddersfield."

There was a deathly hush except for Ron's anguished cry. "Why? Why did that have to happen to our Paul? His mates as well! One of his mates was one of my best ones as well." Ron buried his head in the pillow and his shoulders shook uncontrollably.

"Is there anything I can do, or we can do?" I asked after a bit.

"I have got to get my things together and they are ..." Ron tailed off as he was overcome by another fit of sobbing.

"O.K. mate" this from Phil who was still sat beside Ron with his arm around his shoulder. "What are they going to do when you have got your things together?" "They are arranging for someone to take me home by car" he replied. "They told me to be ready in half an hour."

Pomeroy turned away and I could see tears pouring down his face. Robin kept dabbing at his eyes and I found myself welling up. The tragedy of the moment was broken by Alex who said "Come on chaps, let's get his things together." Solemnly we all mucked in. We emptied Ron's cupboard, bedside locker and stuffed all of his things, tidily as we could, into his kit bag and suitcase.

Promptly on the half hour a sergeant and an airman turned to pick up Ron and to collect his things. We all gathered round to help him carry his belongings to the car.

I had never seen a more touching scene than that of Ron's departure. We all hugged him in turn and said daft things like "Don't worry mate, it's all going to be alright." "We'll be thinking of you." "Keep in touch." "We'll miss you."

Ron tried hard not to cry but was shaking and clung to each of us in turn without saying anything. We bundled his things into the boot and the sergeant opened the car door and indicated that Ron was to sit in the back beside him. With a final "Cheers mates" and now tears coursing freely down his cheeks, he waved as the car drove out of sight.

We all went back into the hut. It was such an eerie feeling and suddenly felt very quiet. I don't know why but all of us sat together clustered on Ben and Gareth's bed which were adjacent to each other.

It was a very personal and intimate time that we spent huddled together. Ron's tragedy had deeply affected us all. It was the first time I had seen men cry. We discovered a lot about each other as our emotions came to the surface. It was abundantly clear that we had forged relationships and unconsciously bonded together in a way we had not realised. What happened to one affected us all.

The whole thing with Ron had somewhat dampened our enthusiasm for the Bank Holiday weekend but we knew that life for us had to go on. It didn't take Keith very long to outline his plans for the forthcoming dates.

We checked our finances and considered we had enough for the bus fare to Warrington, something to eat, a couple of drinks and the evening entertainment. We decided the girls could choose whether we went to a dance hall or to the pictures. It was doubtful that we could afford both.

Since I had not been anywhere to spend much money I was the better off of the two of us. I thought I would be called upon to subsidise the evening but Carol was earning and known for her generosity, for providing jam tarts at least. The prospect of a good day was more than promising.

The rest of the lads in our billet realised Keith and I had something planned for the weekend but we refused to satisfy their curiosity. We didn't want any hangers on or jibes about the girls so we made a pact to keep silent.

Saturday finally arrived. As I lay in the bath I mulled over my blind date. I was beginning to have misgivings. A lot of questions were going through my head. Why couldn't the girl get a boyfriend of her own? What if she turned out to be horrible and I had to spend the rest of the day with her? I voiced my thoughts to Keith but he was confident that I had nothing to worry about.

First thing after lunch I applied my second generous splash of after shave and combed in the extra layer of Brylcreem on my hair. Keith did likewise and feeling like a million dollars we headed for the bus stop.

We felt the excitement mounting as we took the bus to Warrington. Keith had arranged for the girls to meet us at a stop near the railway station and the nearer we got the more nervous I felt.

As the bus drew into the station approach Keith pressed his nose up against the window. I peered over his shoulder but didn't know what I expected to see. "They are not there" he muttered and shielded his eyes from the blinding sun as we stepped off the bus.

There seemed to be a lot of coming and going at Warrington Station that Bank Holiday Saturday but no sign of Carol and my blind date. We must have watched every person passing by for at least a quarter of an hour before Keith grabbed my arm and said, "Look, over there - that's them."

Carol seemed taller than I remembered her and she was looking lovely in a pretty green dress with white edging to the neck and puff sleeves. My attention was swiftly drawn to the slightly shorter girl standing beside her. She was clad in a very colourful floral dress and wore flat shoes. A black bag which looked as though it had seen better days hung on a strap over her shoulder.

Keith, like Jack the Lad, left me to dash off to meet Carol, who got lost to view in his massive embrace. It was obvious that their relationship was going at a pace.

Presuming that the dark haired companion was my blind date, I approached her cautiously.

"Hello", I smiled. "I'm Ken." I felt a bit awkward as I offered to shake her hand. I was immediately impressed by the fact that when she shook my hand she wouldn't let it go.

"I'm Penny and I didn't think you would come" she said in a matter of fact way, her big blue eyes smiling directly into mine. "I'm the one that usually gets let down."

I was about to ask her if she had been on many blind dates before when Keith and Carol came up for air and realised that Penny and I were there.

Keith just stood and stared at Penny because he had not seen her before, obviously admiring the view. He stared at me and winked. It was Carol who came to the rescue and introduced us to each other.

Penny and I continued to hold hands. It seemed the natural thing to do. The other couple kept stopping to kiss and I thought Carol was much louder than the last time I met her. Some of her conversation was quite coarse too.

I thought I would start with a bit of small talk and addressed Carol first. "A lot of things have happened since you bought us those jam tarts" I said brightly. "Yeeees" she said, dragging out the word slowly and then made a very hollow laugh. "I know you like tarts - well, I bet when this day is over, you will go back to Camp and say you have been out with a couple in Warrington." I fell silent as the trio giggled and I began to wonder what I was letting myself in for.

CHAPTER 18

Bank Holiday shoppers seemed to be out in force in Warrington. The blazing sun shone down from a cloudless sky and everybody looked hot and weary.

Penny and I started to saunter down one of the main streets following Keith and Carol, stopping every now and then to peer in a shop window. A blouse was admired here and a pair of shoes there but none of us bought anything. It looked like it was going to be a window shopping day for the ladies.

Penny and I stopped and laughed loudly when she told me about her job. She said she stuffed mattresses in a local factory. It sounded very funny when, in her broad Lancashire accent she said, "I am a stuffer. I stuff mattresses." It appealed to my sense of humour.

I wondered if she had anything to do with the one I had dived on at the Bren Gun exercise. If so, she had not put much stuffing in that one. When I asked her if she was any good at stuffing a turkey, I got a clip around the ear for my trouble. It was all good fun and we were enjoying ourselves immensely.

We went into several shops but none of us bought anything. Keith liked sifting through pop records and kept arguing with Carol about which pop songs were the best. All that he liked she rubbished and vice versa.

It wasn't long before we jointly decided that it would be good to pop into a cafe for a snack.

"I want to get a newspaper first" announced Keith so Penny and I took up the rear again as the two in front headed for the newsagents.

I was warming very much towards Penny. She seemed so open and natural and laughed a lot. When we sat down at the table in the cafe she handed me the Menu. "Choose what you want" she said, and then quickly added, "I will pay!" The four of us held a little discussion and came to an agreement. We would all pay for our own snack but Keith and I would share the expenses of going to the pictures in the evening. That is what the girls wanted to do.

Keith spread his newspaper over the table and started to study the form of the horses. Apparently this was something Carol and he did on a Saturday afternoon. We looked fascinated as Keith muttered, "Yes, yes. I am going to do that one, and that one and that one!" Each time he said "that one" he jabbed his finger at the name of another horse in different races.

"I am going to put a bob on all three" Keith announced and then looked across at Penny and me. "Are you going to have a bet?" he asked.

Penny shook her head and Keith laughed. "Go on, Ken", he insisted, "Put a bob on a horse and see if your luck is in." I gave the matter some small consideration and decided a shilling wasn't too much to lose if the horse didn't win. The girls tut tutted in disapproval as I handed Keith my shilling.

Immediately after finishing the snack we had to go to the bookmakers to place the bet since Keith was betting on an early race. He suggested that I put my money on a horse called Prince Regent. He had placed money on that horse previously and it had won. It had good form he said.

Carol, Penny and I waited a long time outside the bookmakers. I guess we would have waited a lot longer if the girls had not insisted I went in to hurry him up.

The room was dingy and full of tobacco smoke. At one end of the room was a high counter behind which stood a couple of male bookies. Both had pencils stuck behind their ears and folded newspapers, turned to the racing forecast, in their hands.

There were a lot of men in that room. Some were studying lists of horses that were running in the races. The lists and betting slips were littered around the walls on the narrow shelves. It was very hot and airless in there.

Some of the men, pencils poised, were studying the newspapers. A radio, going full blast, was giving a commentary on the current race. I found Keith at one of the shelves. When he saw me he hastily scribbled on his betting slip and I noticed he had increased his bets to five. Looking a bit sheepish he emerged with me having handed over five shillings to the bookie.

The afternoon went by very quickly. When Carol started to complain that her new shoes were making her heels sore, we decided to sit on some grass by a canal.

Keith prised off Carol's offending shoes and proceeded to tickle her feet whilst Penny and I threw pebbles aimlessly into the water.

Keith and Carol had very little inhibitions. Penny and I might as well have not been there as far as they were concerned. It didn't take them long to kiss and cuddle and fool around. I was embarrassed when they started rolling over each other but Penny didn't seem to mind. When I mentioned it to her in private later, she admitted Carol was a very forward kind of girl.

My embarrassment for Carol was eclipsed by all the flattering compliments Penny gave me. She said she loved everything about me and she wanted us to be friends forever. My ego was well and truly boosted.

Eventually Keith got down to his last cigarette and suggested we move on so that he could buy some more. Penny pulled a face at this and whispered in my ear. "I wish we could spend some time on our own." Keith overheard the remark and gave me a broad grin and a wink.

On the way for cigarettes we paused to see what film was showing at the cinema and what time it was due to start. We decided to have an early tea and go to the first house pictures since Keith and I had to be back on Camp by ten thirty.

After tea and before our last visit of the day to the bookmakers, the ladies went off to powder their noses and Keith and I took the opportunity to visit the Gents. It was the first time that he and I had opportunity to talk in private.

"What do you think of Penny?" he asked. "She's a stunner." Before I could reply he went on, "She fancies you like mad. You can tell in the way she looks at you. I've heard all the gooey stuff she has been saying to you. Without doubt you are in there mate."

I tried to change the subject and pointed out that Carol was very nice too. I knew it was what he wanted to hear. I declined to say that I wouldn't change Penny for her any day.

I was rather shocked when Keith said "Carol is alright for up here but I've got a better bird down in Bournemouth. She satisfies me and that's good enough for me." Then he went all serious as we washed our hands and shared the grubby towel.

"After the pictures Carol wants us to go to her place to change her shoes before we go to the Club" he said.

"Club?" I asked. "What Club?"

"It's something to do with the printing shop where Carol works" Keith went on. "It's good for dancing and they don't do a bad pint there. Carol and Penny go there quite a bit and I know you will enjoy it."

Keith looked at me for some kind of reaction and when I didn't respond he continued. "You will get to meet Carol's brother there. Funnily enough his name is Ken too. Ken has got a van and he will get us back to Camp by ten thirty but try and keep sober. We don't want any trouble with the guard on the gate."

I nodded in agreement but said nothing, anticipating that there was more to come.

"It pays to be careful on these nights out" Keith suddenly began to look very wise. "By the way that reminds me, are you equipped?"

"Equipped?" My face must have put on a quizzical expression.

Keith gave a deep sigh. "I thought not" he muttered as he put his hand into the inner pocket of his jacket and retrieved his wallet. Fumbling within its folds he withdrew two small pink packets. One of these he transferred to the breast pocket in his shirt and the other he pushed into my hand. At a quick glance I saw the packet contained a condom. Without a word I hastily stuffed it into my back pocket as another fellow came into the Gents.

"Now for the bookies" said Keith breezily when we met up with the girls again outside the loos. Then, throwing me a knowing wink he exclaimed, "I think this is going to be our lucky day!" I left the bookmakers five shillings better off because Prince Regent romped home to win his race at five to one. Keith called it "beginners luck." He was a bit over a pound better off and would have reinvested some of this on other races if he had the time. Thankfully we had to move quickly to get to the pictures.

My mind wasn't too intent on the film and I'm sure Penny's wasn't either. No sooner had the lights gone down and she got very amorous. Now I understood why couples usually went for the back row in the cinema.

All too soon the film ended and Carol started complaining about her feet again.

She had slipped her shoes off during the film and now she was having difficulty in getting them on again.

"I am going home to change these uncomfortable things" she moaned when we got outside the pictures and I couldn't fail to notice how Keith was eager to get her there.

"I have had a good win on the horses" he said. "Come on. I can afford a taxi.

It's not far."

It was Carol who decided that the taxi should make a short detour to drop Penny and me off at Penny's home first. Carol explained that she was going home to change and put on some more comfortable shoes. She was also going to arrange for her brother, Ken, to pick Penny and I up in his van to take the five of us on to the Club in about an hour's time. It seemed she had got the evening's arrangements very carefully planned.

The taxi dropped Penny and I off first. She was very quick to assure me that we had the house to ourselves. Her father had taken her mother and little sister to visit relatives out Wigan way.

"Do you want a drink?" Penny asked quickly and I shook my head. "What do you want?" she asked provocatively and threw her arms around my neck.

We stood in the middle of the room kissing and cuddling for a long time. It was a nice feeling to be wanted and a very pleasant change from the rigours of Service life.

"I am going upstairs to change my frock" said Peggy. "You can get yourself a cup of tea if you want."

I declined the tea and sat on an old settee which was littered with magazines and newspapers. I idly picked up one and started to read when I was called from upstairs.

"What do you think of this frock, Ken? Do you think it's too tight on me?." I went half way up the stairs to give my considered opinion. Penny was wearing a red skin-tight, low neck dress, which revealed more than it covered. It looked far too tight and really uncomfortable and I said so.

Penny laughed and said something which I didn't hear. On the bed lay a black frock with a check collar. It was short sleeved and looked far smarter than the red one which she was wearing. I suggested the black one was the more classy one of the two. I didn't bargain for her next move.

Peggy turned to the bed, snatched the frock from it and unceremoniously threw it at me with the words, "it's a lovely frock, not cheap, but Carol says it reminds her of a waitress's uniform."

As I lifted the frock from my head where it landed, Penny had slipped out of the red one. Turning, she walked towards me with hand outstretched for the black garment. Except for a very scanty pair of white panties, she was naked.

Gentlemanly I turned my head and proffered the dress. Penny laughed again.

"Am I embarrassing you?" she asked. "You don't give me the impression you're the shy type."

A lot of thoughts were buzzing in my brain and I found myself talking very quickly. I think I said something about Keith and Carol would be there any minute with Ken to collect us."

"You must be joking" Penny pouted. "If you use your imagination you can guess what they are up to at this very minute." Why do you think they were so anxious to get rid of us? You don't want them to have all the fun do you?"

Like an innocent schoolboy being led into school by the hand, she led me to the bed.

CHAPTER 19

The pressure on our military training increased more every day. We were spending a lot of time on the parade ground which was alright when we were in shirt sleeve order. It wasn't too bad when we were in number two dress, trousers, battle dress and beret. It became unbearably hot when we were in number one dress which was a thick tunic, pair of trousers and a peaked cap. Most of us felt strangled by the necessity of wearing shirts with collar studs and a tie as we marched up and down endlessly in the blazing sun.

Our legs felt like they were made of lead at the end of each day. Heels and toes were blistered where boots rubbed, some of us had heat rashes and every day we had stinking socks.

As soon as we were allowed to return to our billet, everybody went through the self-same ritual. Rip off tie and collars with the stud, ease off the boots and lay exhausted on the bed. The problem was that when we bent down to put the boots on again it was always with difficulty. It seemed as though our feet had swollen or the boots had shrunk which added to our misery.

Two things kept us going through the hardest time of our training so far. It was the constant thought that all the extra drill and training was because we were rehearsing for the final Pass Out Parade which was now on the horizon. Secondly we knew that when that day came our time at Padgate was finished and our mental and physical torture would come to an end. The prospect of going home for two weeks leave prior to being posted to our next trade training camp was the incentive and uppermost in our minds. Even so, the days seemed long and the constant jibes and yelling of our instructors unending. Much was expected of us. I was very sad and disappointed to receive a letter from my parents turning down my invitation to come and watch the parade. Neither Mum nor Dad had ever ventured so far away from our home in Berkshire. Lancashire, as far as they were concerned, could have been on the other side of the world.

Most of the lads had someone coming to the parade which made it even harder.

Then I had a brain wave. I would invite Penny so that it wouldn't look like I had been entirely abandoned. I told Keith about my idea and he was horrified.

I was dumbfounded when he revealed that he had told Carol the parade was a fortnight later than it was. He had got it all worked out. The Pass Out Parade would come and go, we would disappear from Padgate for our new postings, and the girls would never set eyes on us again.

There were to be no tender farewells or promises of undying love. No promises of keeping in touch and certainly no leaving forwarding address. It was a callous thing to do.

Keith, who had an irritating habit of calling me "Kiddo" spelt it out to me.

"Kiddo" he said, "let me put it this way. We have had some fun haven't we? There's no flippin' way we can carry on a long distance relationship. We could be posted anywhere for trade training and then abroad somewhere. You don't want a pen pal, do you? We wouldn't like it if they did that to us" I protested. "They are going to be very hurt and I can't just switch off my feelings like turning off the electric light."

"You're too sentimental Ken" Keith replied. "Love 'em and leave 'em I say. You need to keep your options open and see what talent there is on the next posting. Off with old and on with the new."

I had to agree that the distance and serving in the RAF would make contact difficult. I voiced my feelings that to leave without so much as a goodbye was a bit harsh. I knew we would have to make a date knowing that we had no intention of keeping it. Leading Carol and Penny to believe the Parade was a fortnight in the future was a low down thing to do.

I eased my conscience by convincing myself that the girls' were probably expecting something along the lines that we were planning anyway, During times that we spent together we heard that they had dated other airmen in the past. I recalled something Penny said on our very first date "I'm usually the one who gets let down."

The thought of not seeing Penny again made me feel a bit depressed. Keith, on the other hand, was jubilant. He had cheated on so many girls in his short life time and he always had, as he so aptly put it "My bird down in Bournemouth."

"Better to have loved and lost than never to love at all" Keith breezed. "There will be plenty waiting in the future."

Any thoughts for our future never ventured any further than the Pass Out Parade. Every piece of uniform was double pressed, every bit of webbing blanco'd, every button polished and re-polished. As for my boots, you could see to shave in them. Every night I laboriously made little circles of polish dampened with spit on the toe caps. I heated a spoon over the flame of a candle and applied the heat to the polish.

With a piece of rag I made little circular movements to form a layer of gloss.

Vigorous rubbing with a soft duster brought a glow to the toe caps and soreness to my fingers.

It was so important to get everything just right for the parade. Apart from being immaculately dressed, our drill had to be perfect and our behaviour praiseworthy. We were expected to be a credit to the RAF and our instructors. Impressive to the very senior officer who was taking the salute and inspecting us. Finally we had to earn the admiration of the public who had come to watch.

Our billet was a hive of industry the night before the vital parade. Our emotions ran high and our nerves were at fever pitch. We began to bicker amongst ourselves. Frustrations boiled over when we all wanted to use the one iron at the same time.

There was a frantic searching when a piece of kit went missing and a groan or two when buttons were found to be missing off shirts, and holes had appeared in the heels of socks.

I was in despair every time I worked on my webbing belt. It seemed impossible not to get Brasso on the webbing bits and blanco on the brass buckles. I must have spent the best part of an hour putting both Brasso and blanco on and then taking it off again.

Robin came and peered over my shoulder to see how I was managing. He suggested putting pieces of paper between webbing and buckles but it didn't work. It was Pomeroy who butted in and ungraciously snapped at Robin "Don't be daft! Go and blanco your collars" Robin, looking decidedly crestfallen wandered off muttering something unintelligible.

Pomeroy took over my offending belt and made a good job of it for which I was very thankful.

More arguments broke out over the use of the iron. Sweating and cursing could be heard in the bathroom where there were loud complaints about the water running cold for baths and showers. Everybody was clock watching because of the ten thirty lights out rule. There seemed to be so much to do but so little time. All the tension and with emotions running so high it was inevitable that trouble struck.

As Pete sat on his bed polishing his boots, an angry exchange of words broke out between him and Phil who was trying to adjust a brass buckle on his belt. Phil, for no apparent reason, just snapped. He shot off his bed and began to rain blows with the belt on poor Pete's unsuspecting head. We watched open mouthed as Phil went berserk and continued bringing the belt down on Pete and shouting and swearing. Pete was stunned and hastily curled up on his bed trying to protect his head from the blows that fell mercilessly upon him.

When Phil continued to whip Pete and made his nose bleed, Alex went to fetch the Corporal from his bunk but he wasn't in. If he had heard the noise and saw what was going on, I hate to think what the outcome might have been.

A short struggle followed as about four of the lads dragged Phil off. He was hysterical and sobbing as they threw him roughly on to his own bed. We looked at each other, shrugged, and decided to leave him to recover on his own.

No sooner had each one of us returned to our own tasks when pandemonium broke out again. With some vicious remark Phil leapt off his bed, snatched Pete's boots out of his hands and hurled them into the fire bucket of water standing next to the ironing table. The same fire bucket that had been responsible for breaking Ged's toe weeks before.

This was the final straw and our Senior Man, Bill, grabbed Phil by the throat and shook him like a rabbit. He swore at him several times and then slapped his face. Not content with this he then twisted Phil's arm up his back and made him yell. Holding him with one hand he then fished Pete's boots out of the bucket with the other.

Bill threw the soaking boots in Pete's direction and then frogmarched Phil, with his arm still twisted up his back, towards the door and into the bathroom.

"Come on guys. You're needed." This special command from Bill suddenly spurred us all into action. Like a flock of sheep we followed Bill and the hapless Phil, still struggling and protesting, into the bathroom.

With a mighty thrust of his shoulder Bill knocked Phil backwards into the shower. "Get in there and cool off" he said.

But Phil was not having any of that and swearing, punching at anything that moved and still struggling he tried to get out of the shower. This time he was out numbered and we all came out strongly on Bill's side. Together we over powered Phil and held him under the shower whilst someone turned on the tap.

Icy cold water cascaded down on Phil and he struggled to get out but was overpowered. Fully dressed he was forced to take his unscheduled shower.

"Let that be a lesson" Bill growled and unexpectedly gave his cheek a resounding slap. As one we all turned our back on Phil and, trundled back into the billet.

It all ended as sudden as it began. Pete was on his bed where we left him with his head still in his hands. Alex went and sat down beside him and put his hand on his shoulder. "We will sort your boots out, mate" he said kindly. "Don't upset yourself. That guy is a nutter".

It was about a quarter of an hour before Phil ventured to come back in to the billet. His head was bowed and he never said a word or looked at anybody. He had stripped to his vest and underpants and went to his locker where he took out a towel and his pyjamas and returned to the bathroom.

Tears started to trickle down Pete's face and his shoulders were shaking. By now everybody had gathered around his bed to sympathise and to see how we could help. All this upheaval was the last thing we needed the night prior to the Pass Out Parade.

Bill picked up Pete's sodden boots and looked at them ruefully. "How are you going to wear them on parade tomorrow morning?" he asked. Pete sniffed, shook his head and didn't reply.

For the next ten minutes or so several suggestions were made. None of them sounded feasible however. None of us could see how the boots could be dried and bulled up in just a few hours.

As the deliberations continued a very dejected Phil entered the room carrying his wet clothes which he dumped in a heap on his bed. Then surprisingly he elbowed his way through the group of us who were still trying to console Pete, and to our astonishment, he knelt down in front of him.

"I'm sorry Pete" he said very quietly. "you can have my boots if they will fit you. What size do you take?"

A single word escaped Pete's lips. "Eight."

"That's alright then", Phil continued, "I take size nine and we can stuff some paper up the toes to make them fit." It was quite touching to watch how Phil was looking up at Pete from his position on his knees. A thought suddenly occurred to Pete and he managed to raise a smile and asked the obvious question.

"If I am going to wear your boots, what are you going to wear on the parade?"

Phil didn't have an answer but it was all he could think of on the spur of the moment. He was feeling ashamed at what he had done and anxious to make amends.

"I reckon we can get the boots dried and bulled if we put our minds to it." This coming from Robin came as a shock to us all. Robin was not well known for making suggestions or coming up with good ideas. He looked a bit embarrassed - as we all gaped at him in silence and then he came up with a classic statement.

"Why don't we have a go with the hair dryer?"

For once Robin had come up trumps. He was, after all, the only one in the billet who owned a hair dryer. It was a leaving home present from his Mum and he guarded it like a treasure. No-one was ever allowed to borrow it.

Ever faithful Rob enjoyed the attention he received as he withdrew his hair dryer from his locker. He plugged it in the socket beside my bed and reached for one of

Pete's boots. We all gathered round to watch the procedure.

Robin pointed the head of the dryer inside the lace gap of the boot. A strange sickly smell emerged and a trail of vapour which increased by the second.

Pete began to panic. "Go steady, Rob!" he exclaimed. "I reckon you are burning the leather."

"Should keep your feet warm" added Den with a grin.

I thought it was the hair dryer itself that was over heating and said so but no-one took any notice. Someone suggested the dryer should not be held too near to the boot.

More than half an hour later, with us all taking a turn to manhandle the boots, they still remained decidedly damp and stinking of burnt leather and polish. In the end Pete took over the job of drying his own boots with the dryer.

Every now and then Phil wandered over to see what progress Pete was making, even volunteering to do some drying. When Pete got bored with the boots he dumped them and the dryer on Phil's bed. "You can finish 'em off" he said.

"He probably will!" growled Pomeroy as the rest of us returned to titivate every bit of uniform and kit. None of us felt confident that we were up to standard personally, but, we complimented each other on a high standard.

As we finished off all we could do before lights out, one by one we crept to our beds except for Phil. He looked pathetic as he was still trying to make Pete's dull toe caps shine. His head was nodding and he was almost falling asleep as he continued to spit, apply polish and make the little circular movements with a bit of rag.

I looked around the room and thought this is the last night we shall be together.

Tomorrow, hopefully, I would be back home on leave and in my own bed. I was excited with that prospect but dreading what the morrow would bring prior to that happy event.

Would we be a well turned out squadron in the morning? How would we compare to the lads from the other two billets? Most of all, would all the weeks" of toil and tears produce a fine body of trained men or would our incompetence and weaknesses show? We knew that in just a few hours all would be revealed.

CHAPTER 20

I thought I had been hit by a steam roller. 'My slumbers were rudely interrupted as simultaneously I heard a yell, a lot of swearing and felt a crushing weight fall across my chest.

Ron had slipped on some water on the lino by my bed space and landed right on top of me as I lay in my bed.

Every night I had moved the fire bucket from beside my bed after Ged had broken his toe on the thing. Last night was no different. I had as usual moved the bucket, but with all the pandemonium with Pete's boots earlier on, I had forgotten to mop up the puddles which Ron now found to his cost.

As I sleepily protested about the invasion of my dreams, Ron pulled the covers off me. "It's time you got up" he declared, "today is the big day."

One by one the lads arose from their beds. The billet was unusually but noticeably very quiet. Instead of the banter and swearing and ribald comments there was a silence. I guessed everyone was busy with their private thoughts and worried about today's all important Pass Out Parade.

For once we didn't have to make up our bed packs because first thing after breakfast we had to return all our bedding to the store. Providing all went well with the parade we would all be heading for home.

I was so pre-occupied with all my own thoughts for the day that I ignored what Robin was saying as he shaved at the next sink to mine, I came to when he nudged my arm.

"I am ever so pleased Pete's boots are alright" he said, "nobody is laughing at my hair dryer now."

Between us we had to admit a grand job had been done on that pair of boots. Pete was delighted, Phil relieved and the rest of us very thankful. I hoped the boots wouldn't change colour whilst Pete was wearing them. There was no knowing what hot feet might do to damp shoes that looked gleaming on the outside.

For the first time ever we were all very early for breakfast. The Mess Hall was still closed when we arrived and Pomeroy began to swear. "They do it on purpose" he fumed, but we didn't have to wait long before we were admitted.

After breakfast we were assembled by Bill, our senior man, and waited for Corporal Brown to march us off to the store to hand in our bedding. Once that was handed in it felt like we were going home.

From the bedding store we were marched to the armoury to collect our rifles, and, we actually ran back to the billet with them to prepare for the parade.

Our billet was a hive of activity as we had less than an hour to make our final preparations.

To save time we had put everything we should need on our beds before we went to breakfast. Now it was time for a quick change into our best uniform, put the slings on the rifles and breathing on the boot toe caps for the last time. A quick brush of the teeth, assuring cases and kit bags were packed and nothing was left behind ended the ritual which was undertaken at great speed.

One by one we emerged as the smart airmen we were. There was a real sense of pride and comradeship between us. It was amusing how we inspected each other.

A tie was adjusted here and a speck of dust brushed off there. We wanted each other to be on top form because we realised how much we needed each other. We were a team.

About twenty minutes before we were due to assemble for marching to the parade ground, Sergeant Tubbs and two of our corporals came into the billet.

Gone was all the aggression and shouting. It seemed uncanny in the way they smiled and chatted pleasantly without any hint of sarcasm. We were congratulated on our turn out and encouraged to do our best.

Everything seemed to be ideal for the parade. The sun was shining but there was a cool breeze. We had worked so hard for weeks and we were determined that nothing was going to go wrong in this last one hour. On that we were agreed.

Most of the lads were worried about being charged for their personal appearance. I didn't worry about that. My chief concern was that I would do something foolish like getting out of step whilst marching, or, turning the wrong way on command.

We could hear the Band playing in the distance as we assembled outside our billet. Minutes later our Flying Officer and Sergeant Tubbs were marching us smartly to an area not far from where the parade would be held on the main square. At this point we were halted and given last minute warnings and instructions as the Band marched to form up with us.

This was it. With the Squadron Leader out in front, the Band following and we three companies of airmen being led by the Flying Officer, Sergeant Tubbs and the three corporals. The parade had begun.

"Left, right. Left, right." The commands were loud and clear. It was much easier to time the marching with the beat of the Band. We were all in step, very upright, and our arms swinging high.

A special stand had been erected for the VIP's and all the guests and there seemed to be a very large gathering watching us come on to the parade ground.

"Left, right. Left, right." We were marched into the centre of the square and halted in front of a red-carpeted dais.

The RAF Standard fluttered in the light breeze beside the dais as we received the order to "Stand at ease", and then "Stand easy." For the next five minutes it was good to take deep breaths and relax.

Some of the guests recognized relatives and friends on the parade and were calling them by name and waving. It was embarrassing some because they were not allowed to wave or call back, Discipline was paramount. I was just a little bit sad that I didn't have anyone there watching out for me.

"Squad ..... Attention!" The command was drawn out and pronounced. Feet clicked together as one and bodies straightened swiftly and smartly. For the next three or four minutes we stood like rocks staring ahead and not moving a muscle.

The VIP's and guests stood up and an air of expectancy prevailed. Almost immediately and almost silently the Inspecting Officer's car, flying a pennant, glided to a halt next to the dais. The chauffer emerged to open the back door and the Inspecting Officer stepped out in brilliant sunshine to be greeted by the Station Commander and other officers in waiting who smartly saluted each other.

The parade was ordered to "Present Arms" and with a flash of rifles in unison, the move was very smartly executed whilst the Band played The Royal Air Force Fly Past March. The Senior Officer returned a salute and was then informed that the Recruit Pass Out Parade was ready for his inspection.

The Band played on as the Senior Officer was escorted to our Company first.

Slowly he walked up and down each column of men, his glance sweeping every man from top to toe.

I felt my heart beating fast as the Inspecting Officer came to our line. Gold braid stood out on the' peak of his cap and a row of medals clinked on his chest. The sun shone on the Adjutant's sword as he held it aloft as he accompanied the Officer and Station Commander. I took a deep breath and attempted to hold it as the Inspector approached. He looked and passed without a word although he did stop and ask some of the airmen questions. He asked Pomeroy where he came from and smiled when he said, "Beg your pardon, Sir?" He had not heard the question.

The Senior Officer moved on down the line and, thankfully for all of us, Pete's boots passed the inspection.

When our Company had been inspected the Officer stopped for a brief chat with Sergeant Tubbs and the corporals before moving on to the next Company. We were ordered to "Stand at ease!.."

I knew the worst was over. We had been inspected and no fault found as far as we were aware. As long as our drill and marching were good from this point on, we could soon expect to leave the place forever.

It took a long time for the entire parade to be inspected and the Band continued to play throughout. Eventually, as the sun seemed to be at its hottest, the Senior Officer climbed the steps to the dais and awaited the final march past.

We were really beginning to perspire now as the Band was brought into line and the Companies formed to follow it. A series of drill moves followed as we assembled for the formal salute and march past.

My shoulder was very sore from the weight of the rifle but I was carefully concentrating on the command "Eyes right." This meant we had to move our heads sharply to the right and look at the Senior Officer as he stood on his dais and we marched past him.

In rehearsal I never found it easy to march forward in a straight line whilst looking sideways. It all went without a hitch and the Officer saluted as we marched past.

Soon we were well clear of the parade ground and back at the spot where we had formed up with the band earlier on. Our Flight Officer was clearly very pleased and kept repeating his favourite phrase. "Well done, chaps. Well done!" After what seemed like some considerable delay we were marched back to the armoury to hand the rifles in. When this was completed we had to form up again and the Flying Officer, Sergeant Tubbs, and the three corporals from our billets shook our hands very warmly and wished us all good luck for the future.

I looked closely at Corporal Brown and remembered how he had almost strangled me. He had wanted so much to impress his superiors and improve his reputation for turning out a fine body of men. Obviously he had succeeded this time judging by his wide smile.

Everybody knew that we were anxious to get across to the large hall where the relatives and friends were waiting. The RAF had provided a fantastic buffet for the occasion and it was the place where we would receive our posting orders and learn where our next destination was going to be.

The RAF had done us proud. There were wild scenes of exuberance, cheers and some tears as families and friends were re-united again. Although I didn't have anyone to greet, most of the lads introduced me to their folks. There were a lot of hugs and everybody was clearly excited.

Keith strutted about as proud as a peacock with his girlfriend on his arm. The girl he always referred to as "My bird from Bournemouth" was a stunner. She was very scantily dressed so it was a good thing it was a hot day. Lovely blonde hair, big blue eyes and long lashes and tall and slim. Davie summed it up for us all when he remarked "Trust Adonis to land himself a bird worth dying for" Clearly Keith was giving no thought of Carol but I had a twinge of conscience about Penny.

The officers and the senior NCO's mingled with the gathering and a lot of light hearted banter went to and fro until the Squadron Leader entered. He entered with a large pile of posting orders in his hand.

Suddenly the room went very quiet and it seemed like the Squadron Leader was enjoying the sensation his entry had caused.

"I'm sorry to interrupt your party" he began, "but it is necessary to combine business with pleasure." He waved the posting orders aloft.

"Please step forward when your name is called. Abrahams .... Aldridge ....." The Squadron Leader began calling the names in alphabetical order and it took some time for him to get to S for Stallard.

I joined up with a little group consisting of Robin and his parents and Steve who was showing his girlfriend his official letter. "Where are you going?" Steve asked as I approached the group.

I tore open the envelope. "RAF Credenhill, Hereford", I replied "How about you?"

"Weston Super Mare" he muttered and we both looked expectantly at Robin. Robin made no comment but his mother was swift to cut in. "Robin is going to Ventnor on the Isle of Wight, that will be nice don't you think?" It didn't matter what we thought but the prospect of pastures new made Robin look decidedly miserable until he found Davie was going there too.

At last it was time for our farewells. We hugged each other, made rude comments, joked and swore someday we must have a reunion.

A RAF photographer took an official large group photograph of the three companies combined and promised we would receive in in the post by and by. It would be a lasting memorial of the time we had spent together and then we were gone.

On the train later I watched the ever changing scenery slip by as I headed south for Oxford. I was looking forward to going home and being with the family again.

It would be good to have my own bedroom again and get up in the morning when I wanted.

I had two whole weeks of leave in front of me and that seemed like an eternity before I needed to think about RAF Credenhill.

With recruit training now a thing of the past, I had to look forward to a three month stint of trade training in

Herefordshire. I had decided to go as a Provisioning Clerk so I reflected on the fact that I would be spending some considerable time in a class room.

I leaned back and relaxed in my train seat. I closed my eyes and a big smile came across my face. I thought about the last three months. My mind focused on the Reliability and Initiative Test and how we left Bunce on the bus. I thought about capturing my own officer on the exercise, and, I almost laughed out aloud when I thought of the Squadron Leader dangling in the derrick seat. The escapades with the rifles and guns would stay in our memories for ever. We had a good bunch of lads in our billet. Sorry that old Ged had to get re-flighted for breaking his toe though. I wondered, if by contrast, Penny would be nursing her broken heart? So much had happened in the past three months with recruit training: What, I wondered, would the next three months of trade training entail? A new Camp, a new way of life and a set of new friends.

At Padgate I had almost been struck by lightning and strangled by a Corporal. It surely could only get better at Hereford. Just before I fell asleep through sheer fatigue I thought on Keith's words. "Kiddo, it's off with the old and on with the new."

CHAPTER 21

I watched in amazement as my mother did a whole loaf of sandwiches. Half of cheese and cucumber and half of corned beef.

"I am not going to feed a whole squadron" I said as she proceeded to pack the lot into a biscuit tin.

"You can take some cakes and some crisps and a bottle of orange squash" was her prompt reply. "Oh, and I almost forgot, I have made you some mince pies." "Mince pies in October?" I asked but my question was met by silence.

The day had arrived for me to catch a bus to Oxford Station and then proceed to Hereford by train. Hereford was the nearest railway station to RAF Credenhill where I was due to report today for three months trade training.

Standing on the platform at Oxford Station I surveyed my luggage. I clearly had to make some adjustments in order to be able to carry all the gear. I had a bulging kit bag with my name and service number emblazoned on it for all to see. One very large suitcase, a holdall with a broken zip fastener which was bursting at the seams and the larger than large tin of sandwiches.

I felt awkward and very self-conscious in my greatcoat which had been far too large for me since it had been issued at Cardington. Now it was looking grotesque with both pockets bulging. One with a pint size bottle of orange squash and the other stuffed and overflowing with the cakes and mince pies. I tried unsuccessfully to transfer items between the luggage but to no avail. I decided to give up and was very thankful when I had heaved all the gear on to the train and shoved as much of it as I could under the seat.

There were a couple of lads in RAF uniform in the carriage. One of them was blond and the other had a shock of bright ginger hair. I noticed the blond guy elbow the other and nodded in my direction. I smiled and nodded back whereupon they stood up together and came and sat down beside me.

"You going to Credenhill?" Ginge enquired.

"Yes, it's my first day for trade training" I replied. "Are you going there too?"

"We are" the blond guy cut in. "I am Tim and I'm from London." Then with a wave of his arm towards the other lad he said "This is George and he got on the train at Reading. There are some more lads in uniform in the other carriages as well."

I revealed that I was Ken from a village near Wantage in Berkshire and soon the three of us were giving our life and RAF histories as though we had known each other forever.

Further conversation was cut short when Tim with his nose pressed against the window announced "It's snowing!" Snow had been forecast and the past couple of days had been bitterly cold even though it was only October. I was glad to be wearing the bizarre great coat and reflected how different first day at Credenhill was compared to the first day we sweltered on Warrington Station when we were on our way to Padgate.

I was surprised to see at least a couple of dozen airmen getting off the train at Hereford. We kind of grouped ourselves together and it seemed like everyone was talking at once.

"Anybody know how we are supposed to get to Credenhill from here?" "Have they put on any transport for us?"

"Why is there no-one here to meet us?"

At this point one of the station staff came up to us.

"I presume you lot are going to RAF Credenhill" he said, "they will be sending a coach for you anytime now. The coaches are usually here in time to meet the trains. They picked up a coach load about an hour and a half ago so don't give up hope." In less than a quarter of an hour the coach arrived and we were met by a young corporal and a much older sergeant.

I was impressed. The sergeant addressed us as "Gentlemen."

"Gentlemen" he said, "sorry we were not here to meet you but we got held up by the police and an ambulance at Sugwas where there has been an accident."

We were ushered on to the coach and I was only too conscious that I appeared to have a lot more luggage than everybody else.

It was a very grey day and the snow continued to fall and the flakes got bigger.

We went through a couple of villages and very soon we swept through the gates of RAF Credenhill.

The Camp resembled Padgate in many ways. There were the customary couple of guards on the main gate. The all too familiar Guard Room and a white flag pole flying the RAF Colour and the Station Commanders flag. Classrooms were dotted about here and there but I failed to see any buildings that looked like our billets. The coach drew to a halt near the cookhouse. We disembarked from the coach and were ushered inside the cookhouse which was in semi darkness. The only occupant was a very unfriendly cook who made it very clear that tea had ended ages ago and then promptly disappeared.

Minutes later the same cook re-appeared with some loaves of bread and two large cartons. One contained margarine and the other marmalade. "You can make yourselves some toast" he said and disappeared this time for good.

There was a general scramble for the bread and a small queue formed in front of the toasters. Some of the lads spread the margarine and made marmalade sandwiches not content with joining the toast queue. It was now that I was most thankful for all the food my mother had prepared and sought out my new found friends, Tim and George, to share the luxuries.

It was getting quite dark before a Warrant Officer arrived and ordered us to form up in parade style in the car park. We were allocated accommodation by building number and sent off in the direction of the billets. It was a very long walk and most of it uphill and in the dark.

I was hampered by all the stuff I had to carry and was one of the last to arrive at my allocated billet. It was not welcoming in any way at all.

It was an old wooden hut with a tin roof and looked like something left over from World War I. Inside it had wooden rafters and eight iron beds on each side. In the centre of the room was an old tortoise style coke stove sitting in the centre of a concrete base and surrounds complete with a very black chimney.

There were some bedside lockers and cupboards and a few old wooden chairs. It smelt musty and the lighting was extremely poor.

Unlike our billets at Padgate here we had to go outside and enter another building for washing, baths and toilets. Not a comforting thought with it presently snowing and winter months to look forward to. Then we figured out that the central heating simply consisted of that very old central coke stove. The only thing that was central about the heating was that it stood sadly in the centre of the room.

Any further moans and complaints that we had were silenced by the return of the Warrant Officer who returned with a van containing our allocation of pillows, pillow cases, sheets and blankets. We proceeded to make up the bed we had chosen and I added my greatcoat as an extra blanket because I was so cold. Once the lights were out I sneaked the mince pies out of my pocket and under cover of darkness and the blankets enjoyed a midnight feast when most of the others went to bed very hungry.

Next morning in the cold light of day reality hit us. It had stopped snowing but it was still bitterly cold.

We dashed the short distance from the billet to the wash room but the water was only tepid. No one was going to have a bath for sure.

As I entered the wash room I was confronted by two elderly men who were cleaning the sinks. They were civilian cleaners from Hereford who were employed to clean the wash rooms and toilets and the classrooms but not the billets.

Clearly they did not enjoy their work and swore and complained about the Camp and the conditions that they were working under. I was not a little alarmed when they explained there was a shortage of coke and the billets would be freezing. The small supply of coke that was left was for heating the classrooms only but airmen of the past had been known to break up the wooden chairs and use them as the only means of fuel. I could only imagine that would bring some recriminations and punishment.

Whilst we were at breakfast we were confronted by half a dozen teachers and instructors designated to be our tutors on the Clerk Provisioning Course that we had chosen as our RAF trade. We were called in surname order to an allocated classroom. I was delighted that both Tim and George who I had met on the train were in the same class as me.

Our Sergeant Instructor was called Bill Redfem and he was a most likeable chap. Friendly and with a great sense of humour he never lost patience and was painstaking in explaining every minute detail of the subjects we were studying.

We got on well from the very beginning when he discovered that I was from the Wantage area of Berkshire and he was from Wallingford which is only about eighteen miles away in the same County. He announced to the class amidst great laughter that we were Berkshire born and Berkshire bred, Strong in the arm but weak in the head! Sergeant Redfem's very first question was, therefore, directed at me. "Why did you choose to join the RAF as a Provisioning Clerk?" he asked.

I explained that prior to joining the RAF I had been employed by the International Grocery Store chain as a grocery shop assistant. I was experienced with dealing with all kinds of provisions. I listed Tea, Sugar, Butter, Cheese, Flour, Bacon and Eggs as examples. I concluded therefore that as I was conversant with "Provisioning" that this would keep me in good stead for provisioning for the cookhouse which would need all the items just mentioned.

Sergeant Redfem smiled broadly. "So you think you are going to provide all the provisions for the cookhouse do you?" he asked. I nodded.

"Well, Stallard, I've got news for you" he replied. "You and the rest of the class are here, not for the provisioning of the needs of the cookhouse, but you will learn to be competent in provisioning for all aspects of parts for aircraft. From nose to tail, from wings, engine, propeller to wheels and undercarriage."

I was stunned. Everything seemed to sink into oblivion as he went on to explain. "We are taking on board a new aircraft which is currently on the Secret List. It is the pride and joy of our Canadian friends and we shall be privileged to keep it in the air for Britain. It is called the Sabre Jet. When the aircraft is grounded for the want of a part you will be the one to provide that part and get the 'plane back in the air on active service."

Suddenly it felt that I was like a non-swimmer who had been thrown into the ten feet deep end of a swimming pool. Intricate parts of the aircraft panel, navigation and electrical systems seemed so very far distance from raisins, butter, sugar and flour ingredients for the provision of a fruit cake. This is not what I had bargained for at all. It is a long route from a cookhouse to jet travel.

Berkshire born and Berkshire bred, strong in the arm and weak in the head I surely must be. My head had been so much in the clouds when I volunteered to join the RAF but somehow I couldn't imagine that the Sabre Jet would be up above the clouds because of my provisioning skills. Only time will tell.

CHAPTER 22

Whack! A sudden sharp blow suddenly hit me on my neck which almost made me jump out of my skin.

Our Class Sergeant Vaughan had thrown the missile which was no other than the wooden backed sponge for cleaning the blackboard. It hurt a lot.

"Wake up, Stallard" he yelled in his strong Glaswegian accent. "Next time I will throw you at the blackboard." Everybody giggled until he further explained "And that goes for the rest of you who don't pay attention."

It was my turn to be on the receiving end of his tongue lashing again. "Well, laddie" he continued, "so what does A.O.G. mean?"

The blank look on my face must have conveyed the fact that I didn't have a clue so he took large exaggerated strides over to my desk. I suffered further indignity as he twisted my ear and hissed "If you had been listening you would have known it means Aircraft on Ground." He almost lifted me off the ground by my ear as he repeated "Did you get that? Aircraft on Ground!" The Sergeant went on to explain that when we were on occupational and active duties, any demands received from other RAF units endorsed "A.O.G." meant these had to be treated with the greatest urgency. It was vital that a grounded aircraft was supplied with whatever it needed to get it back into the air as soon as possible. It was emphasised that in war time it could lose valuable time and lives if what the aeroplane required was not available. Timing was vital.

I quickly discovered that Tim and George had understood the demands system fairly well and were more than happy to explain it to me in greater detail when we had a break for tea.

There were six other lads with us in the Class. Mick and Joe had paired up because they both came from Lancashire. Geordie, well we didn't have to guess where he came from, and, the tallest goofiest bloke I had ever seen from Wolverhampton was called Gerald. The last remaining guy was Raymond, who hated being called Ray but everybody insisted that was what he was going to be called so he had to put up with it. I always thought Ray had some sort of an affliction because he had a constant running nose which he was always dabbing with a handkerchief.

Three days into the Course and Shaun was drafted in to join us from Belfast. Shaun was typically Irish and his Irish accent and non-stop humour kept us continually entertained.

I suppose, all in all, we must have given Sergeant Vaughan nightmares. We were hardly Battle of Britain material but at least we had all volunteered for this Course and were determined to do our best.

We were always glad when the afternoon sessions ended and we could escape to the Airmen's Mess for late tea.

The food was better than we had at Padgate but sadly it appeared to be in short supply. The portions served were very small and Shaun was forever complaining because at every meal something was not available that should have been.

It was cereals and no milk or milk but no cereals. Apple pie and no custard. Finally Shaun's humour turned to rage when it was announced cottage pie had no gravy and he discovered maggot holes in the potatoes.

"You couldn't organise a booze up in a brewery" he complained to the chief cook. "Every day dare is someting missing" he raged.

"Look at teas taters." The plate of half cold potatoes was unceremoniously thrust under the cook's nose. "I have seen better taters in a pig pen!" The cook appeared unruffled and suggested he could serve Shaun with some corned beef but there were no other potatoes. Somewhat appeased Shaun handed the offending meal to the cook and agreed to accept corned beef sandwiches instead.

Later on as I was at the tea urn filling my mug I heard a roar and a resounding crash and much swearing. Looking over to where Shaun had been sitting with Geordie and a couple of lads I didn't know, I now saw him standing, ranting and stamping his foot on a broken plate and a pile of corned beef sandwiches.

Much more swearing and still more swearing. I heard him yell "Who do you tink I am?" "Do you tink I am an idiot? I know dat when der bread is blue it's mouldy. It's bad. You give me gut rot wid dat muck."

Oh dear! I couldn't face another blast off from Shaun or be a witness to a murder so I decided to walk back to the billet in the dark. I cupped my hands around the mug of tea to keep them warm as the wind was bitter. I shivered as I climbed the hill back to the billet and thought of my folks back home. They would be sitting by a nice log fire. I knew the billet was going to be cold again tonight and I couldn't make up my mind whether to revise on the Course work in preparation for tomorrow or try and get warm in bed.

Most of the lads were in bed when I arrived at the billet. A couple were propped up on their pillows going over the Course notes, a couple were smoking and apart from three sitting around the old coke stove the rest appeared to be asleep.

The trio sitting around the stove were in the process of tearing up some old newspapers and stuffing them in the top of it. Shivering all the time they stretched out cold hands towards the flames. The sudden rush of warmth and the glow from the flames didn't stay very long and brought forth a lot of grumbling and swearing. After about ten minutes the newspaper supply was exhausted and Ray enquired if anybody had any old comics or newspapers or anything made of paper that we could set on fire.

Geordie, one of the lads sitting by the side of the stove suddenly had an idea. He got up and pulled out a large battered old cardboard box from under his bed.

"Cor, that cardboard will burn and last a bit longer." observed Mick but Geordie shook his head.

"No" replied Geordie. "I need the box to keep my magazines in. I have got some old copies of my fishing mags we can use." He brought quite an armful over to the heating apparatus and dumped them in the well precariously close to the hot metal. I drew up a chair and helped to tear up the magazines as we took turns to stuff the pages in the top of the stove and through the small aperture at the bottom of it.

The glossy pages were slow in burning but went well once they caught on. Wisps of grey smoke emerged from the join in the chimney but no-one cared. Inevitably the supply of burning material came to an end and George asked Geordie if he had any more magazines he wanted to get rid of. Geordie muttered "No, you've had your lot" and now on his knees proceeded to push the box of remaining magazines under his bed.

"Oh, come on Geordie" Tim called. "You've got stacks more in there. You don't need to keep all them. Come on, mate, give us a few more."

Geordie's reply was short but final. "No" he said.

Tim and George went together to Geordie's bed space thinking in unison. Two of them together could put more pressure on him to release some more fuel for the stove. It ended up with Geordie complaining and struggling with Tim and George as they tried to grab at the box which disintegrated and spilt its contents on to the floor.

"Blimey look at these" said Tim "I'm all for fishing if these are the manuals." "What you got there?" asked George as a frantic tug of war for the magazines went on between them both and a very agitated Geordie.

"Cor, you dirty old man" added George to Geordie "you've got a stash of porn here!" Geordie fell silent as other lads joined the group and started rummaging amongst the pornographic magazines which were still on the floor. "Cor, look at this." "That can't be natural", "Wow" "Have you seen this?" there was a chorus of ooh's and ah's as pages were turned and the magazines tilted at different angles for added effect.

By now the fire was forgotten. Geordie's unscheduled library was now well and truly open and causing a sensation. It was late into the night before library closing and a lot of bleary eyed individuals dragged themselves in to class the following morning.

Today we learnt all about U.R.R's. I was keeping very observant now because each time we had a mock test I came in the top three. For two consecutive tests I had the highest mark and I was very keen to keep up there. To pass the final course exam meant promotion to Leading Aircraftsman and I was anxious for that and the extra money that came with it.

U.R.R's meant Urgent Repair Requirements. These demands for aircraft spares were considered urgent but not so urgent as the A.O.G's which were vital to get grounded aircraft airborne. The U.R.R's ordered spares that were important for routine repair purposes but the aircraft was still flying.

The supply chain for ordering specific parts was difficult to grasp. Determining what part was required and in what quantity was even more so. The Course was getting more intensive by the day and I longed for a break from the constant stress of learning.

The break came in a way I could not have envisaged.

Joe and I had to take our turn for Guard duty and it had to be from teatime to breakfast time. It was now dark by 5 o'clock and we would have to patrol the Camp through a whole night of darkness and protect it from enemy forces, terrorists and whatever threat presented itself. A daunting thought since each of us was issued with a rifle but no bullets.

The night started cold and eerie. The first hour or two dragged and it got worse as the night drew on. Huddled in our greatcoats we shivered. The rifles felt heavier by the minute and tiredness and yawning set in.

We chatted and stopped and listened every now and then. We heard voices near the wire perimeter of the camp but it was only a courting couple going by. Every now and then a car passed. We saw a shadowy figure of a man approach one of the concrete pillars that supported the wire fence by a light of a passing car. He looked furtively right and left and then drew nearer to the pillar. We held our breath and watched and listed carefully. My heart was thumping and I felt a bit afraid.

We need not have worried. The bloke urinated against the pillar and made off in the darkness.

Joe and I laughed. "The phantom piddler piddles again and moves on" he said and we laughed some more.

The night got darker and the temperature dropped to freezing. With aching feet we trudged from classroom to classroom making sure each one was locked as we had been instructed. Then, almost in relief, we came across a classroom door that yielded when we tried the knob. It was unlocked, open and inviting. We hurried inside in silence and closed the door.

In the safety and relevant warmth of the classroom we stumbled in the darkness until we fell almost exhausted in to chairs next to the desks. In whispers we confirmed that we would stay awhile, go sleuthing later on and return every now and then for warmth. So much for guarding the Camp! It must have been about 3.30am when it happened.

Joe and I were having a whispered conversation and we began to laugh again.

Why were we whispering because there was no-one there to hear us? We concluded that it was our guilty consciences and that by some unguarded chance we might be discovered abandoning our responsibilities. It was then we heard the thump and movement coming along the side of the classroom. Someone was there. Someone was edging forward and then stopping.

I jumped in the darkness as Joe nudged my arm and whispered "Shush" even though I wasn't making a sound. I was trembling, feeling very dry and very afraid. Whoever it was was being very cautious and moving slowly, hesitatingly and coming closer to the door. I think it was at that point I went rigid and held my breath in fear and waited for the inevitable.

CHAPTER 23

Silence. Nothing seems more frightening and eerie than a prolonged silence. Seconds seem like hours. Real fear of the unknown causes the mind to work overtime. Imaginations go into overdrive as the heart is felt thudding in the chest. I could hear Joe breathing in spasms. I felt as though I couldn't breathe at all and I was physically shaking.

We waited in the inky darkness, glad of each other's company as we remained motionless and our ears straining.

I started to think rationally. We were inside a building which surely must be an advantage. We had a weapon albeit a useless one because we didn't have any ammunition, but, whoever was outside was not in a position to know that.

Whoever was prowling had darkness as cover but we had torches and could provide light when necessary.

Thinking about the torch I started to fumble in the depth of my voluminous greatcoat pocket and in doing so let my rifle slip and it clattered to the floor. I froze with fear and Joe swore.

We stayed very still and listened but nothing happened. We didn't move, whisper or make any further sound at all. Finally after about a quarter of an hour Joe whispered "We have got to get out of here."

"Shall I switch the torch on?" I whispered.

"No" was the hoarse reply.

Negotiating our way to the door in utter darkness was no easy feat as we knocked against desks and chairs on the way. When we did eventually reach it we took some time to pick up enough courage to open it.

Gingerly Joe turned the knob and pulled at the door. It squeaked on its hinges as it opened and I heard Joe take a deep intake of breath. We waited.

"Come, on, let's go!" he said.

We stepped out into the darkness and the freezing air. Joe pulled the classroom door shut and for a few seconds we stood waiting for our eyes to become more accustomed to the darkness.

Tip toeing together with Joe taking the lead we furtively moved forward away from the classroom. The next one was only a few feet away and similarly we tip-toed along the side of that one also.

Now clear of two classrooms we quickened our pace and headed for the airmen's mess which was some distance away illuminated by two street lights. Neither of us spoke until we were within a couple of feet of the Mess.

"Whoever was prowling up at the classrooms must have scarpered" said Joe. Then as an afterthought he added "Do you suppose it was some other guard looking for somewhere to get in the warm?"

"Dunno" I replied. "Since guards have to do different areas no-one should be anywhere near our territory."

Joe and I agreed that we wouldn't mention what had happened to anyone in the billet. You never know who you can trust one hundred per cent and someone might innocently mention the incident and get us into a lot of trouble. It could possibly be seen as desertion from duty or something and we didn't want to find ourselves on a Court Martial.

Since we had used up so much adrenaline with the stress of the night we decided to wend our way back towards the Guardroom. The area was reassuringly floodlit and it would be good to see the Guards on the main gate of the Camp. It was ironic that we prepared to say there was nothing to report to the night duty sergeant.

Duty done Joe and I headed back in the greying light of dawn to our billet. The other lads would be up by now and preparing for another day in class. We could look forward to the luxury of a few hours in bed since we had been up all night and our presence would not be required in the classroom until the afternoon session.

We were almost at the billet when we saw a fox standing motionless looking in our direction. Joe put his fingers to his lips and motioned me to stay still. We stood and watched the beautiful animal which didn't seem to be afraid or make any attempt to move. Then almost immediately a second fox jumped down from a pile of old wooden pallets quickly followed by a third and headed for fox number one. For a few seconds the three animals stood together which was a beautiful sight.

Then, one behind the other, they ran off towards the ablutions.

"There's your answer" muttered Joe. "I bet we have been hiding from foxes half the night. I reckon that was what we heard outside the classroom." I agreed in the absence of any other explanation.

Once in the billet I took off my greatcoat and fell on to my bed and within minutes fell asleep fully clothed. It was nearly five hours later that I awoke, very cold, hungry and still very tired.

The time seemed to drag through the afternoon. The adventures of last night and tiredness was catching up on me. I could not concentrate on the Course and watching Mick flick paper clips from an elastic band was about all I could manage.

Sergeant Vaughan's voice was monotonous and he droned on relentlessly. It was a very welcome relief when Sergeant Bill Redfern arrived to take over and to change the subject. Bill did have a good sense of humour and his presentation was much clearer.

As the weeks passed I became very conscious that I was doing well on the Course. I supposed it was because I am blessed with a good memory and retain knowledge that some folk find easy to forget. I also made notes on just about everything which I referred to constantly.

Every Friday we had mock tests on what we had learned so far. I excelled in these and most weeks I came top or was within the top three. I was just hoping that it would be the same when we did the final exam at the end of the Course.

The three months at RAF Credenhill seemed to drag time wise but it was not all learning and trying to exist in Hell Hole. The latter being the name we adopted for our billet.

The freezing nights found us in bed or still huddled around the coke stove. Under cover of darkness we nicked half a dozen of the pallets we found when the foxes appeared. Any paper available was retained for lighting the stove even toilet rolls. From time to time we raided Geordie's stash of pornographic magazines and committed them to the flames. He never seemed to notice.

Some of the pallet wood was very wet where it had been exposed to rain and snow and consequently was difficult to burn. Then the unthinkable happened. Gerald thrust an old torn bed sheet beneath the wood and lit it with his lighter.

The sheet didn't burn but began to smoulder. What a stink it caused and smoke began to billow out in three very distinct places. It came out of the top and the bottom of the stove and we had never seen so much emitted from the join in the chimney. It literally billowed out into the billet and the smell of burning rag was overpowering.

Ray bravely had a go at pulling the sheet through the small aperture at the bottom of the stove but it was too hot and too tight to be salvaged. It did absolutely nothing for his constant running nose and in the end he gave up with a fit of coughing.

It was almost impossible to see the furthest end of the billet. There was a lot of coughing and swearing and Shaun insisted goofy Gerald was illegitimate for burning the sheet.

With the doors and all the windows now wide open the room was like a refrigerator and the situation just got worse by the minute. In spite of all the confusion, however, some humour was evident.

Somebody started singing "London's Burning", "London's Burning" and others joined in with the chorus "Fetch the engine! Fetch the Engine!" George said "Seeing all this smoke, someone will think we have elected a Pope." Tim had the bright idea of wafting at the smoke with a pullover. It did help to drive the thick cloud towards the windows so we all had a go until the situation was improved. We could still smell the smoke on our clothing and our beds reeked of it when we finally called it a day.

Speaking personally I found my time spent at RAF Credenhill was not all doom and gloom. Classes were broken up with some forty eight hour passes and I was able to go home for some weekends. I felt sorry for the lads who lived too far away from home like Mick and Joe who lived in Lancashire. On a couple of occasions they came home with me.

On the weekends that I could not go home I was happy to catch a bus into Hereford and go to Church. This came about because I accepted an invitation from one of the Camp civilian cleaners.

I enjoyed the Services and the suppers that the cleaner's family always provided in their home afterwards. The thing that I enjoyed most was the luxury to relax in a nice warm home.

I was often on the receiving end of barter and jibes from my mates in the billet because I went to Church. Tim said "The reason he does so well in the mock tests is because he goes to that Church. No doubt God likes answering his prayers." A couple of weeks before the end of the Course and the vital examination that would determine our promotion and future, I stayed longer than usual at the Church family home.

I missed a bus and I had to wait a long time for another one because the Service on a Sunday was very poor.

By the time I was dropped at the main gate of the Camp it was well after lights out time. I walked the long walk to the billet through freezing fog which swirled around me as I blew on my fingers because they were so cold. I wished I had brought my gloves.

When I arrived at the billet it was in complete darkness as I expected. During my walk I had worked out a strategy in my mind. I would open the door gently and close it behind me again. I would not put any lights on. I would tip toe to my bed, undress in the dark, and then get into it. We had an unwritten rule that if anyone came in after lights out that was always to be the procedure. No-one wanted to be awakened by light or sound.

My strategy plan started off well. I opened the billet door very gingerly and stepped inside. I closed the door behind me and started to tip toe in the general direction of my bed. There were the usual sounds of snoring, creaking springs and coughing.

I edged towards my bed and then .... calamity! I bumped into two chairs that had been left by the stove which threw me off balance. As I tried to go forward I tripped and fell against a third chair in the dark and felt myself twist as I fell headlong. I had forgotten the deep concrete well lip that surrounded the stove and fell over it. I vaguely remember the impact as my head hit concrete, seeing a blinding flash of stars and nothing else.

Sometime later I regained consciousness. I was laying on my bed fully clothed and soaking wet. My head throbbed with pain and I was shivering and feeling very sick. I was aware of the fact that there was a lot of light which seemed too brilliant for me to see properly. I could hear voices but not very clearly and my breath seemed to be sucked out of me as the top half of my body received a torrent of water. It was a deluge and extremely cold.

I must have passed out because the next thing I knew was a voice demanding to know if I could hear him speaking. It was a young Flight Lieutenant. I could only groan as my head felt as though it was on fire and I was conscious of having a pain every time I moved my shoulder. I seemed to be looking at him through a haze. The saga of events were made clear to me by Mick and Joe who visited me in the sick quarter the next morning.

Apparently I had tripped over the chairs and hit my head on the concrete lip which had knocked me out. The lads that were sleeping were awakened by all the commotion and joined those who were not sleeping to see what had happened.

Once they switched the lights on they found me face down and between them decided to pick me up and lay me on my bed. I was not conscious of any of this. When I made no sign of coming round Shaun decided I needed water throwing over me in an attempt to revive me. He grabbed hold of the fire bucket full of water and threw the lot over my top half. When I did not respond to the Niagara Falls treatment panic set in. Someone decided further action was required and seemingly Geordie and Ray ran together to the Guard Room to report what had happened to the Duty Sergeant. The incident was passed to the Medical Officer who arranged for me to be moved to the Sick Quarter.

I was in too much pain to laugh but I did manage a smile when Geordie said "The Medical Officer was concerned because your bed was soaking wet and he said you couldn't sleep in it and that was why you had to come in here." There was I thinking it was because I might have concussion or a dislocated shoulder! I tried to sleep during that day but every time I closed my eyes the pain in my head intensified. I looked up at ceiling and tried to figure out what the next course of action would be.

With less than two weeks to go I needed to be well and spend all of that time revising and studying for the Trade Training exam. If I was not in a position to sit the exam, or if I failed it, it would mean staying at the Hell Hole for a further three months. I would have to go through the entire course again with the next intake of men.

I had to get better. I just had to pass that exam for which I had worked so hard. With these very disturbing thoughts I eventually fell into a restless sleep.

CHAPTER 24

The fact that I had a very sore shoulder, a black eye and a bump on my head as big as an egg failed to bring any form of sympathy from the Medical officer.

"You are as good as new" he announced "you can report back to class after lunch." I started to complain about my severe headache and argued that my head coming into contact with concrete could be serious. I reasoned that I could develop a haemorrhage of the brain and it might be safer for me to stay in under observation. "Nonsense!" he snorted. "You have to have a brain before it can be damaged. Anyone who is daft enough to wander about in darkness when light is available is not using their brain."

"I could still study and revise from the text books from here!" I ventured. The comfy hospital bed and the warmth of the building were much more appealing than the thought of my old hard mattress and the unscheduled water bed I had left.

The Medical Officer was a man of few words. "Classroom at one thirty" he snapped, scribbled something on a board at the bottom of my bed and left. Although reluctant to return to the class room I was in for a surprise. The lads greeted me like some long lost hero and informed me of the latest new rule for the billet. The last person sitting by the stove before lights out was responsible for removing all chairs from that vicinity.

I realised it was like closing the stable door after the horse had bolted but it was the thought that counted. I had already made up my mind that henceforth I would learn from my mistake and I would not be going for a repeat performance.

I was also greeted with the good news that a load of coke had been delivered for the stove.

Geordie had called the lads together and insisted that we should ration the coke on a daily basis. "It's not worth bunging a lot on at a time and running out in a couple of days" he explained. "It's better to have a little bit of warmth every day rather than being sweltered a couple of times and then freeze for the rest of the time."

What he said made sense. He never once mentioned his missing pornographic magazines that we had burned so perhaps he was safeguarding his assets.

We had a bit of a problem transferring the coke from outside the billet to the stove in the absence of any form of a shovel. We cupped our hands and brought in handfuls like it was gold.

It was a very welcome change to sit around the stove with hands stretched towards some warmth. There was a lot of banter and jokes and laughter but every now and then we got really serious.

Someone would bring up a topic that we had been going over in the classroom. If the topic was not clear then someone in the group would clarify the meaning. We would ask each other questions and much was learnt from each other. If we could not decide on a certain matter we would look it up in the text books or go back over our Course notes. Those late night sessions around that old fume and smoke leaking stove was every bit as important as what we had learnt in the classroom.

For once I wanted an early night. The lump on my head was just as big and ached as much as ever. The pain in my shoulder seemed to be worse and I needed to catch up on my sleep.

For the first time I noticed that the blankets on my bed were not placed as I usually placed them. Instantly I suspected that the lads had done me a favourite "apple pie bed." Basically this is when the sheet and blankets are only folded halfway down the bed. All is well until you go to get in your bed and you discover that your feet can only go down a short distance. There is no alternative but to get out and remake the bed. Sometimes the lads would sprinkle toast crumbs between the sheets which if endured could be very uncomfortable.

As though he was reading my thoughts Tim came over. "We have sorted you out some blankets because yours were soaked" he explained, Ray came over with a pillow. "Here you are mate" he said "I don't need two!" I appreciated the help and concern and gingerly ran my hand down beneath the sheets. No apple pie bed. I got undressed and climbed thankfully into it. Then suddenly I became aware of the wetness.

"Oh No!" I hollered and quickly added "my bed is soaked."

The billet went silent as I swung my legs out of the bed and threw back the sheets and blankets. There for all to see was a large area of saturated mattress.

When the lads had kindly shared their bedding and made up my bed they had not noticed the wetness. I had to admit that it looked stained rather than wet but as soon as I laid upon it I felt the difference.

The ribald comments that followed were not appreciated as it was suggested I had wetted the bed. There was more joking and further silly suggestions and even a hint that I could sit up all night.

Finally it was Shaun who came up with what we thought at the time was a great idea.

"If you've got a wet bed, you will have to dry it" he said in his lovely Irish accent. "Just be thankful you're not in der Navy cause you might get washed overboard." Mick and Joe had kept quiet during most of the banter and then Mick had an idea and both of them came to my rescue.

"Let's dry the mattress by the stove" said Mick.

"Give us a hand lads" said Joe and between us we hoisted the mattress off the bed and carried it towards the stove.

Three of us held it quite close to the heat and the smell that arose from the mattress was awful. It was difficult to hold it rigid because it sagged in the middle and now vapour was ascending in a cloud. What with the smoke leaking from the chimney and the steam coming out of the mattress it was like some horrific poor man's sauna. We couldn't stop laughing.

After ten or fifteen minutes our arms were aching with the weight of the mattress as we struggled to keep the thing rigid. It was only then that we decided to prop it up against three of the chairs as everybody in the billet decided to get into bed and as far away as possible from the stink of my damp smelling, musty, camphorated mattress.

Feeling totally dejected I fell on the springs of my old iron bed which twanged beneath my weight. I watched the steam continuing to rise from the mattress and wondered how long it would be before I could sleep on it.

I must have dozed off because the next thing I knew Gerald had invaded my bed space. I quickly came to realising that only one of the electric lights had been left on.

"Ken, I think something is burning" he said.

Sure enough there was now an extra smell of singed material added to the other aromas that came from the mattress. Together we approached it cautiously. Gerald's face was a study. "Crikey" he said with eyes almost as big as saucers. "It ain't half scorched."

Another few seconds and I am convinced the mattress would have burst into flames. There was a burn about three feet across and red bits were glowing on the edges. We tried to ease the thing away from the chairs but it sagged further and came very dangerously close to touching the stove.

As Gerald and I struggled with the bendy mattress it seemed like it was coming alive. It sagged all the more and we were heaving and puffing in our attempts to lift it over the concrete lip which surrounded the stove. Apart from the weight it was very hot to handle and we had to be careful not to burn our hands. In the process of lifting and tugging the thing we knocked over a couple of the chairs which crashed on to the floor.

Then the murmurings and moaning started. It was evident that we were keeping the rest of the lads from their slumbers. The day, or rather the night, was finally saved when Joe leapt out of his bed totally starkers and helped us haul the mattress back on to my bed. On the way back to his bed Joe flicked the switch and plunged the billet into darkness. I was left to make my bed as best as I could in the dark and was surprised to find that there were still damp patches in the mattress and an overpowering smell that wafted from it every time I moved.

Surprisingly no mention of the nocturnal events were mentioned the following morning as most of us blundered about bleary-eyed as we washed and got dressed and ready for another tense day in class.

The days were passing quickly now as the day of the final exam drew near.

Our Class Sergeant Vaughan was painstaking in explaining every detail that was discussed. He had a good idea of the type of questions we would be asked and did his very best to guide us in the right direction.

"This is the last course I shall be teaching before I leave the Service" he said. "I have never had a one hundred per cent pass and I want all of you to work hard so that I can fulfil that ambition before I leave."

I was still doing well and coming in the top three every Friday when we had the mock tests. I intended to do my very best in the final exam because so much depended upon it. It would mean promotion to Aircraftsman First Class and a good chance of a posting outside Britain. I was also keen to do my bit so that Sergeant Vaughan could achieve his ambition to get a whole class through the exam before he left the RAF.

The day of the exam finally dawned and thirty two of us sat down to the task of remembering what we had learnt and to convey that knowledge to paper.

I found the exam less demanding than I had feared and imagined. The rest of the class thought the same and we were jubilant as we shared what we had written with each other.

We eagerly awaited the results.

I shall never forget standing in a hangar whilst the Commanding Officer climbed up on to a platform to announce the results.

He cleared his throat and began. "This is the very nearest thing we have ever had to a one hundred per cent pass" he began, "you worked very hard indeed and only one of you has let us down!" A short silence followed and we all fidgeted and then he glared at me and pointed and said, "You! Stallard is the only one amongst you to fail the Course."

I was stunned as a murmur ran around the group. I felt humiliated, baffled and sick.

It was hard to take in that I was the only one out of thirty two airmen to fail the Course. What must they be thinking of me? I had let Sergeant Vaughan our instructor down too with his hopes of a hundred per cent pass dashed. What would happen to me now? I was only vaguely aware of all the congratulations which were being poured forth between the lads and my eyes smarted as I listened to the Postings.

The entire Course was being sent home that very day for seven days embarkation leave prior to being posted to 401 Air Stores Park at Eindhoven in Holland.

The lads all came around me to commiserate, some of them slapping me on the back and wishing me well for whatever the future held. I felt very emotional as I said my goodbyes to the lads especially Mick and Joe, Geordie, Gerald and Ray and Shaun from Belfast. We had gone through so much together and now they were all going and leaving me behind in isolation. I had never felt so abandoned. Farewells over, the lads dispersed to hand in their bedding and pick up their kit and head for home. I stood alone to face the Commanding Officer.

"You did exceptionally well during the Course" he said, "I can only think exam nerves must have let you down."

I said I didn't suffer from nerves and then Sergeant Vaughan butted in.

"Sir", he began, "Since Stallard did so well throughout the Course, would it be possible for him to sit another exam at a later date? I am leaving 'the RAF in a couple of weeks' time and I would be willing to give him some private tuition in between settling my affairs."

The officer was not altogether sure this would be allowed but promised to make enquiries, and I was sent back to an empty billet.

It was strangely quiet, dark and cold. I didn't have any enthusiasm to light the stove but threw myself on to my bed and wept bitterly.

I looked around the room at fifteen iron beds with the mattress rolled over as if to say I am vacant. My single bed in the middle of the room looked strangely out of place.

I went to tea and returned from it alone. The wash house was eerie and silent and I was already missing the laughter and banter that usually went on.

Early because of the cold I crept in to bed with the lights on. No need to worry about keeping anyone awake now.

I laid on my back and stared at the ceiling. Heavy rain descended making a noise on the old tin roof and I began to sob.

I thought of all the lads in their homes in the warm and with their families. They would be looking forward to a week's leave before going off to Holland.

The Commanding Officer had instructed me to report to the Cook House early next morning for domestic duty. No-one had any idea what was going to happen to me at this point.

My overwhelming sense of failure and the uncertainty for my future was almost too much to bear. I just could not face another three months in Hell Hole even if I was accepted to start another new Course.

There was every likelihood that I would be what the RAF called re-flighted. This meant some other job would be found for me in the Service. But where? What else could I be fitted for? I knew for certain that the coming days were going to be desperately hard and I cried myself to sleep.

CHAPTER 25

The Flight Sergeant in charge of the Cookhouse looked at me as though I was mad and for the third time asked me why I was there.

For the third time I tried to explain that I was the only one to fail the Clerk Provisioning Course the previous day. The rest of the Course personnel had been sent home on embarkation leave and the Commanding Officer had ordered me to report to the Cookhouse that morning.

"Well I don't know anything about it!" he snapped. "Are you supposed to be a kitchen assistant or what?"

"I don't know why I am here" I continued, "I only know that the C.O. said I had to report here this morning."

The Flight Sergeant snorted and went off to make a telephone call. He returned minutes later looking and sounding more than a little frustrated.

"Neither the C.O's clerk or the Adjutant knows anything about it. Are you sure you were told to report to the Cookhouse?"

"Yes" "Why the Cookhouse."

"I don't know!" "Are you sure he said the Cookhouse? "Definitely." Suddenly from outside of the Cookhouse came the sound of a vehicle sounding its horn repeatedly which brought an abrupt end to any further interrogation.

"Supplies have come" he explained and quickly added, "you can help us unload the van."

An airman wearing kitchen type cotton trousers and a white tunic appeared and I was delegated to help him unload a mass of boxes of supplies. The Sergeant ticked off each box of items on a clip board. This was familiar territory for me and served as a reminder of the days when I helped unload the supplies at the International Stores shop in civvy street.

The airman turned out to be a guy called Gus but I had no idea if that was an abbreviation of a Christian name or a nickname.

Gus asked me to help him transfer the contents of the boxes to the shelves in the storeroom. He was a very cheerful chap with a tendency to keep talking to himself. The time passed quickly and the Flight Sergeant seemed satisfied with our efforts.

The noise of the kitchen was almost deafening. There was a continual clatter of cutlery and crockery and pots and pans. Oven doors slammed, the dishwasher was noisy, steam gushed from boiling saucepans and there was an overpowering smell of onions.

Later on a couple of other airmen appeared with a civilian lady who was laden with a large tray of salt cellars and vinegar jars. The latter being dumped unceremoniously on one of the kitchen surface tops.

"Hello dearie" she said with a smile. "and who might you be?"

I introduced myself and for the umpteenth time that morning explained why I was there.

"I am Lottie" she went on. Another name I was unfamiliar with, but, I decided she was very friendly especially as she was more than a little sympathetic about my circumstances. She was old enough to be my mother and I think I must have brought out a motherly instinct.

"If you are going to work here you will have to wear the kitchen uniform" Lottie explained. "You can't stay here dressed like that!" Any further conversation was cut short by the return of the Flight Sergeant carrying tee shirts, light weight trousers and tunic as though on cue.

"Put these on now" I was ordered, "and report back to me" I changed in the staff room and returned as instructed. The Flight Sergeant was in deep conversation with three or four of the kitchen staff and Lottie. It was obvious they were deciding what duty they could line up for me next.

I was very aware of the sniggers of the little group when the Flight Sergeant led me to the porridge boiler and said "You can clean that!" I hated the job. The old porridge was stuck to the boiler like glue. It had a horrible smell and a lot of detergent and elbow grease didn't have much effect. After half an hour I had only managed to clear a very small area and my fingers felt numb. Lottie brought me a mug of very sweet tea and tried to be encouraging.

"You are doing very well" she said peering with her head on one side at the area where I had cleaned. "You will have got it all off and cleaned before tea time." Tea time was five hours away but she only laughed when I reminded her of that. Clearly she was trying to convey that the process was going to be very laborious and time consuming.

Lottie left with a laugh but not before she made a very cutting remark. "It is bound to get easier every day."

Lottie's remark brought me down to earth with a bump. Was this how it was going to be day after day? Was I destined to a future of porridge boiler cleaning? I had to wait three more days before I got the answer.

I had by now spent four days on boiler cleaning duties. The Flight Sergeant had in the meantime received confirmation from the C.O. that I was there on temporary duty only. Consequently the kitchen staff gave me the worse job in the kitchen which no-one else wanted to do. They had already agreed between them that they would use me for the porridge boiler task whilst they had opportunity.

Just before lunch on the fourth day Sergeant Vaughan, the instructor from the Clerk Provisioning Course, arrived at the Cookhouse.

He was a personal friend of the Flight Sergeant and they exchanged pleasantries before giving me the best news ever.

Authority had been given for Sergeant Vaughan to give me some private tuition for being a Provisioning Clerk. I was told to meet him in our old classroom after lunch.

I did not wait for any lunch. I rushed back to the billet and changed back into my normal uniform and returned to the Cookhouse to hand in my kitchen garb and make my farewells.

Lottie insisted on giving me a bag full of cakes and assured me that I would be missed.

Sergeant Vaughan was true to his word and was waiting for me in our old class room. He was extremely kind and pleasant and said many encouraging things about my work on the previous Course. He was just as mystified as I was for the reason of my failure. We agreed to go back over the lessons and he was very thorough and patient in explaining every detail of the things that I had struggled with.

It was made very clear to me that the next examination would be held on the following Monday, I could not expect the same questions and this was the final chance to prove whether or not I was destined for a clerical job in the RAF.

The five days passed quickly. Sergeant Vaughan did not spend a lot of the time with me. In fairness he was finalising his own departure from the military. He was handing in various items of kit and equipment and celebrating with his mates in the Sergeant's Mess. Christmas was only a fortnight away and celebrations were already taking place.

The Sergeant often set me passages to revise from the text books and gave me handwritten questions to answer whilst he went missing for hours on end. Every night I studied in the billet because there was no no-one to speak to. It helped to shut out the loneliness and I curled up in my bed and read and re-read until I knew the text books almost like a script.

The Saturday before the exam I went into Hereford to do a bit of Christmas shopping. I wandered around the shops looking for inspiration for a gift for Sergeant Vaughan. Pass or fail I knew he had worked very hard and sacrificed a lot of time and energy on my behalf. I wanted to show in some small way that I appreciated all he had done.

I changed my mind often but in the end decided to buy him a military book. I reasoned that as he had spent most of his working life in the military he would at least be interested in some aspect of it. I was delighted to find a book about how the R.A.F. was formed in 1918 by the merger of the Royal Naval Air Service and the Royal Flying Corps.

The day of the second exam dawned bright but still bitterly cold. The classroom was already lit when I arrived and I found Sergeant Vaughan there with a Warrant Officer who was a stranger to me.

I sat at my desk and Sergeant Vaughan introduced the Warrant Officer. The latter kept looking at his watch and the tension and efficiency of the couple was just as intimidating as the first actual exam had been. My first question paper was placed upside down in front of me and I had to wait until the appointed time before I could turn it over and start on the questions.

No-one spoke throughout. There was a short gap between two papers and at noon the task was complete and the three of us sighed a huge sigh of relief.

After being questioned at length by the couple, I could only say that I did not think the questions were too difficult and I had answered every question with some confidence. I had felt just the same after completing the first exam and we all knew that had ended in failure. Only time would tell the outcome of my second attempt.

The Warrant Officer left almost immediately with my answers in his brief case. Sergeant Vaughan said "You will get the results the day after tomorrow. Until then feel free to come and go. It's not worth you going back to the Cookhouse."

I thanked the Sergeant for all he had done and he was visually very touched to receive the gift I had bought for him. He turned the pages of the book and explained the pictures of early military uniforms and weapons. There were pictures of famous leaders and lots of facts concerning the formation of the R.A.F. "I will treasure this" the Sergeant said. "It will be a lasting souvenir of my time in the R.A.F." and he rewrapped the book and put it in his bag.

"You must be back in the classroom on Wednesday but not until 1.30pm" he went on. "We should have the results of your exam then. Be sure to pack up all your Kit because if you pass you will be going home on leave, but, if you fail you will be moved elsewhere. Your billet will be required for the next Course." Wednesday morning I bundled all my kit together in my kit bag and suitcase. My mind was in turmoil. I was both very excited and yet very nervous.

Today I could face the bitter disappointment of a Sergeant who had put so much faith in me. That would be unthinkable on his very last day of a long service career.

I could be a very disillusioned young man not knowing where next he would be accommodated. National Service was mandatory and not an option. I had no idea where I would be sent or what I would be doing. A dilemma and not a nice position to be in. On the other hand I may well have passed and this evening I could be in the comfort of my own home with my family.

Sergeant Vaughan came promptly at 1.30pm and we chatted about everything except the exam. If he knew the result he wasn't giving anything away.

He seemed a little irritated when some time had gone by but there was still no sign of the Warrant Officer. When some thirty minutes later he did arrive Sergeant Vaughan muttered "About time!" The Warrant Officer breezed in with a huge smile, full apologies for being late. He blamed his delay on a belated meeting with the Commanding Officer.

"I am glad you are both here together" he said, "I can drive you down to HQ because the C.O. wants to see you both" "How did he do in the exam?" this from the Sergeant.

"Sorry, I can only say the C.O. wants to see you both together."

The trip to HQ was made in silence and after a further brief delay we were ushered into the C.O's office.

I was greeted with a stern look and I heard him say, "Stallard, what is the matter with you?"

"Oh no!" I exclaimed, "please don't say I've failed again?"

"Failed" he echoed, "you've passed with a very high mark indeed and put all on that last Course to shame. Your perseverance has been rewarded. Now hand in your Kit and your bedding and get your rail tickets from the Admin Office. You are going home on seven days embarkation leave" "Sir" I butted in. "Will I be going to 401 Air Stores Park at Eindhoven in Holland and meet up again with all the others on the Course?"

The Officer shook his head. "I'm afraid not" he replied. "The Air Ministry, for reasons best known to themselves, have decided to send you to 402 Air Stores Park at Wildenrath in Germany instead."

I found it difficult to contain my joy and relief. The C.O. shook my hand and wished me well and then turned to thank Sergeant Vaughan for all of his efforts. Calling him by his Christian name he said "Congratulations. As you leave the R.A.F. today you can do so with the knowledge that you got your wish and your one hundred per cent pass with your last Course. Well done!" Outside the office we all began to speak at once. We were thanking each other and Vaughan said he had had faith in me from the start. As he shook my hand he wished me good luck and urged me to get on my way.

I ran all the way to the billet to collect my bedding and struggled with the load to hand it back in at the bedding store.

I raced back to the billet again to collect the rest of my things and one last nostalgic look at the old coke stove and my vacant bedstead. I wondered who the next poor unfortunate airman would be to have the privilege of sleeping on my half burnt mattress and endure the pure delights of the Hell Hole.

As for me I had beaten the odds. I had achieved something. I only wished that the other lads could know that I had finally made the grade.

I stood at the bus stop outside Credenhill Camp and waited for the bus to take me to the railway station at Hereford. I kept looking at the leave pass and the warrant for the train journey to Oxford. When I boarded the bus I put the documents safely in my wallet and transferred the brown official envelope to my kit bag. There it was as plain as day. Her Majesty's Service envelope contained rail tickets from Oxford via Kings Cross, London, to Harwich to connect with a troop ship bound for the Hook of Holland and then onward journey by train into Western Germany.

I pressed my face against the window of the bus and saw the lights of Christmas trees and decorations on the way to the railway station. I was on combined embarkation leave and Christmas Grant leave.

I reflected on the past six months and how my life had changed so much. I had successfully passed my drill and physical training and now I was a qualified Provisioning Clerk. I was going home for Christmas and a well-earned break. I was eagerly looking forward to being with the family for the festive season.

I was just as eager with the prospect of going to Germany three days after Christmas.

I smiled to myself and thought some more about Christmas and the coming New Year. A new year, new surroundings, new friends and above all new experiences. I decided this was going to be the best New Year ever.

CHAPTER 26

Christmas came and went very quickly. Relatives and friends gave me money as Christmas presents in anticipation that I would need extra cash whilst out of the country.

My excitement grew with the prospect of going abroad for the first time. A couple of days after Boxing Day and I was on my way. Dressed in full second dress uniform and carry the inevitable kitbag on my back and a suitcase in each hand.

I took a train from Oxford to Kings Cross in London via Paddington and had to wait some time before catching the onward train to Harwich.

I made the mistake of walking past a Squadron Leader Padre at Kings Cross Station without saluting him. He was quick to remind me of the fact and I felt very embarrassed at his reprimand in front of the other travellers.

Standing on the platform I noticed a lot of other military, Army and RAF, waiting for the same train. By the time it arrived I realised it was full of military personnel only.

It was middle evening before we arrived at Harwich in the dark and the temperature was well below freezing. It was chaos with no-one knowing where to report.

There were several Army non-commissioned officers but a clear evidence of an absence of RAF personnel. We were herded like cattle from one area to another until eventually we were ushered into a large mess hall where we received tea and sandwiches and biscuits.

Then everything began to happen at once. We were lined up outside on the quay in the biting freezing wind and began to embark on to the troop ship which I seem to think was called Aurora. I recall staggering up a sloping gang plank as I struggled with the suitcases in either hand and a kit bag which had a habit of slipping off my shoulders.

The contrast from the heat inside the ship from the icy winds outside was amazing. Each of us was allocated a canvas bunk, very similar to a hammock but static.

We were crowded together like sardines in a tin.

The stink was unimaginable. Stinking feet, sweaty bodies, stifling heat and the overpowering smell of oil from the engines.

After a considerable wait as more and more lads joined the ship and kit bags and suit cases were stacked, we suddenly felt the boat shudder and head out to sea.

I was among some of the first to go up on to the upper deck. The air was really freezing now. I watched the Harwich lights recede into the distance and for the first time felt really nervous and alone within a crowd. I whispered "Goodbye England" to myself and a lump came up into my throat. I had no idea how long it would be before I would be coming home again.

The cold soon forced me to return below deck to the sleeping quarters. I had never seen so many people lying on narrow bunks side by side in so small a space. The smell seemed to get worse. Someone broke wind and somebody else swore. Some were sleeping whilst others snored and others chatted incessantly. We all slept in our clothes except for tunics and boots.

I slept most of the night through sheer exhaustion and was rudely awakened by the roar of the ship's siren.

I heard someone say we were coming into dock but no-one was allowed to go up to have a look.

Yet again it was the turn of the Army to give the orders. Around us was a sea of khaki uniforms which outnumbered the RAF by about four to one.

When we were finally called up on to the top deck we were segregated by the colour of our uniforms.

I saw abroad for the first time. I don't know what I was expecting but the quay at the Hook of Holland didn't look any different to the quay back at Harwich.

We were given tea, sandwiches and yet more biscuits in a large mess hall like the one at Harwich. Then in no time at all we were lined up on the platform and put on a train to head east across Holland.

Now it seemed for the first time that I was indeed in a different country. My eyes opened wide when I saw the large heavy and old fashioned train engine, the hard wood and leather seats and foreign writing on the signs which seemed to be everywhere.

We went through miles of very flat country and I felt quite excited when I saw my first windmill. The train chugged its way past a level crossing and I saw my first foreign street and observed cars driving on the right side of the road.

The journey seemed very slow and I began to feel hungry, unwashed and unkempt. We were all airmen together now and a couple of RAF sergeants, hitherto unseen, toured the corridors of the train to assure us that we would soon be arriving in Germany. Our first overnight stay would be at a RAF Station called Goch where we could shower, eat, and have a proper bed for the night.

The sergeant went on to explain that the following day we would be grouped together in a large hall and receive our postings to whatever area of Germany we had been assigned.

There was some considerable delay as the train arrived at the Dutch German border but eventually we were on our way until we arrived at what looked like an ancient village railway station. We had arrived at Goch.

It was a very long drop from the train to the platform. Pandemonium instantly broke out as bodies, kit bags and suitcases descended on to a very small platform not designed or built for such a large intake.

When a convoy of coaches arrived we boarded them starting from the front of the queue regardless whether we were soldiers or airmen.

It was a short ride to RAF Goch. On arrival we were segregated. Airmen on the left and soldiers on the right.

The soldiers were marched away and we never saw any of them again. The airmen were formed up in lines of three and a pasty looking Flight Lieutenant came along the lines handing out building and room number cards. Half an hour later we had found our room and bed.

There was an instant stampede for the ablutions and showers. Two days without washing, shaving and not changing our clothes, and being confined in cramped places, had been an extremely unpleasant experience.

We had neither bedside cabinets nor wardrobes. These were not necessary since we were only staying one night. After breakfast the next day we would receive our posting orders and be on our way to the allocated RAF station.

In the morning the Commanding Officer at Goch welcomed us to the main hall and explained that we had come to the 2nd Tactical Air force for military service. He explained that four RAF Stations were known as "Clutch Stations" and these had been formed at Bruggen, Laarbruch, Geilenkirchen and Wildenrath. None of us had any idea where these stations were in Germany and a large map was unrolled and the officer pointed them out with a pointer. The Station Commander went on to explain the role of the RAF Stations Squadrons until someone asked why so many soldiers had undertaken the journey from Great Britain. We were told that they would be joining various Army Units at Monchen Gladbach and other stations as part of the British Army of the Rhine. "Listen carefully as your name is called" the officer was very brisk now. "Your name will be announced in alphabetical order and along with it your onward destination."

I already knew that I was going to 402 Air Stores Park at Wildenrath because the Commanding Officer at Credenhill had said so before I left there. I listened carefully and sure enough the posting was confirmed. Standing among so many I listened to the venues. Bruggen seemed to head the list closely followed by Geilenkirchen and Laarbruch but apart from my posting I didn't hear Wildenrath mentioned. Not surprising that when we were ordered to form up by destination that I stood alone apart from the crowd. Three large groups of men gathered and waited for their separate transport to the main stations. I saw two weary looking airmen standing together apart from the rest and then there was me standing alone.

A friendly Flight Sergeant came over to me. "Are you Stallard? he asked. "Yes, Flight Sergeant."

"Right! Get yourself over to tweedle dumb and tweedle dee" he nodded in the general direction of the other two airmen. "I will drive them to the RAF Hospital at Wegberg and then I will take you on to Wildenrath."

I sauntered over to the other two lads and repeated what the Flight Sergeant had said. The lads were reporting to RAF Wegberg as Medical Orderlies and I explained that I was on my way to Wildenrath for clerical duties.

The Flight Sergeant duly arrived in a minibus and I sat beside him in the front of the vehicle whilst the lads plus baggage went into the back.

The roads were very icy and snow was very evident all the way. It seemed very odd to be driving on the right side of the road.

The Flight Sergeant and I chatted all the way but not a word was spoken by the medical orderlies in the back. They seemed reluctant to leave the minibus when we arrived at their station and the Flight Sergeant had to tell them twice that they had arrived. The couple did not utter a word as they lugged their gear out and on to the road and looked decidedly dejected as they trudged towards the main gate.

The Flight Sergeant laughed. "They will go a long way to cheer up the sick" he joked. "I hope I never have to go in there and be on the receiving end of their care."

It was only a short drive to RAF Wildenrath and I was not left at the main gate as the medical orderlies were at Wegberg.

I was ordered to stay in the minibus whilst the Flight Sergeant ducked under the bar beside the Guard Room and went in with one of the guards from the gate.

He emerged a few minutes later with a piece of paper on which was written my Hut number. It seemed that billets were called huts in Germany. The paper also gave details of the whereabouts of the bedding store and the airmen's mess where I would be entitled to get an evening meal. The Flight Sergeant asked me to choose where I wanted to be dropped.

I reasoned that it would be best to be taken to the Hut. I wanted to get rid of the kitbag and suitcases and free myself up to collect my bedding and to get something to eat.

The Flight Sergeant wished me well and a happy new year which was now only a couple of days away. With a cheery wave he drove off.

I liked the look of the concrete huts which were far superior to the old wooden billets at Credenhill. They were shaped in the form of the letter "H". Two accommodating rooms on one side, washbasins and toilets on the other side, and, bath rooms and showers in the middle part.

I tried the handle on the door of my hut and was not altogether surprised to find it locked and unyielding. I dumped my kitbag and cases on the doorstep and went to peer through one of the windows.

The sight that met me shocked me to the core. I was expecting to see a row of beds and wardrobes and bedside cabinets. I was looking at a pub type bar, umpteen chairs, crates, boxes and a lit Christmas tree. Decorations were hanging from the ceiling and the place was festooned with balloons.

I was still gazing through the window, shielding my face with my hands and making a mist on the glass panes with my hot breath, when two lads in civilian clothes came along. I could not see the face of one which was hidden inside a thick fur hood. The other spotty youth had missing teeth. They both carried steaming mugs of tea and were clearly on their way back to their hut from the mess.

"What are you up to mate?" asked one of them. "You on your way home?" asked the other.

"No" I replied. "I have just been posted in and this is the hut I have been assigned to."

The two lads swore in unison. "They have converted this hut into a beer bar for Christmas and New Year" said the faceless guy with the fur hood. "Are you sure you've got the right hut number?"

I showed them the piece of paper with all the details written on it.

Spotty looked wistful and then grinned and came up with a brilliant idea.

"The Mess is still open" he said. "Why don't you go and get some grub and tell the Sergeant in charge there what has happened. Ask him to 'phone the Duty Officer and get you sorted." I was quite touched when he rubbed his fingers around the rim of his mug and offered me a drink of his tea. I accepted, thanked them for their assistance and made my way to the airmen's mess.

The Sergeant at the mess was a jovial soul and thought my predicament was hilarious. He just kept laughing and cracking jokes and kept repeating my circumstances to each cook and catering assistant that appeared. I had to ask him three times to 'phone the Duty Officer which eventually he did.

I must have waited nearly an hour and consumed half a dozen pieces of toast with jam before a very dozy Pilot Officer appeared.

"You cannot go into that hut because it has been converted to a beer bar for the festive season" he said stating the obvious. Then he looked at his watch. "The bedding store will be closed now as well. Why have you been posted here alone?" I could not see why the last question had any bearing on getting a bed for the night. It was quite obvious that he was out of his depth and I was an unwanted encumbrance.

I stood in silence watching his growing agitation as he hummed and hawed. Finally he turned to the Sergeant cook. "Have you any idea where we could put this man until the hut is put back to accommodation, Sergeant?"

Before the cook had chance to open his mouth one of the assistants butted in. "We've got two or three spare beds in our room" he said. "Some of our guys have gone home on Christmas Leave and will not be back until the New Year." The Pilot Officer sighed with relief and asked me my name. "Stallard" he continued, "you can stay in the catering block until your billet is put back to accommodation." Turning to the catering assistant he gave him permission to go off duty and show me the way back to his hut.

I helped myself to a knife, fork, spoon and mug whilst the Sergeant kept chuckling and keeping up his banter. I left the mess with new found mate with the sergeant's words ringing in my ears. "And I thought it was only Jesus who had no place at the inn!" The catering accommodation block was spacious with a dozen beds in our room. I was given the choice of anyone of four beds. I chose the one where the sheets looked the cleanest. I was not very happy about sleeping in somebody else's bed but I was glad of somewhere to stay.

The catering assistants greeted me with a lot of enthusiasm and made me feel very welcome straight away. My new found friend explained to everybody that I was only there on a temporary basis since I was not in the line of catering.

A very tall Scottish lad occupied the bed opposite to mine. He came across and shook my hand. "Are you hungry?" he asked. "We've got plenty of rations in here but mum's the word mind!" He bent down and heaved a large cardboard box out from under his bed.

"Do you fancy a tin of pineapple?" Scottie asked. "You can have a tin of condensed milk with it. Perhaps you would prefer peaches or oranges?" More rustling went on inside the box. "How about some corned beef with Cream Crackers? You can have cereal if you want or fruit cake or jam tarts."

It was clear that I was about to be the receiver of stolen goods. Under every bed was a box of goodies which had been transferred from the cookhouse to the billet. There was no shortage of food and drinks in this place. Scottie smiled and said it was one of the perks of the job.

I consumed a whole tin of pineapple and condensed milk before I remembered that all my kit and personal belongings were still on the doorstep at the newly formed pub. Scottie insisted on showing me a short cut to the place and helped me carry all my gear back to the catering block for which I was very thankful. Everybody seemed in a good mood and still full of Christmas cheer. I was looking forward to a lie in. I didn't have to go on breakfast duty because I wasn't in the catering business.

I didn't have official accommodation for the time being or an allocated office to go to. I was in no man's land.

As I lay in bed reviewing my situation I was suddenly aware of a deafening noise as a jet aircraft flew over the hut. It was so close that it seemed like it was heading direct for the building. I shot up in bed as I heard the panes rattle in the windows. The guys laughed when they saw my startled look.

"You will soon get use to the jets" said the chap in the next bed.

It was at that point I realised that the New Year was going to bring a lot of new experiences. I had already come a long way in a few short months but there was much further to go. I yawned, stretched and braced myself as a second jet screamed its way skywards over the billet.

CHAPTER 27

The raucous singing of Auld Lang Syne saw the old year out and ushered the new one in.

I had arrived at the converted beer bar to be met with a record player that blasted out music unfriendly to the eardrums.

The central heating was sky high for a building that was packed with lads. A long trestle table was laden with sandwiches that had gone dry and were beginning to curl at the edges. Sausage rolls and crisps were in abundance so I helped myself to a plateful.

A haze of cigarette smoke hovered above us and there was a very strong smell of beer and pickled onions.

I elbowed my way to the bar and picked up a can of beer. As I made for some vacant chairs on the far side of the room I felt a grip on my shoulder and a voice blasted in my ear above the music.

"Give us a hand mate. You new here? What section you with?"

I turned to find a lad trying desperately hard to keep his mate upright on his feet. It was obvious that he had had too much to drink and was sagging at the knees.

I put my hands under the victim's arm as instructed and between us we manhandled him to the chairs that I had been heading for. He was dumped on the first available chair without a word.

"I'm Ken Stallard and yes I am new" I explained. "I have come to 402 Air Stores Park and this is the hut I am supposed to be billeted in. I am at present in the Catering Block until this building is restored."

The drunk passed wind and then had a fit of coughing and the airman I was chatting to kicked his foot and swore before paying me any further attention.

"I'm Jimbo" he said. "I am an Admin Clerk in the Orderly Room and we thought you were coming last week. We have allocated you a bed in the next block. We are all on extended Christmas and New Year break and we have got to get this place back into shape the day after tomorrow. You will be in here and then in three days' time we start back at the office at 8.30am."

I thought it very fortuitous that of all the airmen in that room my first contact was with Jimbo. As an Admin Clerk he was responsible for the records of all airmen posted in and out and where they would be accommodated. He was a. mine of information and during the evening explained a lot about the comings and goings of the unit locally known as 402 ASP.

During the evening Jimbo introduced me to several of the guys I would be sharing the hut with. They seemed to be very friendly and high spirited but not too impressed when I said I had decided to stay in the Catering Block until Hut 51 was back to normal. I was, after all, acting on the instructions of the Pilot Officer who met me on arrival. It also meant that I would miss all the manual labour of moving the bar out and all the beds and furniture back in.

My short remaining time left at the Catering Block went very fast. I was sorry to be moving on as the catering assistants had made me most welcome. The never ending food they brought from the Airmen's Mess was an added bonus. Without doubt the crème de la crème was when one of the senior men, Mac, brought back a whole roasted turkey. My last night with them was celebrated with turkey sandwiches, mince pies and some left over cans of beer.

My arrival at Block 51 brought a few surprises. First of all the transformation was amazing. All evidence of Christmas festivities had disappeared and the bar, chairs, tables and decorations had all vanished. In their place was a row of eight beds on either side of the room interspersed with wardrobe cupboards and bedside cabinets.

An overpowering smell of disinfectant and floor polish filled the room. I was surprised to find only nine of the beds were occupied and I had a choice of seven to choose from. I elected to sleep in the fourth bed on the right hand side which was in the middle of the line.

It was good to be able to unpack all my belongings and place them in the cupboard and locker. Unless a war broke out or some emergency posting cropped up, this was going to be my home for the next two and a half years.

Jimbo had already introduced me to seven other occupants of the room when we first met at the beer bar. There were two Andy's which were known as Andy one and Andy two, Tony (the drunk I met at the Christmas festivities), Colin, Pete, Taffy whose proper name was Bill, and, Matt so called because he came from Matlock but his real name was Clive. A new lad transferred in the very day the billet re-opened was a chap called Dennis which made up the ninth occupant of the room.

Jimbo explained that 402 ASP would be taking on a lot of extra work in the coming weeks and that was the reason we had so many vacant beds. When the extra work arrived more personnel would come with it and therefore need the beds.

I will never forget my first morning in the office. A great guy called Geoff was given the task of teaching me the system of receiving demands for the aircraft spares and how to process the documentation.

I had to number and record every individual demand and put on it the location of the item in its appropriate store. When I had batched twenty such demands I then had to deliver them to the store sheds on the site. The store men selected the items and sent them on to another shed for packing and onward transport to whichever RAF station and aeroplane was waiting for the specific store or piece of equipment.

It was a monotonous but very easy job. Each demand voucher came in three copies and an allocated reference number had to be entered on each copy by the means of a numbering machine. It was a very heavy metal machine containing an ink pad. Geoff repeated time and time again that the machine had to be set so that the number changed after every three strikes on the voucher. That was the most complicated part of a very uncomplicated procedure! It was made quite clear that the same number had to appear on each copy of the voucher for identifying and accounting and, not least of all, for costing every item. Each of the three copies ended up in different places and the number was the only means of tracking every transaction.

"Just imagine the problem it would cause if you stamped 003 on two copies and 004 appeared on the third copy" said Geoff. "You would wrongly number every batch and cause chaos. Always check that the same, I say again same, number appears on all three copies."

I laughed. "I am not that stupid" I replied. "A child could do that!" Strangely the whole procedure was not as simple as it sounds.

The machine seemed to have a mind of its own and sometimes the catch that dictated the change of number slipped. Banging away with the machine constantly, thinking all was well, sometimes revealed that successive numbers appeared on each page of the voucher. It was not changing after every three! At other times the machine jammed and the same number appeared on every voucher in the batch. I found the most frustrating and time consuming part of the job was deleting most of the inked machine numbers and over writing them by hand. Inking the felt pads from bottles of thick black goo was a mess in itself and very difficult to wash off your hands. Worse still if it splashed onto your uniform.

So there I was carrying out the very vital task of keeping aircraft flying. As Flight Sergeant Moon often commented "We are all links in a very vital chain."

Flight Lieutenant Pallett our Officer in Charge always put it another way as only an officer could. "Well chaps, always remember, you may think you are a very small cog in a very large wheel, but, the large wheel cannot turn without you little cogs."

Little cogs we might be but a large disaster would be much nearer to the truth. Pranksters were very much in evidence in our office and the two other large offices in the headquarters building. It was continuous banter and laughter day after day.

There was not a single day that went by without a reprimand or threat from Flight Sergeant Moon, Flight Lieutenant Pallett or both.

Pete and Matt were without doubt the stars. They were the best of friends but constantly arguing and winding each other up. They were cheeky to the bosses and always up to mischief. Everybody knew who the pranksters were but when challenged they would put on very serious faces and protest their innocence. They could put on the most angelic appearances.

There was one lad they didn't like at all but none of us knew why. I think it was because they suspected him of drinking from their bottles of pop.

"I'll teach him a lesson" said Pete and left a bottle of urine on his desk. Half the bottle disappeared but we never discovered who the thief was.

Sometimes Matt would come in to our office and wipe ink all over the earpiece of the telephone. "I am going next door to 'phone Pete" he said. "Make sure he answers and don't tell him there is ink all over his ear!" Sadly it all went wrong because as soon as Matt went to make the call Flight Sergeant Moon came in and answered it. "Somebody mucking about as usual" he said "or somebody has got the wrong number." We all sniggered as we saw the Flight Sergeant's very blue ear.

To make matters worse the Flight Lieutenant came in to speak to Moon. Whatever they discussed meant that he had to make a 'phone call and he too ended up with a blue ear. Both of these bosses suddenly stared at each other and the Flight Lieutenant stepped slightly side-wards to take a further look at the Flight Sergeant. He smiled.

"You have got ink all over your ear Flight Sergeant" he said. There was a short silence as the Flight Sergeant glanced at the Flight Lieutenant and said "So have you, Sir." At this juncture Matt came in grinning to see if Pete had received the ink treatment but when questioned by the bosses put on his angelic act and said he could not think how anyone could be so juvenile.

Everybody it seemed played tricks on everybody else. I was constantly on the receiving end because I confess I often played jokes on the others. Consequently someone would attack me with my own numbering machine and stamp numbers in triplicate over areas of my body, sometimes in sensitive places. It was so difficult to wash off.

I enjoyed walking around the site delivering the batches of vouchers to the store sheds when the weather was fine. It got me out of the office and I loved to chat to friends I had made in the sheds. Even the Flight Lieutenant and the Flight Sergeant came in on some of the jokes. I think it was to break the monotony.

One day the Flight Sergeant sent me to a shed to collect a "long weight." I duly went to collect it and waited for ages before the chap in charge returned to me. "What did you come in for?" he asked. "A long weight" I replied. "Well you've had a long wait now laddie and you can go back to your office" he said.

On another occasion he sent one of the lads for a sky hook and another for a left handed screwdriver.

All the lists and prices of the aircraft parts were listed in bound vocabularies which were called vocabs for short. The Flight Lieutenant would often summon me to his office and ask me to collect the CP or CX vocab because he needed some information.

One morning he summoned me and said, "Right Airman, I want you to go to Shed F and collect the N.I.V. Vocab that they borrowed from me."

"Yes Sir", a smart salute and I was off to Shed F where I asked for the return of the Flight Lieutenant's N.I.V. Vocab."

A Warrant Officer in the shed, called Percy, asked "Are you mad? Do you know what N.I.V. means? I shook my head.

"It means Not in Vocab" he said. "You are asking me for a Not in Vocab Vocab." The Flight Lieutenant laughed until he cried when I returned to his office. That day I learnt from him that if an item was not listed in a vocabulary it could be found in other Manuals and Catalogues.

So each day was a process of learning the trade, learning to try and keep one ahead of the next joke, and, be as efficient as possible with each task that came to hand.

We were paid once a fortnight when we assembled on a pay parade and we were paid in alphabetical order.

We were not paid in German Deutschmarks as I had expected but what was known as BAFFs. British Armed Forces Finance vouchers. These were very similar to play money with varying coloured pieces of paper valued at pennies, three pence, sixpence, one shilling, and so on. These could be exchanged for German currency on camp if we were going off camp to buy outside.

I did not receive much pay because I was of lowly rank and I did allocate a small allowance home. I was thankful that I was a regular airman because we did earn a bit more than a man doing ordinary national service.

First pay day and I was anxious to get some German money and get off camp. It was a Saturday and Colin and I decided to walk the four miles into Wassenberg to see the shops and maybe get a drink and some food.

Wassenberg is a small German town just a couple of miles from the Dutch border. It has the remains of what looks like an old ruined castle with steps and beautiful rose gardens leading down from it.

Towering above is the large Berg Hotel with wonderful scenic views. Yes Wassenberg is a very picturesque place but very spread out with steep hills to go down and seemingly steeper hills to come up, especially after a glass or two of schnapps or potent German beer.

At the lower part of Wassenberg was a very large public swimming pool with a nearby shop that sold sweets, crisps and ice cream. On the opposite side was a very large pond surrounded by tall trees with small rowing boats for hire underneath. It is such a lovely and peaceful place.

A large Roman Catholic Church stands a little way above the rose gardens. Colin and I went in and between the pews saw a skeleton under glass. Later on we discovered that someone had died at that spot when the Church was bombed during the last war. There were some nice shops for such a small place. We found a very good shop that sold cameras and films and came across a very small cinema, some pubs and just what we were looking for. A pub come restaurant called Zur Hotel Post that had a menu in the window written in English. This was accompanied by a picture of our Queen Elizabeth the Second and the British Union Flag.

Colin and I saw the words "English spoken" and "Egg and chips" which cost far less than we expected. We went in.

There was a small bar on the left and a juke box and a one armed bandit machine straight ahead. There were about a dozen tables with chairs at each one. Each table sported a crisp white table cloth. An ancient piano was stuck in the corner.

Two business type men sat smoking and drinking at one of the tables. Sitting with them was a lady, probably in her early sixties, who rose and greeted us with a smile and a hand outstretched to shake ours. She was the owner.

It was an amazing afternoon that we spent at Zur Hotel Post. The lady introduced herself as Frau Schmitz but she said everybody calls me "Momma." In faltering English Momma explained that her husband had died a few years previously.

"That's him" she said nodding to a large picture on the wall that had a respectful black band across the corner of the frame.

Momma was tall and very thin and clad in a long white overall. She looked very pale and stooped forward from the shoulders. She coughed every now and then which indicated some form of chest complaint but during the afternoon we watched her drink several drinks of spirits and smoke a lot of cigarettes.

Lifting a half full glass of brandy Momma smiled at us and pronounced "This is Momma's penicillin" indicating that she drank it for medicinal purposes.

Colin and I were very pleased to hear of her interest in us. She explained that the picture of The Queen and the Union Flag in the window was her way of encouraging the local British military to become her customers. Hence the menu's being written in English.

Momma went on to say that she had one beautiful daughter called Puppi who lived with her. Puppi had a very handsome young Dutch boyfriend called Reiner and the three of them cooked, served food and manned the bar. Puppi and Reiner came in during the afternoon and we all sat at one table chatting.

The meal was beautifully cooked and so large. Momma suggested that we had cutlets with our egg and chips which turned out to be the biggest pork chops we had ever seen. As a very special welcome she said we could also have a large schnapps each for free. They wanted us to always feel welcome and urged us to bring as many friends along as we could. We were not so naive as to realise she was using us to drum up extra custom.

Colin and I giggled and chatted and discussed our new friends as we walked back the four miles to Wildenrath and our camp. We had already decided that Zur Hotel Post was a must for future visits.

I had no idea then that that establishment would play such a very large role in my life for the next two and a half years whilst stationed at Wildenrath. Or indeed, that it would play a big part in my personal and private life for decades to come.

CHAPTER 28

Colin and I wasted no time in telling all the lads in the hut about our visit to Zur Hotel Post. Without exception everybody was enthusiastic about giving the place a visit. The only drawback was that transport was a problem. Local public transport was almost non-existent, and a four mile walk each way was not very appealing. Andy One said "We could only venture when the weather is alright. You would be like a drowned rat by the time you got there or back if it rains."

"Yes" added Taff, "and it does restrict how many pints you could drink as well. If you get a bit tipsy you could never stagger all that way back."

There were, of course, several other factors to be taken into consideration. Some of us were under the age of twenty one and the rule was that we had to be back on camp by 11 o'clock. The biggest problem of all was that we did not have very much money to spend.

A group of about seven or eight of us went together on the next visit. Momma, Puppi and Reiner were thrilled to see us and made sure that we were well and truly looked after. The meals were excellent and we bought a couple of bottles of whisky to share which we decided was cheaper than buying by the glass. The only problem was that Momma kept helping herself to her "penicillin for Momma's health" and very discreetly plied Colin and I with glasses of cognac because we had increased her custom.

The night wore on. Local customers came and went and some came and joined us.

Everybody seemed friendly, laughed and raised their glasses and one middle aged chap started singing something in German. The song appeared to have a chorus because at the end of each little piece he sang, all the rest burst into song and together slapped their hands on the table. Well that was too much for us British and we were not going to be beaten. Someone started singing the hokey cokey and we arose unsteadily on our feet to perform with the song. Those Germans looked on with amusement and some of the younger lads tried to join in.

I knew I had had too much to drink because my speech was effected, my legs felt light and I couldn't stop laughing. I can play the piano though and Colin knew it. As far as I can remember he lifted the lid and asked me to play.

I would never have volunteered to play in public in a pub back home but sadly when the drink is in the wits are out. Young people far away from home often do things they would never dream of doing otherwise.

I had my share of the whisky, Momma's glasses of cognac and now the Germans were lining up small glasses of beer on top of the piano for me. The inevitable had to come. For the first time ever I got very drunk.

Zur Hotel Post did not have any closing time but stayed open as long as customers kept coming in. Several years later after I had left the RAF and I was back on holiday in Wassenberg, I invited Momma to come to England. She thanked me for the invitation but shook her head. "I don't want to come where the public houses close at 11pm" she said.

It was getting on for midnight before any of us gave any thought about the long trek back to the Camp. No-one was keen to venture out into the bitter cold. When we decided it was time to leave Momma embraced and kissed us all in turn and made it very obvious that I was her favourite.

From that evening until the day she died she always called me "Momma's best boy!" I felt worse when I got out into the fresh air. I didn't sense the cold but I was very conscious that my legs felt funny and didn't want to walk as they should. There was a lot of laughter and singing along the way. The more we walked the worse I felt and I just wanted to keep sitting down but I was literally pulled along by one and another.

The other lads seemed to be in a far better state than I was. I reckon the odds were that I had consumed more alcohol than the rest of them because of my stint on the piano.

The well-lit camp gate at Wildenrath was a very welcome sight. A couple of military police were on Guard Duty as we approached.

Jimbo and Andy Two walked very close on either side to support me and fished in my pockets to produce my Pass. Jimbo said "If they ask you if you are twenty one Ken, say yes!" To the consternation of everybody else I lumbered up to one of the policemen and said "I am twenty one but I am not really" and went off into peals of hysterical laughter.

One policeman shook his head. The other looked at the group and simply said "Take it away." They did so as fast as they could before I was let loose to cause any further embarrassment. We still had at least another mile to walk once inside the main gate.

I felt so ill the following day and I vowed that I would never get in a state like that again. I never did except that I got very close to it on a later special occasion.

401 Air Stores Park at Eindhoven closed and many of the lads I had been on the Course with at Credenhill were transferred with all the stores to Wildenrath. It was a time of great rejoicing when my old mates Mick and Joe from Lancashire, Geordie, Gerald, Ray and Shaun arrived at Block 51.

The reunion caused for celebration and the very first weekend I introduced them to Momma Schmitz, the family and new found friends at Zur Hotel Post. This only added to my popularity with all at the hostelry because trade had never been so good. It was the second and last time that I got really drunk.

All the personnel at 402 Air Stores Park were taken to RAF Wildenrath airfield at regular intervals to view the aircraft for which we were provisioning the spares.

First of all it was the Sabre Jets which had come to us through some arrangements with the Canadians. Later on a squadron of Canberra's flew in.

We heard rumours but had no facts of why these aircraft were at Wildenrath. In the fifties it was alleged that we were matching the Russian MIG's buzzing the air corridors. This was never confirmed or denied.

The transfer of stores from 401 Air Stores Park at RAF Eindhoven meant a large increase of the work for our offices. More air squadrons joined the Stations at Bruggen, Geilenkirchen and Laarbruch so there was a much larger demand for aircraft stores and maintenance.

Vouchers arrived daily by the hundreds and my poor old numbering machine was working at capacity.

The Air Ministry in its wisdom decided that 402 ASP needed to be a mobile unit. In the event of war or emergency we would have to transfer all the items of stock from the shelves of sheds to racks inside vehicles. We should all be prepared to move out and away at very short notice. To be a mobile unit meant that all the personnel needed to learn to drive the 3 ton Magirus Deutz lorries which had been adapted for the purpose of storing and transporting aircraft spares.

Then two important things happened in quick succession.

I was promoted to L.A.C. which meant I had become a Leading Aircrafts man. I was very happy to sew the two propeller badges on the sleeves of my uniforms. I was also given the date for my first driving lesson.

Three of us had to report to the Mechanical Transport Section the following Monday morning. Known as the MT Section for short it accommodated several 3 ton Magirus Deutz lorries, pick-ups, lifting gear and the Commanding Officer and Adjutant staff cars. There were three or four motorbikes for courier purposes, and, a large area which was used for maintenance and repairs and for changing tyres. On one of the walls of the Office was a display of very large photographs of the most gruesome nature. Every picture depicted the scene of an accident. One of the photographs showed a decapitated woman sitting in the driving seat of her car. A lorry load of metal pipes and ladders had reversed into her car and the extended pipes and ladders had smashed through her windscreen and took her head off. It was a horrific sight. Other pictures were ghastly showing wrecked vehicles and mangled bodies and lots of blood. It certainly was not for the squeamish hut served as a warning to all learners that mobile vehicles are just as lethal as weapons.

Three sergeants were assigned to us three airmen as driving instructors. For the rest of the morning we filled in official papers for driving on the German roads, insurance and so on. Then we got to see the lorry and the feel of sitting in the driving seat.

The lorry was not so big as I had envisaged. It consisted of a cab with a high step to get up into it and was covered by a canopy. A drop tail gate completed the rear of the vehicle.

Sergeant Gifford, my instructor, was a portly man with a handlebar moustache. He had a very round face, a jovial nature and wore his beret looking something like a mushroom or a flying saucer. We got on well from the start.

I was shown how to open the coupling cover to reveal the engine underneath and taught where to put the water and the oil and then we were off.

The sergeant drove the short distance to an apron near one of the air runways and then he handed me the keys and we changed places in the cab. I was taught a few manoeuvres and then instructed to drive for the gate and out on to the road heading for Wassenberg.

It seemed strange to be driving on the right side of the road but I felt confident and Giff, as the sergeant liked to be called, was very patient and encouraging. I was disappointed that there was no sign of life at Zur Hotel Post as I drove by.

It was intensive training and getting driving experience for seven days. We ventured as far as Monchen Gladbach to get experience in town traffic.

The most anxious moment for me was when I was told to stop the vehicle half way up the steep cobbled hill by the rose gardens in Wassenberg.

Giff took the watch off his wrist, jumped down out of the cab and placed the watch next to the rear wheel of the lorry.

"Right mate" he said, "this is where you get your hill start."

My heart missed a beat as he continued by tapping his forehead with the tip of his fingers. "Think!" he continued. "Think carefully about what you are doing. You have practiced this before but not very successfully. Remember it's all about throttle and clutch control. Hold your hand brake until you feel you are pulling forward, then release it and drive slowly forward. Remember this too, if you go back and wreck my watch you will have to buy me a replacement."

I had never concentrated so much in my life because there was so much counting on it. I did think carefully and co-ordinated my thoughts, hands and feet to do exactly what was required of me and went forward. What a relief "Well done" said a grinning Giff as he retrieved his watch, strapped it back on his wrist and climbed back into the cab.

He looked at my very serious face and laughed out loud. "Cheer up!" he said, "It's an old busted watch. You didn't think I would put a good one under there did you?"

I learnt that day that all the instructors produced broken watches for the hill starts. It did the trick. They also chalked crosses on the rear windscreen to help line up the vehicle for three point turns and reversing around corners.

All three of us passed our tests at the first attempt and received our BZ Licences. These important documents allowed us to drive anywhere within the British Zones of Germany.

Several times over the next year we went out on short weekend exercises. It was simply a case of selecting a lot of stores off the shelves in the sheds and storing them on the racks in the vehicles. We drove in convoys of six or eight lorries and parked in some isolated places where we tried to operate as though we were back at base camp.

On one exercise our star duo, Pete and Matt, had no opportunity to ink the ear pieces of telephones but got up to just as much mischief away from the offices. After a heated argument about missing cigarettes, Pete snatched Matt's beret from his head and threw it to the top of a very tall holly tree.

Matt tried hard to climb the tree to retrieve his beret and was badly scratched as we all stood, watched and laughed.

Flight Lieutenant Pallett could not have chosen a worse time to appear on the scene with his brisk word of command.

"Well chaps, muster! Return to your vehicles immediately and prepare for imminent departure."

Matt stuck at the top of a holly tree was in no position for any imminent departure.

"Sir" he called from the tree, "Can you do us a favour please?"

The Flight Lieutenant's face was a picture as he gazed upwards. "Favour? Entwistle, what are you doing up there?"

"I'm getting my beret, Sir."

"Beret? What's your beret doing up there?"

Pete, with a straight face, explained to the Flight Lieutenant that it had blown up there whilst the rest of us were doubled up with laughter.

"Come down immediately, we are just leaving" Pallett continued. A very forlorn Matt was now close to tears, bleeding and pleading.

"Please Sir, do us a favour" he tried again. "Could you have one of the lorries pull up against the tree so that I can get out on to the canopy? I'm bleeding to bits through coming up. I will have no skin left if I've got to climb down."

"For goodness sake" Pallett was growing impatient now. He turned to Geordie and said "See to it. Get him down."

Pete just could not help stepping in at this juncture. "I'll get him down" he said and raced off to get his lorry which he practically drove into the tree.

Matt cautiously edged his way to where the canvas canopy had come to rest between the spiky branches. He heaved himself over the metal support and lay face down on top of the canopy. We all cheered to see him there but this was just the cue for Pete to drive off. Now clinging precariously on the top of the canopy Matt was screaming for Pete to stop.

Pete gathered speed and Matt screamed all the more. There was no knowing what the outcome might have been if it had not been for Flight Sergeant Moon. He arrived in the nick of time and stopped Pete's imitation of being at a grand prix. A frightened, blood splattered and very cross Matt slid down the side canopy of the lorry and confronted Pete. Pete listened with a grin as Matt called him all the names under the sun.

"I thought we were mates" moaned Matt as he tugged his beret back on his head. "We are" replied Pete with a smile as he snatched Matt's beret again and ran off with Matt in hot pursuit. There was a tussle, a lot of swearing, and lo and behold Pete tossed the beret to the top of another tree where it remained.

All of us were well aware that Matt would be getting his own back on Pete and sure enough he did a week later back at the hut.

Matt was usually one of the first to go to bed every night. This particular night, however, he was not in at midnight and all the lights were out. No-one heard him creep in in the early hours but there he was in his bed as large as life at dawn.

To see sixteen lads get up out of bed first thing in the morning is not a pretty sight. Nightwear comes in various guises. Pyjama tops only, or bottoms only, underpants and tee shirts and more often than not no clothes at all.

Pete was modestly dressed in his underpants on this occasion. In normal fashion he crawls out of bed, usually swearing at something or somebody, yawns, stretches and opens his locker for his uniform or whatever.

Half asleep and still yawning he opens the door of his locker and immediately bedlam is let loose.

There is the sound of a lot of rustling, flapping of wings and a cock a doodle doo as a trapped cockerel is released. Pete goes as white as a sheet and almost faints with shock whilst Matt sits up in bed singing "Got my own back! Got my own back!" No prizes for guessing why he was late going to bed.

Billet capers seem to run in cycles and every one of us got caught out in one way or another. If I wasn't a victim I was usually a participant.

Mick and Joe, the two Lancashire lads, were often on the receiving end of some prank or other.

I never knew anyone snore so loudly and so persistently as Mick. When he went to bed and to sleep it was just as though an earthquake would fail to raise him.

Well, I had heard that if someone is sleeping, and subsequently snoring, you can wake them up by slowly pouring water from one mug to another. The sound of running water apparently makes you want to wee and makes you wake up and head for the loo.

We decided to give it a try on Mick and I volunteered to do the bit with the water and the mugs.

So there I am in my pyjamas beside his bed, and in complete darkness, pouring cold water from one mug to another whilst everybody is sitting up in bed, listening and laughing.

I can't see what I am doing and I am spilling cold water down my pyjamas and on to my naked feet whilst Mick slumbers on.

I proceeded to fill two mugs with water and kept up my bedside vigil, gently pouring the water from one mug to the other.

"Ken, the sound of that trickling is making me want to wee" says Ray and shuffles off to the loo. I never did succeed in waking Mick but, one by one, almost all the lads had to go off to the urinals.

Joe was very protective of Mick and the closest of friends. He made a bit of a fuss because we were playing a joke on his mate and turned quite miserable. In fact his complaining that we had kept him awake most of the night was beginning to get on all our nerves. We decided the next night we would retaliate on him.

Whilst Joe was sound asleep the rest of us hatched up a cunning plan. The funny thing was that although Joe came out in Mick's defence, it was his mate Mick that was the instigator of what we were about to do.

We surrounded Joe's bed and lifted it up together and headed for the door of the hut with him fast asleep in it. It was decided to place sleeping beauty complete with bed in the middle of the car park.

We had a bit of difficulty when we got to the door because the doorway was narrower than the bed.

Between laughter and whispers we had to tip the bed sidewards whilst a couple of the lads pressed on Joe to save him toppling off it.

Joe sniffed and grunted but didn't show any signs of waking up.

Very cautiously we eased the bed through the narrow doorway, opened the outside door and carried our cargo to the middle of the car park where we left it and hurried back inside.

All of three hours must have passed by before our dark billet was flooded with light and we were awakened by a lot of shouting.

In the doorway stood Joe soaked to his skin wrapped in a blanket. His face was as white as milk and pouring rain had made his hair look like ringlets. Water ran down his face as he shivered and shouted at the top of his voice.

"I don't think that's funny. No, I don't think that's funny." He called us a lot of very rude names suggesting that we were all illegitimate.

The hut went very quiet and someone went over to hand Joe a towel and then somebody else did the same. Blankets were offered and a couple of the lads went out to collect the sopping bed.

The sad sight of Joe gave us all a very guilty conscience and one by one we tried to apologise and appease him.

After some time Joe calmed down when he saw how contrite we all were. He laughed but begged us not to do anything like it again and we all agreed.

Something happened in Hut 51 that night. That isolated incident seemed to make us all aware of how much we needed to support each other. We realised we were a team - comrades - mates.

We all went very serious and solemn. It was like we had grown up overnight.

CHAPTER 29

Every single day someone would ask "How many days are there before pay day?." The pittance pay didn't allow for many luxuries. Whenever a money gift was sent from home we rejoiced. We shared the good fortune of gifts received and loaned to each other and economised where-ever we could.

Any chance of earning an extra shilling or two was eagerly accepted.

The RAF had a scheme whereby they held back some of our pay each fortnight and put it into credit for us. If we caused any damage to the hut or equipment it was paid for from our credits. This made us very careful. Every three months or so we had a sizeable refund of our credits if we had not caused any damage. There was dismay and an outcry if someone broke a window or a fitting.

At Wildenrath we had two extremely good institutions. There-was the Navy and Army and Air Forces Institute (N.A.A.F.I.) and the Malcolm Club. Both of these served food and drinks, sweets, crisps, toiletries etc. In fact the N.A.A.F.I. provided almost everything an airman could possibly want at good reduced prices. These were places where you could play various games and snooker, billiards and darts were always the favourites.

We often met up at the N.A.A.F.I. as our main social outlet or went to the Astra Cinema to watch the latest release of films. It was not a great expense but sometimes our finances forced us to make a choice.

The N.A.A.F.I. had a mobile van which used to call at 402 ASP every morning at 10 o'clock. Lads would stream out of the offices and sheds and queue up to buy bottles of pop, rolls and cigarettes. I always think of that N.A.A.F.I. van every time I have a cheese and onion roll. No-one ever put so much cheese and onion in a roll as the N.A.A.F.I.

Whoever drove the van and served the goodies charged an extra two pence on each bottle of fizzy pop. This ensured the return of the bottle to obtain the two pence refund which you could put towards the cost of some other luxury. I always took good care of my bottles and saved them up. I was always short of cash on the second week before pay day and survived at the van by trading in my bottles and any I found around the site.

I had accumulated about a dozen empty pop bottles and these were lined up on the window sill next to my desk. This worked out to be as good as two shillings in real terms. Enough for a couple of rolls and another couple of bottles of pop at least. Tony from the office kept pestering me for my bottles. He wanted to trade them in for some cash for cigarettes but I refused.

After two or three days of pleading I still refused to hand over the bottles.

One day when I was out of the office, Tony more in fun than revenge I suspect, opened the window and dropped them one by one on to the grass outside. Now I had a real problem.

All of the windows had vertical metal bars outside at about three inches apart.

These had been placed there to safeguard our offices which contained secret files and information concerning the aircraft and the provisioning of the spares. It was a wonder that Tony had managed to squeeze the bottles through the narrow bars. To make matters worse the grass area where the bottles were was enclosed by a high inaccessible fence.

The only window that did not have bars on that entire side of the building was the one in the Commanding Officer's office.

I looked at my empty window sill in dismay. I could see no way of recovering the bottles through the bars. The only possible way to get into the area where the bottles were was to climb through the Commanding Officer's office window. I watched his movements very carefully all the morning but he didn't budge. During the early part of the afternoon I saw the CO drive off in his car. This was my opportunity! It had to be now or never and so I went with speed to his office. I opened the window and it was necessary to pull his posh leather chair up to it in order to have a stepping stone for climbing through.

I scurried along to where the bottles were but there were too many to carry in one go. I ran along to the CO's window and put what I had picked up on the inside sill and returned to pick up the remainder.

Dennis peered through the bars and made a hissing sound. "Ken" he whispered, "the old man has come back." This was his way of saying the CO had returned.

He tried to give me a warning. I laughed but didn't believe him. I had seen the CO drive off only ten minutes previously. Then I heard voices coming from the area of the open window and the next thing I knew the CO, a very quiet and unassuming Squadron Leader, was leaning out and staring at me in disbelief. "Airman, what are you doing?" he asked. He didn't look too pleased.

I had to think quickly. "I am just clearing up these old bottles" I replied and decided the truth was the best policy as I did not have time to hatch up a lie.

"I am sorry I had to get through your window, Sir, but it is the only way I can get out here." I stammered.

"Well hurry up" the Squadron Leader said and transferred the bottles sitting on his window sill to his desk. Then to cap it all, realising that it was quite a drop from his window to the ground, he leaned further out, extended his arm, took the bottles I was holding and then helped me back through his window. It was hilarious! I was further embarrassed when the CO apologised to his visitor for my intrusion. The visitor was another Squadron Leader and I later learnt that the CO had only driven to the main gate to pick him up, hence his quick return.

Flight Sergeant Moon nearly had a fit and could hardly believe his eyes when he saw our boss hauling me up through his window. I expected to be in a lot of trouble but the whole thing went off without a fuss. I learnt from the experience and never hoarded bottles in the office again.

Always on the lookout for earning cash, getting a bargain or embracing some economy, I thought my luck had well and truly changed when Flight Lieutenant Pallett asked me if I would like to earn five shillings.

He and his wife were going out for the evening and he wondered if I would be willing to baby sit for his two young children, aged eight and six, in their married quarter. Not only was he willing to pay five shillings but they would leave some eggs and bacon and I was at liberty to get myself a meal.

I considered the tempting offer but was reluctant to do it on my own. I asked if Colin could do the baby sitting with me.

"I don't mind at all" he said. "Five shillings is being over generous so you can share it. You are getting fed as well!" In the early part of a very dark evening Colin and I walked the two miles to the Officers Married Quarters. We were more than happy to have a night out together to get half a crown apiece with a meal thrown in as a bonus.

Pallett had a really lovely wife and she showed us where the utensils were for the fry up that we were going to have later on. She had already put the boys to bed and she didn't think they would wake up or cause any fuss whilst they were away. Pallett called us into the kitchen and said we could have a couple of cans of beer but he did not want us to smoke. That was no problem since neither Colin nor I smoked anyway.

The older boy called out once and asked for a drink but apart from that we never heard another sound out of either of them throughout the entire evening.

We listened to music on the radio and had several goes with the electric train set that was laid out on the living room floor. We more than helped ourselves to eggs and bacon and used up nearly half a loaf for fried bread.

Colin and I enjoyed the time relaxing and spent a lot of time going through the books in the bookcase. Then we came to a decision about the cans of beer.

We didn't fancy any after the amount of tea we had consumed but we decided that we could take a couple of cans back to the billet. There was every possibility that we could sell them on to our mates and earn a bit of extra cash.

The Palletts had dozens of cans of beer in boxes. Not surprisingly because beer and cigarettes on Camp were extremely cheap. So cheap in fact that the cigarettes were generously rationed to the airmen. The rationing was imposed to stop airmen selling them locally or hoarding them to take back to Britain.

"They will not miss half a dozen cans of this beer" said Colin. "Let's have three apiece."

"We can't just carry them out in front of them when they come home" I replied.

"How can we conceal them?"

Colin came up with an idea. "I know" he said, "let's put them by the hedge just inside the gate now. We can pick them up when we leave. Nobody will see in the dark." So we strategically placed six cans of beer by the gate.

It must have been nearly five hours that Colin and I had been babysitting. It was getting on for midnight and both of us were almost asleep when the Palletts breezed in looking considerably wet as Mrs Pallett shook her umbrella and tossed her wet hair with her hand. "So sorry we are late" she said.

"We are in the Wildenrath Drama Group" explained the Flight Lieutenant. "We have been preparing for the dress rehearsal and that is why we have been out longer than usual." He sniffed. "I see you have had a fry up. Everything gone OK? Thanks lads for helping out." He fished in his pocket and mustered up the five shillings in Baffs and went on to say "I will drive you lads back to the billet because it is absolutely pouring with rain."

"Thank you very much Sir, that's very kind of you" said Colin.

"No, no it's alright. We like a breath of fresh air and often go for a walk before we go to bed." I lied.

Colin looked at me as though I was mad.

"We will get soaked" he said, "we will take your offer of a lift Sir. Thank you very much."

"I wouldn't dream of you walking all that way in this weather" Pallett went on and ushered us out to the car and drove us the couple of miles to our hut.

"We would have been mad to walk all this way in the rain" scolded Colin as the Flight Lieutenant drove off. "Whatever possessed you to suggest it?" "Half a dozen cans of beer propping up his gate" I replied.

Colin clapped his hand to his mouth and gasped.

"Oh no. I had forgotten about the beer" he said. "What are we going to do? In the morning Pallett is going to see it and know that we have pinched it. We will be in a load of trouble and he will never invite us to baby sit again."

"Only one thing for it" I muttered, "we will have to go back and get it" and so we did. A four mile round trip in the dark and pouring rain at midnight to pick up six cans of beer. Truly it has been said that crime does not pay and be sure your sins will find you out! When you live together and work together and spend so much time in each other's company you do forge close friendships. Time spent in the Forces taught us to look out for each other, to be loyal, to bear each other's burdens to be there for each other when needed.

For instance we all gathered around Ray's bed when he burst in to tears after reading a letter from his girlfriend. "It's a Dear John" he explained. We were all familiar with "Dear John's" it was the Forces slang for receiving a letter to say some wife or girlfriend back home wanted to break a relationship because they had found somebody else. Long periods of separation often took their toll. Sometimes a "sprog" letter would arrive. A sprog was the nickname given for a baby. When a letter arrived from a girl back home to say she was pregnant there was always a serious discussion about it between the lads.

"Is it mine or has she been playing the field since I've been here?" a lad would ask. We could only try to reassure and urge him to contact the girl as soon as possible. Although Germany wasn't on the far side of the world, it seemed like it was when problems cropped up at home.

Sometimes we were prone to help each other too much. Our good intentions were often misguided like the time I operated on Shaun's boil. For days he had complained about a large boil in the middle of his back which looked red and angry.

I had heard that if you get a bottle and fill it with steam from a kettle and place it over the boil, the steam will draw the boil to a head and cause it to burst. I fished out one of my concealed pop bottles and put it under the long running hot bath tap and applied it to the centre of Shaun's spine. He fainted. I can confirm it works! Sometimes we were misguided about the way we dealt with hygiene problems, or rather very big hygiene problems.

At one time we had a big strapping lad posted in who was nicknamed Thumper. Thumper was so called because he had a reputation of getting drunk frequently and was known to thump anyone who tried to help him or got in his way.

It was not unusual for Thumper to come in late from a long drinking session at the N.A.A.F.I. Drunk and tired he would kick off his boots and often climb into bed fully dressed. He didn't wash very often and the stink of him caused a lot of complaints especially from those who occupied the beds each side of him.

After a couple of weeks our patience was exhausted and we held a billet council. We decided that the next time he went to bed fully clothed, we would yank him out of the bed, strip him in the shower and give him a good scrub down with a birch broom.

Pete and Matt were at the forefront of the event. They approached Thumper and told him what they intended to do but he only swore at them. They pulled him off the bed and he started throwing his arms about so much that we all came in to help restrain him. He was frogmarched to the shower, stripped naked, and thrust beneath the hot water and scrubbed. He started yelling and his skin got red and then he went quiet, swayed and slumped to his knees.

Two things stopped us in our tracks. Thumper's eyes grew large and he stared without blinking. It was uncanny. We were most concerned when suddenly he started choking and gasping for breath. He could not stand on his own feet. Between us we carried Thumper and laid him soaking wet on his bed. He just stared at the ceiling but was strangely quiet except for the sound of his breathing. After some time he rolled over and pulled his blankets over him and started crying. No-one spoke to Thumper about the incident the following day although some of us talked about it amongst ourselves. When we relayed what we had done to Flight Sergeant Moon at the office he did not see the funny side and told us off. He explained that we could have killed Thumper. Excessive hot water on the outside of the body and alcohol on the inside was not a good mix and said something about the effects it has on blood pressure and the heart. We never attempted to do anything like that again even though the experience didn't change Thumper's attitude to hygiene.

Regular kit inspections were a nightmare. Every item that we possessed had to be exceptionally clean, even pristine, and laid out in order on our blanket covered beds. The night before a kit inspection was a hive of activity in our billet as we spit and polished our boots, blanco'd our webbing belts and back packs and used endless Brasso on our brass buttons and buckles.

It took ages to place everything in order and in the prescribed way on our beds. It was only at kit inspection time that we often discovered we were missing something, usually pairs of socks or gloves. The "housewife" a little linen pouch containing needles and thread together with combs often went missing.

The inspections were always carried out by an officer with a non-commissioned officer like our Flight Sergeant in tow. They would peer at the layout on the beds and make more adverse comments than good ones. Sometimes if one of the lads was short of an item, we would toss the item across to his bed behind the inspecting officers' backs. In this way the same shirt, underwear or socks et cetera would often reappear to be inspected several times on different beds. We had an answer for everything! Every autumn the Unit went off on a special two week exercise.

The Squadron Leader called us together on the parade ground and informed us that the entire Unit would be going by convoy to a wooded area near to Zandvaart in Holland.

A large percentage of the stores had to be transferred from the sheds to the 3 ton Magirus Deutz lorries adapted for the purpose. Other vehicles would transport tents, sleeping bags and cooking facilities. Washing and toilet facilities would also be made available.

Our Commanding Officer spoke of the tremendous responsibility the Second Tactical Air Force had put upon us. Our vehicles converted to store sheds and offices would be concealed in the depths of a large wooded area. We were to be camouflaged so that we could not be spotted from the air. That was vitally important but just as important was the work output.

We would be required to receive, action all documentation, and provide more stores whilst on exercise than we did back at base where every facility was available. Every airman would be scrutinised at his job. We had to tackle the exercise as though we were at war for real. It all sounded exciting but rather daunting at the same time.

I started packing all that I thought I would need both at the office and at the billet. In just a few hours we would be leaving Germany for Holland and the unknown. We were bubbling over with high spirits and enthusiasm. Perhaps we would not have been so keen if we had known then what was to come.

CHAPTER 30

In less than two days all our store sheds were stripped of their stores. A line of 3 ton Magirus Deutz vehicles had been loaded with them in readiness for departure. All our office equipment, typewriters, four drawer cabinets, boxes of forms and documents all neatly labelled in cardboard cartons were loaded also.

All we left behind was our desks and chairs. We had obtained several long trestle tables and light weight stacking canvas chairs for use on the exercise at Zandvaart in Holland. We were travelling as light as possible.

There was no need to load any tents, cookhouse or toilet facilities as all of these had been taken and put into place the weekend before our full scale departure. Each one of us was responsible for taking our own uniforms and personal clothing, lightweight portable Z beds and sleeping bags. No other creature comforts were allowed.

I made sure that my most important tool of the trade was with me. The vital inked numbering machine together with spare pads and bottles of ink. All in readiness for endorsing all the store demand vouchers that we expected to receive.

I was thankful that I was a passenger instead of a driver. It was a long way to drive over the border of Germany and across the country of Holland. We enjoyed the scenery as we went and the hospitality of the Dutch people when we stopped for breaks along the way.

We knew we were going to a large wooded area but we had no idea that it would be as large as it was.

There were several entrances and exits to the gigantic forest. The lanes through the forest were straight but very narrow. The canopies of the lorries brushed against many of the branches as we spread out in different areas amongst the trees.

We were looking for the parts of the forest which were most dense, conscious of the fact that we needed a lot of foliage cover to avoid being seen from the air.

The paths crisscrossed like a maze and it was both confusing and difficult to find where each vehicle and tent was situated. The worst part was finding each location you wanted by poor torch light when it was dark. The covering of the trees making it exceptionally so. The paths and wooded areas were very dark even during the hours of daylight.

I shared a tent with three other guys. Joe and Gerald from the hut back at Wildenrath and a new lad called Philip or Pip for short. I was in charge of the three of them for numbering and processing all the vouchers when we set up in another cramped tent serving as our office.

My chief concern was that all the vehicles containing the stores were spread a long way apart and in all directions. I envisaged long trips to deliver the paper work for the selecting of the stores. Then on the second day the rains came.

Did it pour! For the entire fortnight we had rain every single day. The accommodation and the office tents were waterproof but the rain seeped in under the canvas. Our

Z beds were sitting in pools of water and it was horrible to step out of the sleeping bag and paddle before you could find a dry spot on which to stand and dress. Pip made us laugh when he said "We are all in the same boat" because that was how it seemed. We got up and dressed one at a time to have a small square dry spot of ground in the centre of the tent on which to stand.

The demands came in thick and heavy every day. Then tragedy struck on the second day when we had a message to say that Gerald's mother was dying and it was necessary for him to go home on compassionate leave. That left three of us to do the work.

Pip was new and seemed to be very slow in learning the procedure. He made so many mistakes and held me up whilst I tried desperately hard to show him what to do and lost valuable time by correcting all his mistakes.

Joe complained continually about the positioning of the vehicles. He ran from one to another to find the right one and got soaked by the rain every time he went out. On the fifth day he was gone a considerable time and the vouchers I had numbered and batched piled up waiting to be delivered. I was frustrated because our section officer and the Flight Sergeant kept coming to complain that we were holding up the supply of the stores because we were delaying the paper work.

Joe should have completed three runs in an hour and a half but had not returned from the first one. I was getting more cross by the minute by Joe's non-appearance and every five minutes answering Pip's enquiries or correcting his mistakes. I had to renumber a whole stack of vouchers because he had forgotten to change the numbers on the machine. He also put too much ink on the pads so that when the machine hit the paperwork the ink splattered and sometimes obliterated what was written on it.

The situation worsened when our Flight Sergeant arrived with a medical orderly to say Joe was on his way to Wegberg Hospital. Running through the trees on a flooded and muddy path he had slipped and broken his ankle. He had been found trying to hobble in great pain. The vouchers he had been carrying were soaked and practically unreadable and the Flight Sergeant had brought them back all muddied and to be resorted.

The situation couldn't get worse or so I thought. There was only Pip and I left to bear all the responsibility of dealing with the demand documentation and the delivery of it to the store vehicles. The Flight Sergeant appreciated the crisis and persuaded the Squadron Leader to give me another couple of lads to ease the situation. But instead of improving the situation it only made matters worse. There was no time to teach two new lads the job. Pip could not cope with working under pressure and only made more mistakes.

To add to the misery of the situation was that it seemed like a monsoon season had started. Everywhere was soaked. The tents that we lived in and the office tent were wet and cold. The trees gave very little shelter when it poured with rain. The squelching muddy paths had to be negotiated with care as we remembered what had happened to Joe. It was a very miserable and wretched time.

Towards the end of the first week I was confronted by the Squadron Leader who was our C.O. for the exercise. He was extremely angry that we were holding up the entire proceedings. He complained that the severe delays we were causing meant the lads in the store vehicles were unable to select the items demanded. Similarly the vehicles on standby for delivering the stores were almost at a standstill.

As we were the source of the chain it was essential to keep the chain running. When the C.O. appeared for the third time in his attempt to speed up our jobs I finally exploded.

"Sir," I began, "I am spending all my time checking and re checking the vouchers and rectifying the mistakes. It is impossible for me to produce anything and teach the others at the same time." Then I added "It would be quicker and far easier for me to do it all on my own."

The Squadron Leader didn't hesitate. He pointed at Pip and the other two lads and said "Right! You, you and you get over to Flight Sergeant Moon and tell him I have sent you as runners." They left immediately.

Turning to me the Squadron Leader continued. "Right, Stallard, from now on you are on your own. I have taken the responsibility of teaching others off you. Now you are experienced in the job. Get on with it. I want those vouchers moved and the stores selected." Then off he went through the squelching mud.

I sat at the table with my feet in a puddle and looked at the heap of vouchers. It was a relief to have the silence of the tent. It was good to be alone without all the questions and moaning and the expectancy of having to teach. Now I was only responsible for myself and so I got stuck in and started to sort and number the vouchers like I did back at the base but with more gusto.

I bundled up the vouchers and ran as fast as I could to the vehicles. Slipping and sliding through the mud and dodging the large puddles in the paths.

The smell of the woods reminded me of the forest near to my home. The large wet ferns soaked my clothing as I ran pass them. I was very thankful for the short dry spells but they were few and far between.

The Squadron Leader looked in from time to time and complimented me on the fact that the work was speeding up. He turned up one occasion with a runner who was instructed to run to some of the vehicles to deliver the paper work for me. Then he was taken off to some other duty and I was back working by myself again. I realised quickly that the only way to keep up the supply of the documentation was to work longer hours. The accommodating tent was not fit to stay in for long anyway. Consequently I was working alone from 8 o'clock in the morning until 9 or 10 o'clock in the evening. I was in solitude except for the occasional appearance of the Flight Sergeant or Squadron Leader to see how I was doing. The programme was moving far quicker without mistakes and I was far less stressed. Late nights and early mornings began to catch up with my energy but I kept going at full speed.

Three or four days after working alone I knew that I had produced more output than in a similar period back at base. I was increasing the amount of processed vouchers every day and this greatly encouraged me. I also knew that if I maintained the time, speed and accuracy for the last few remaining days, I had single handed achieved the goal. It was all due to the relentless long hours otherwise the progress could not have been obtained.

Constant running through the forest kept me fitter than I had ever felt before.

We were very conscious of aircraft flying over the woods trying to spot our activities. As far as I know we succeeded in being camouflaged because we never heard anything to the contrary.

A couple of days prior to the end of the exercise our C.O. the Squadron Leader made a special visit to my office tent accompanied by a Wing Commander. The latter being most charming and complimentary about my performance. "Well done!" he said "To date you have exceeded the average back at base issues by almost eighteen per cent. Maintain this progress for the next forty eight hours and you will have exceeded all possible expectations. Excellent! Carry on the good work" Then the pair were off.

The visit had been brief but was sufficient to give me the boost I had needed. I decided to give the last couple of days my very best endeavours. I could tell by the piles of paper work that I actioned and delivered that my percentage was increasing by the hour.

Then, at last, the final hour of the exercise came and the last voucher had been endorsed and delivered and the stores were on route to their destinations. Then, for the first time in a fortnight, the sun shone.

It was an unforgettable moment when the C.O. called us all together in a large clearing in the centre of the woods.

He congratulated every one of us on our performance and told each section how we had excelled in whatever role we had played. Waving a hand in my direction he went on, "Stallard excelled himself because he was required to work single handed and managed to boost input away from base by thirty nine per cent." It was music to my ears.

We lost no time in packing up all the tentage and equipment and prepared for the long drive back to Wildenrath. We were all nigh exhausted but happy in the knowledge that we had done our unit proud. We had never seen our Squadron Leader look so happy and that was an achievement in itself. We must have impressed him because he gave us the Friday before and the Monday after the following weekend as free leave in thankfulness for what we had achieved. Four clear days to relax and do as we liked. This was a real bonus after the misery conditions we had endured at Zandvaart.

It was a tremendous relief to be back to normal in Hut 51. Life resumed its warm, dry and steady routine. It was good to be back in the thick of things rather than working in isolation. The N.A.A.F.I. seemed to be the most happy and entertaining place that we had indulged in for some considerable time.

It was in the N.A.A.F.I. that Taffy came across all excited to the table where a group of us were sitting. "Hey chaps, how about going on a trip to Amsterdam?" he asked.

We all sat and stared waiting for him to continue.

"There's a notice behind the bar" he explained. "The Families Club is running a coach trip to Amsterdam on Saturday. It's cheap. How about us going? "I'm up for it" said Mick. "Me too" added Ray.

Pip looked at me. "Do you want to go?" he asked. "Might as well" I replied. "I have never been to Amsterdam."

"Count me in" said Pip and Shaun added "Me too! "No-one else wanted to go so Taff went up to the bar and handed in our six names. Taffy, Mick, Ray, Shaun,

Pip and I were already looking forward to going to where the poster advertised the "Venice of the North."

We counted our spending money and decided that we were comparatively better off than normal. We had not spent any money at all during the couple of weeks we had spent in the woods at Zandvaart. There had been no time or opportunity to spend and now our forced savings were going to be extremely useful.

We were going off on a lad's day out. There was safety in numbers. Six of us sticking together couldn't get into trouble. Or could we?

CHAPTER 31

It was the night before going to Amsterdam and Taffy, Ray, Pip and I were a foursome around a table in the N.A.A.F.L We were discussing the trip scheduled for the morning. We had already changed our military BAFF's money into German Deutschmarks and decided the first thing we would have to do when we got to Amsterdam was to find a Bank and exchange the Deutschmarks for Dutch Guilders.

We thought our other two travelling companions, Mick and Shaun would agree to that proposal but they were missing from our meeting. They had cadged a lift with our Flight Sergeant to visit Joe in Wegberg Hospital.

A message received at the office informed us that Joe's broken ankle was causing complications and that he was suffering from bronchitis as well.

"Not surprising is it" muttered Ray. "It's a wonder we didn't all get pneumonia on that exercise."

Any further conversation concerning Joe and his health was suddenly cut short by Pip as he took a very large swig from his mug of N.A.A.F.I. tea.

"Oh no, not again" he said as he pulled a wry face, swore, and spat a mouthful of tea into his handkerchief.

"What's up?" I asked.

KEN STALLARD

"Bleedin' Bromide" he replied in disgust and swore again. "They should be made to stop putting that stuff in the tea especially as we are paying for it."

Our tea seemed alright and we said so. Pip had an obsession that every cup of tea that the N.A.A.F.I. produced was laced with bromide.

It was widely rumoured and accepted that the tea in the airmen's mess and the N.A.A.F.I. was dosed with sodium or potassium bromide. This substance, often given as a sedative, was allegedly given to young male servicemen to reduce their libido and to limit their sexual urges. One of the symptoms was tiredness.

There was never, as far as I know, any actual evidence that bromide was added to the tea. The tiredness and needing extra sleep experienced by almost all the young servicemen was contributed to exhaustion after extra military training.

Ray silenced any further rant from Pip by delicately explaining that he was known to drink far more tea than any of us. Since he was constantly bragging about his many sexual conquests he concluded that either there was no bromide in the tea, or, if there was it had no effect whatsoever.

We decided to leave the N.A.A.F.I. early and have an early night in order to wake up refreshed for the next early morning departure for Amsterdam.

Thankfully Mick and Shaun arrived back from Wegberg Hospital soon after we got back to our hut. We updated them with our plans. The news of Joe was good too in that he was expected to be back at Wildenrath the following week.

Next morning the six of us were all eager, excited and among the first to be waiting at the coach stop. A mixed bunch of folk were assembling. A couple of officers with their wives and about half a dozen non-commissioned officers with their families and their children. The rest of the coach was made up from airmen from other units and squadrons from the Camp.

Judging by the way he spoke we presumed it was a young officer who arrived with a very beautiful girl on his arm. Ray's eyes popped out like organ stops and he was heard to mutter "Cor, she's a bit of alright!" There was a real sense of camaraderie between all the ranks. We were all going out with the common purpose of enjoying ourselves. This trip was no different than any other in civvy street. Everybody wore civilian dress. There were no orders or feeling that we were being watched by the superior ranks.

It was a long journey and we had a couple of brief stops on the way.

A cheer went up when Amsterdam was seen on a signpost for the first time. Minutes later we had arrived and parked in one of the busy thoroughfares.

It wasn't necessary to hang back and let the officers off the coach first but we did. It was a kind of instinct. We were glad that we did this because they had been to Amsterdam before and knew the drill. We meekly followed them to the nearest Bank to exchange our German money for Dutch Guilders.

I was the first to see the van selling chips and we decided that the first priority was to eat. It was the first time I had ever had lashings of mayonnaise on crispy chips. I loved it and that combination has been a firm favourite of mine ever since.

We all decided that Amsterdam is a beautiful city and now understood why it is called the "Venice of the

North." There were endless canals and little islands and a colourful array of boats going up and down their narrow waterways. We stood on a bridge over one of the canals and watched the boats sailing underneath for ages. None of us were very impressed when we saw someone empty a bucket full of garbage into the water from an upstairs window of a building beside the canal Cyclists were in abundance on the busy roads and bicycles were chained up at fences and lamp posts everywhere.

It was a warm and sunny day and we spent some time just strolling and taking in the sights. We kept crossing bridges over the canals and took in all the tall buildings and endless boats. I decided that it would be very easy to get lost in Amsterdam since all the canals and streets looked the same.

"Shall we go and have a look at Canal Street?" Ray enquired. A strange name for a street especially as every other one is a waterway.

We all knew why Ray was keen to see Canal Street. He had been told by an army lad attached to a unit at Wildenrath that it was a street not to be missed. It was in the centre of the red light district. A long street and a surrounding area of brothels and sex shops. Ray had been obsessed with visiting the street and seeing its activity ever since he had booked to come on the trip.

Taffy sighed deeply. "Let's leave it for later" he said. "We know you have got a one track mind but there are a lot of other interesting things to see first" Ray looked sullen but made no reply.

Leaving the canals behind we headed for a wide open square and saw a tall majestic building with arches. A lot of folk were filing into the building. It looked as though it was of some importance and decided it was worth investigating.

Large advertising posters were displayed outside the building and it was evident that some form of an art exhibition was drawing the crowds. We joined the end of the queue and once inside we saw some of the amazing landscape paintings of Van Gogh and brilliant portraits of Rembrandt and several others.

We spent some time gazing at all the masterpieces until Ray got restless and starting complaining that it was too hot inside the building and he wanted to get out into the fresh air.

We all suspected that he was still eager to get to Canal Street and deliberately pooled ideas to do other things to frustrate him. He was obviously unappreciative of our other pursuits, window shopping, buying a couple of souvenirs and watching some street artists doing coloured chalk drawings on the pavements. He cheered up considerably, however, when we went into a pub for some beers.

We had done a lot of walking by now and it was good to be able to sit and just relax.

The beer was cool and refreshing and this pub was quite different to Zur Hotel Postback in Germany because almost everyone talking around us was speaking in English.

Shaun nudged my arm and nodded in Ray's direction. I looked and saw Ray look at his watch for the umpteenth time. He was still fretting to get down to the red light area.

"Hey lads, how about us going to get something to eat?" Shaun asked.

"Good idea" I replied. "It's ages since we had that cone of chips and I am getting hungry."

"You're always hungry!" snorted Ray with another glance at his watch. Everybody else chipped in and agreed with me. We would have a proper meal somewhere because it would be a long time before the day was over and then there was the long journey back to Camp. Ray's face was a study. He glared but didn't say a word as he shuffled along with us with his hands in his pockets. The six of us set off to find another cafe bar.

During the meal Pip suggested that our next move should be to another pub. He liked the beer. I could see at this point that Ray was getting agitated and was having a whisper in Taffy's ear.

"No lads, I think Ray is right" Taff began. "We have only got just over three and a half hours left and it will be interesting to see what Canal Street is like. We can have a couple of beers afterwards before we get back on the coach."

"Yes" cut in Mick quickly. "We can hardly go back to the hut and say we never even saw the place. Let's see if it lives up to its reputation."

"Yes, come on" agreed Ray and started forging ahead with the rest of us trailing behind.

I am not quite sure what we expected but Canal Street was long and narrow and ablaze with a mass of coloured lights. It reminded me of Christmas lights back home but there were far more in this place.

Frankly I didn't expect to see so many people milling in the street, mainly men loitering and gazing at the shop windows.

These were not ordinary shops but lines of brothels and sex shops.

The word SEX was ablaze in lights everywhere you looked. Advertisements for every conceivable kinky activity were clearly on display.

People were pouring into the shops and many were carrying carrier bags boldly displaying the name and nature of the products they had bought. No-one appeared to be even the slightest embarrassed.

Ray was in his element. His comments were coarse and very sexual as he stopped to gaze in every window.

Mostly young girls sat behind the glass completely naked. In the main they looked extremely bored but from time to time smiled, ran their hands over their bodies, and beckoned as their red light twinkled inside the window or above the door.

At every window there were individuals or small groups of men calling at the girls through the glass. The girls called out the price for their favours and everywhere the men were shouting back a lesser fee. It was sad to see the bargaining that was going on. Every now and then a girl would accept the offered fee. The curtain was drawn back from the door and the man went in and the curtain was swiftly pulled to behind him. Seconds later a light appeared at a shuttered window upstairs and you were left to imagine what activity was going on inside.

I was quick to notice that there were burly men everywhere protecting the prostitute's interests. Pimps were extremely aggressive if they saw anyone trying to take photographs. Two or three of them would surround the would-be photographer and there would be a scuffle and the camera confiscated. It was as simple as that. No photography! If a fellow started to laugh at the girls or make some obscene remark the pimps would similarly push him on. Having passed a window no-one dared to look back. A refusal and pass on was almost considered an insult to the girl.

We discovered a larger than usual group of men stood gazing through windows adjacent to each other.

"Struth!" was the only word to escape from Mick's lips. "Gee" added Shaun. "Have you ever seen anything like this?"

This must have been Canal Street's answer to the older or more grotesque women! These were not girls or young women but elderly grey haired ladies of the night. Their painted faces made them look like they were made of wax. Here too were the very fat ladies, the ugly ones and the very wrinkly ones as well.

A group near to us were very uncomplimentary about the girls and I heard one say "I guess you have got to cater for all tastes."

We moved speedily on pass more sex shops, brothels, and in this area some much older pimps.

Ray kept giggling and whispering to Taff since they had palled up together since we left the pub cafe.

We could see them lingering at each window and conferring with each other. They were comparing scores out of ten for all they could see on offer.

"I'll give her nine" I heard Ray say.

"No, I reckon she's only worth a seven" replied Taff. So it went on.

Ray and Taff continued to lead the group of us down the street. Suddenly Ray stopped outside a window and gasped "Wow! That's a definite ten for sure! "We all stood and looked at a beautiful girl about twenty years of age. Unlike most of the other girls she wore a two piece swim suit.

Taff turned to Ray and said "Well, mate, you said you would go for a ten. Is this the one? Are you up for it?"

Ray looked sheepish and smiled at the rest of us without replying so Taff asked again. Ray shrugged his shoulders but did not answer. Sensing our curiosity Taff turned to explain.

"Ever since we planned this trip Ray said he was going with one of the girls" he said. "That is why he has been giving each one he has seen points out of ten. He said he wouldn't go for anyone less than ten and now it seems like he has found one."

"You don't know what you are letting yourself in for" I said to Ray. "Remember all the films and lectures we have had about diseases. Is it worth the risk?"

Ray started arguing that the girls were regularly checked for sexually transmitted infections and had certificates to prove it.

"That don't prove anything" explained Mick. "They could get a certificate yesterday and catch something from some bloke today and pass it on."

"I have not got anything" snapped Ray.

"No, it's too risky" Pip went on.

Ray could not resist smiling at the girl and gave her another little wave. She promptly smiled back and pointed upwards indicating that she was available for going upstairs.

Ray was getting uncomfortable with the situation. By now he was more than keen to go in with the girl and tried hard to persuade the rest of us to find someone as well. He felt awkward that we all refused point blank. He didn't want to be seen as the only one of the group to succumb to temptation but it was obvious that his urge was too persistent to resist.

Ray was getting desperate and almost pleading for someone else to go in with him. The girl he fancied was now joined by two other girls who saw us as a group and no doubt thought that trade and custom was looking up. All three of them started to count on their fingers to indicate the charge in guilders for the services.

A couple of swarthy looking guys came up alongside us but they were not looking at the windows but only at us. Without doubt they were minders to the girls and they looked very menacing.

Ray took a deep breath and made an immediate decision.

"Hold my bag" he said to his mate Taff and handed him the carrier containing souvenirs he had bought earlier on "I am going to give it a try" and headed for the curtained door without waiting to ascertain the charge.

Immediately one of the swarthy guys accompanied him to the curtained door, pulled it aside and Ray disappeared inside.

The five of us that were left went over to the other side of the street and leaned against one of the iron bridges that spanned the canal and waited.

We saw the light go on upstairs in the brothel and the curtains quickly drawn together.

Our little group stood silent and stared at the curtained door waiting for Ray to emerge. He did so in less than ten minutes looking very embarrassed with a bulge under his jacket and his arm up and covering his chest.

"How was it?" asked Pip.

"Was she OK?" this from Shaun.

Ray seemed very agitated and anxious for us all to move on.

"Come on" he said "let's get moving" and started striding ahead. For some distance we almost had to run to keep up with him.

Taff who was Ray's closest mate finally pulled at his arm and dragged him over to a wall that spanned the canal further down the street. We all gathered round. "Come on, Ray. Give us the low down" said Taff "How much did you pay and was she worth it?"

"No she wasn't" Ray replied. She is a con and she stinks. It was nothing more than business to her and she didn't take her eyes off the clock. It was almost all over before it began. She wasn't worth the asking price but I made sure I've got my money's worth."

On saying this Ray dropped his arm from across his chest and opened his jacket. He pulled out a little embroidered wall mat suspended from a wooden hanging attachment.

"This was hanging on the wall beside the staircase" he explained. "I've nicked it" and for the second time went on to say "I've made sure I've got my money's worth."

"You will be able to keep this little mat as a souvenir" laughed Taffy as he popped it into the carrier bag containing Ray's other souvenirs.

"Give him a few days and I bet he will discover he got more than a little souvenir off her" joked Shaun.

"Yes, watch this space" added Mick. Clearly by this time Ray was looking really worried. We were only jesting but he was thinking hard about the possible consequences of his visit. Then he kept spitting on the ground which was gruesome and spitting on the back of his hand and furiously rubbing it over his lips.

It was as though he was trying to cleanse and erase any contact he had with the girl.

I now felt sorry for the guy because it was obvious that he deeply regretted what he had done. He admitted that he was worried and wanted our support.

In true camaraderie fashion we gathered around Ray in his time of need. We agreed we would discuss it further over a few beers during our last pub visit in Amsterdam. Then it would be time to re-join the coach.

Mick urged Ray to go and see the Medical Officer as soon as possible back at Camp and say what he had done. He would get a severe reprimand and it was all very embarrassing but that was better than getting a nasty disease. From all the films and lectures we had been informed that emergency treatment was available and there the matter rested.

Fortunately for Ray there were no problems but valuable lessons were learned. We were all very tired and slightly tipsy by the time we arrived back at the coach. Apart from waiting about half an hour for three lads who had got lost all was well. It was a long trip back to Wildenrath and nearly everyone slept on the way.

I felt cold and tired on the coach and couldn't get to sleep.

I started to wonder where and when we would be able to change our Dutch Guilders back into German Deutschmarks. I thought of my family back at home and looked around at my sleeping mates.

My thoughts turned again to Christmas which was not far away. This would be my last one in the RAF and next summer I would be home for good and looking for a job.

I decided to volunteer to stay on duty over Christmas this year and go on leave in January. There were married men who just longed to go home and be with their wives and children at Christmas. As a single man I could stand in for a married one who wanted to be home for the festive season.

Shaun started snoring beside me and I gave him a nudge and received a grunt in reply. I looked over at Ray and Taffy and they looked a comical couple as they slept with their heads together on Ray's shoulder.

I glanced over my shoulder and saw Pip sleeping with his head up against the window. Mick was fast asleep beside him with his head back on the headrest and his mouth wide open.

I remembered how several of my peers back home had hated the fact that they would be conscripted into the National Service. Some of them had gone to great lengths to try and avoid it. Most of my friends thought I was mad when I volunteered to join the RAF and do the extra year on a regular engagement. I would not have missed the experience for the world.

I made myself more cosy in my seat and thought some more.

I had already done my national service equivalent and was determined to make the most of the last remaining year.

I had already come through a lot of experiences and adventures and felt sure that there were many more yet to come.

CHAPTER 32

There was hardly ever a dull minute at Wildenrath. Every week there would be something to plan or prepare for.

In a short space of time we had V.I.P. visits from Princess Alexandra and Winston Churchill. All boot polished and blanco'd, pressed and pristine we were either on special parades, guards of honour or required to line the route where the dignitaries visited.

. The second year at 402 Air Stores Park seemed to pass far quicker than the first and another Christmas arrived with a flurry of festive activity.

A new lad, Paul, had been posted in. He was older than the rest of us in his mid-twenties and he was first class at organising parties. Paul also became a Member of the Presbyterian, Methodist and United Board Church which was locally known as the P.M.U.B. Church and he was trusted with his own key to the building for organising Church activities. At Paul's invitation I often attended the Services and some week nights I would help him with activities which he had organised. The tea and cakes were free, and came not only as a bonus, but were very acceptable when we had run out of money a day or two before payday.

The Padre was a marvellous man called Squadron Leader Swallow. He was quick to listen and slow to speak. When he did speak it was with compassion and wisdom. We soon became close friends.

Paul was disappointed that the Christmas Eve Service was at 6 o'clock. He was used to a midnight service back home to usher in Christmas Day. We discussed this at length with the Padre who came up with a good suggestion.

"We will leave the Church open all day and night on Christmas Eve" he said. "You can pass the word, and, if anyone wants to join you for meditation or prayer at midnight, please feel free to use the church."

The most outstanding remembrance that I have of that Christmas is that no-one accepted our invitation. Similarly our posters advertising the opportunity were ignored. Undaunted Paul and I made our way to the Church just after half past eleven.

The Church was in complete darkness as we expected and it started to rain.

Paul knew the way in to the building and where the light switches were positioned far better than I did. He opened the outer door and then the inner door to the church with me following close behind.

The moment Paul opened the inner door we could hear sounds coming from inside the church in the inky darkness. The sound was that of someone sobbing and for a moment I held my breath as Paul flicked the switch and flooded the Church with light.

Lying prostrate, face down, in the carpeted aisle of the Church was a young man sobbing his heart out.

He was dressed in trousers and wore a white Arran jumper. He made no other movement but continued weeping as Paul and I stood there looking and feeling like intruders.

Paul and I stood motionless for a while and then approached him. "Are you alright, mate?" asked Paul. There was no reply.

The shaking of the lad's shoulders stopped and he was quiet now but still lay face downwards and we couldn't see his face.

"Is there anything we can do to help?" I tried which did bring a positive response. The lad rolled over and sat on the carpet. He crossed his legs and buried his face in his arms which were now folded across his chest and he continued to weep.

When he did look up at us his face looked awful. He was very pale and his eyes were red with crying.

"I'm sorry" he muttered. "This is the first Christmas that I've been away from the family. I have never known a single year of my life when we have not attended a midnight mass in our Church in Manchester." He then got up from the floor and sat in a chair beside us.

"I'll get us a drink and some biscuits" said Paul and returned promptly with glasses of fruit squash and some ginger biscuits which were always available in the church kitchen. When all else failed you could always depend on squash and biscuits. The three of us just sat and chatted for more than half an hour. No one else came anywhere near us and we assured this new found friend, who was called Andrew, that we didn't think he was silly or emotional because he chose to come to church and fret for missing his loved ones at Christmas.

Andrew enjoyed our company and the chat and cheered up considerably. Paul said a little prayer for the three of us and then for our families and Andrew went off to re-join his squadron accommodation which was some way away from ours.

With the New Year came extra work. This was because of more extensive flying at RAF Bruggen and Laarbruch causing more demands to be placed for our stores. Pete and Matt kept us constantly amused by their comedian antics and although they often got each other into a lot of trouble they remained close friends. Even when Pete tried to give Matt a home-made tattoo which got nastily infected.

I spent a lot more of my free time with my friends Momma Schmitz, Puppi and Reiner at their Hotel Zur Post in Wassenberg. I had now been adopted as part of their family and Momma never ceased to introduce me to all and sundry as "Momma's best boy."

On one occasion I entered Zur Hotel Post to discover Momma with a Cognac in one hand and a cigarette in the other, chatting merrily to an Air Commodore and a lady. I had never met such a high ranking officer in two and a half years in the RAF. Momma pulled out a chair, motioned me to sit down and join them, and, in true fashion introduced me as "Momma's best boy." I felt so embarrassed.

The Air Commodore and the lady were very welcoming and chatty but I just felt like I wanted a large hole to appear and for me to disappear into it.

I am sure the Air Commodore would not have been so friendly if he had known some of the escapades I had often got into in that hotel.

Wassenberg was often put out of bounds to military personnel. Sometimes fights broke out between Army lads that were in barracks nearby and the airmen. More often it was airmen fighting airmen as excessive drinking caused trouble.

In spite of Wassenberg being out of bounds I still kept up my regular visits to Momma and her family. Very often vehicles would appear with the Military Police and they would visit the pubs, cinema etc. to see if anyone was breaking the ban.

I lost count of the times I hid behind the barrels in Momma's cellar or in her bedroom cupboard stuffed full of dresses and an old fur coat that stank of mothballs. I was never discovered. When questioned if anyone from the military had been in that week Momma put on an Oscar-winning performance.

"Momma does not break the law" she would snap. "How dare you suggest I would cover for anyone!" No-one dared to challenge Momma when she was in full flow.

One night there was a big crowd of both Army and Air Force lads in Momma's bar. She had a strange knack of knowing when there was someone there she couldn't trust or was acting suspiciously.

Momma looking in the full length mirror saw one of the young fellows slip a very nice glass ashtray inside his tunic.

Momma strode over to the table where the chap was sitting and to the amazement of us all she gave him one very swift but hard slap on the cheek. She then proceeded to put her hand down the front of his tunic and retrieved the ashtray. "You do not steal from Momma" she bellowed in the young man's ear. By now he is looking both petrified and embarrassed because there is an audience.

"If you want an ashtray you ask me for one and I will give you one. You do not steal! "The chap stuttered out his apologies and Momma gave him the ashtray. A little later on he offered to buy Momma another "penicillin" which she gratefully accepted. True to form Momma kissed the offender when it was time for him to leave with his mates. With a smile she said "You will remember - never steal from Momma", I am sure he never forgot.

I suppose a lot of things happen to us all that may not seem significant at the time but they are brought back to our memory later on. That is what happened to me in a very big way a week or two after the ashtray incident.

It was just another ordinary day in the office when our Squadron Leader summoned me to his office. He was brief and to the point.

"Stallard, get yourself to the Station Headquarters at 3 o'clock" he ordered. "The Group Captain Station Commander wants to see you." I froze and my mouth went dry.

"Sir, what does he want to see me for?" I asked.

At that moment the telephone rang and the Squadron Leader reached for it. He waved me away with his other hand and said "See the Group Captain at 3 o'clock." My boss and the Flight Sergeant were as mystified as I was to know the reason why I had been summoned to see the Station Commander. It was usually something very serious if you had to appear before him.

I was really scared and tried to think hard if I had done anything wrong. Had my hiding from the Military Police in Wassenberg been discovered? Sometimes I lied that I was twenty one when I was only twenty when I came through the Camp gates late. Apart from this I was not aware of any other misdemeanours. I could not think of anything serious enough to get me up in front of the Station Commander.

At 3 o'clock I reported promptly to the Commander's Secretary and had to wait an agonising half an hour before he was free to see me.

As I was ushered into his office he stood up behind his desk and I saluted him. He indicated for me to sit in the chair in front of his desk and smiled broadly. "Stallard, it's good to have you here" he began.

I was in a daze. Whatever was going on? I was soon to discover.

"You will be wondering why I have called you here" he continued. "It is in recognition of all the hard work you did for a long time, single handed, on the Exercise at Zandvaart last year".

I could not believe what I was hearing and simply stared ahead.

"Your Commanding Officer at 402 Air Stores Park has put your name forward for this year's special commendation for meritorious service. You will receive the award from the Air Officer Commanding the 2nd Tactical Air Force when he comes to review the whole station parade on 22nd April. Congratulations and well done, and what do you have to say to that?"

Almost lost for words I lamely replied "It will be my twenty first birthday on that day."

The Group Captain laughed at this. "Well it will be a nice Birthday present for you" he went on, I am glad your efforts have been recognized. The Unit is extremely proud of you", I felt like singing as I walked back through the trees to the office. I wondered how the lads would receive the news. I was happy and excited but already feeling nervous at the same time. Obviously our Squadron Leader did not want any of the 402 Air Stores Park personnel to know about the award before me.

Momma Schmitz, Puppi and Reiner had already promised me a twenty first birthday party to remember at Zur Hotel Post for the evening of 22nd April. They said I could take along as many friends as I wished just as long as they knew how many one week before the event.

This was going to be a great day. The biggest parade I had ever been on. Receiving this prestigious award and then a grand twenty first birthday party with my friends in the evening. This most certainly promised to be the greatest day ever.

CHAPTER 33

As I looked to the left and right of me and behind all I could see was a sea of air force blue uniforms. We were all lined up by flights and squadrons in columns of three on the main parade ground at RAF Wildenrath. It was a very warm and sunny spring day. It was the day for the annual inspection of the Air Officer Commanding 83 Group the Second Tactical Air Force in Germany. It was also my twenty first birthday.

We had marched on to the parade ground behind the RAF Band and we listened to them playing the Dam Busters March as we waited for the arrival of the A.O.C. Our Station Commander was a Group Captain and he and a retinue of other officers patiently waited at the dais for our very important visitor. The Union Flag and the Royal Air Force Standard fluttered side by side in the breeze and the red carpeted area around the dais looked pristine.

In the distance we saw the car, flying a pennant, slowly approaching the parade ground.

It was at this point that I began to feel extremely nervous.

After the parade today I was to be presented to the A.O.C. to receive my commendation for meritorious service. This was an honour indeed because I was the only one selected from our unit, 402 Air Stores Park, to receive the award in recognition of the service I had given on a special exercise in Holland the previous year.

"Parade, Attention!" the command was given loud and clear and the parade came to attention as the A.O.C. stepped from his car and was greeted by the officers awaiting his arrival.

I noticed that our important visitor held the rank of Air Vice-Marshal as he climbed the steps of the dais. He stood very erect and surveyed the parade from his lofty position on the platform.

Another command rang out. "Parade, General Salute, Present Arms!" A burst of music came from the Band and the sea of airmen did their skilful handling of their rifles to comply with the salute. The Air Vice-Marshal returned the compliment with a very smart salute of his own.

It took almost an hour for the whole parade to be inspected. Parts of the parade came to attention whilst other parts stood at ease. Flight after flight came under close scrutiny as the inspecting officer peered at each airman that he passed. A line of officers, and the adjutant carrying an unsheathed sword, escorted the A.O.C. on his inspection.

I had never seen an Air Vice-Marshal before but this one looked very pleasant and smiled a lot. He stopped every now and then to speak to individuals on the parade. It was brief questions that he asked as he enquired where the individual was from or asked what trade he was in.

As soon as the whole parade had been reviewed and inspected the A.O.C. was escorted back to his platform where he gave a speech and said we were all making a valuable contribution in the role we played. Not only were we working a good work for our nation but we played an important role on the wider world stage.

It was a short speech and the whole parade was brought to attention for another salute and lined up for a lengthy march past.

I was spared the march past as our unit Squadron Leader marched up to me and hissed in my ear. "March off to the left when the flight gets to the corner. Go and hand in your rifle in at the armoury and then go immediately to the Station Commander's Office at HQ."

This was the third or fourth time the Squadron Leader had told me what to do. During the previous week he had repeated the instruction. I had to march off the parade ground when our flight was at the furthest spot away from where the A.O.C. was taking the salute. I was glad about this because when the order was ever given for "Eyes right" I could never glance to the right and march straight forward at the same time. If anyone made a straight line look like a snake it had to be me.

As instructed I marched off the parade as we got to the corner. It seemed very strange to be marching in the opposite direction to everyone else. I was going away from the rest of the flight but everything was going to plan.

Everybody of the Unit knew that I was marching away from them all in order to go and receive my award.

When I was a safe distance away from the parade I stopped to take a deep breath. I reflected on the fact that two and a half years earlier my friends had been a witness to the fact that I was the only one among them to fail the Provisioning Clerk Course at RAF Credenhill. I had to stay behind when they had all forged ahead to better things. I had to remain behind in humiliation to clean out the porridge boiler whilst they went off to Holland.

Now I had achieved more than any of them. What more can I say except that God moves in mysterious ways! I watched the parade, flight by flight, marching pass the A.O.C. as he took the final salute. Two Canberra aircraft flew very low over the parade which drowned out any further sound from the Band as I hurried forward towards the armoury to return my rifle.

It was a relief to get rid of the rifle. It feels light enough when you first shoulder it but the weapon feels heavier and makes the shoulder sore when you have had it rubbing there for some time.

It was a long walk to the Headquarters building and I began to perspire in the unusual heat for the month of April. I wished I had had time to return to the billet first for a shower but there was not enough time.

I duly arrived outside the Commanding Officer's office and found that a Flying Officer, a Warrant Officer and a Senior Aircraftsman all from Tech Wing were waiting to receive their commendations, also, a Corporal from the Flying Wing and a Senior Aircraftsman from 88 Squadron. As a Senior Aircraftsman from 402 Air Stores Park I was sixth in line.

The Group Captain spoke at length and the Air Vice-Marshall listened intently to a catalogue of my redeeming graces. I learnt that day that I had given outstanding performance on the previous year's exercise. My commendation had been well and truly earned.

The Air Vice-Marshall shook my hand and said he was very proud of my sterling work and he was confident that I could have a brilliant career ahead of me in the Royal Air Force. Promotion was assured and he reminded me of the many benefits that were available for long serving personnel.

"You may think you are just a little cog in a very big wheel" he said, "but big wheels are useless without little cogs to keep them working." I smiled and wondered where I had heard that before.

"I see from your records that you are due to leave the RAF in seven weeks' time" he went on. "In light of your exemplary service to date and my own personal commendation will you not consider signing on for a further period of service?" "No, thank you, Sir" I replied smartly. "I have almost completed what I set out to do. I have enjoyed my time in the Service very much but I want more freedom to do as I wish. Service life can be very restricting."

The Air Vice-Marshal went on to extol the good points of a regular safe RAF career compared to the many uncertainties of civilian employment. I stuck my ground and said I had already prepared myself for life outside the Royal Air Force.

"You do not have to make a decision here and now" he persisted. "If you do change your mind, you know the procedure for extending your service."

He shook my hand for the second time and wished me well for the future.

One last salute and I was on my way.

I was eager to get back to Hut 51. I was excited with the prospect of opening my twenty-first birthday cards and to see if I had received any presents from home.

I was desperate for a shower and I was getting more excited by the hour with the prospect of the evening's party at Zur Hotel Post.

All the lads were back in the billet by the time I arrived. I had to wait for my turn in the shower because everybody had the same idea after a gruelling parade.

I was disappointed and found it difficult to believe that I had not received a single birthday card or a present. The mail had been delivered because some of the lads were reading theirs.

I was left wondering why I had been so neglected for about a quarter of an hour before Pete lifted up his pillow and brought to light a pile of cards and one small and one large parcel which he had hidden from me.

He grinned as he threw my mail on the bed. "Happy Birthday, mate" he said and everybody came around my bed space to sing "Happy Birthday" and "Twenty One today."

I opened all my cards from family and friends and then turned to the two parcels. The small one contained a real leather wallet with my initials engraved on it bearing some money. This was from my parents with a message that a further gift would be waiting for me at home. The other parcel contained a twenty first iced birthday fruit cake which had been sent by a lady that my mother did house work for.

We decided to put the cake aside as we did not want to spoil our appetites before going to my party at Zur Hotel Post. Momma Schmitz, Puppi and Reiner had promised to put on a party to remember.

What a party that was. Truly I shall never forget it.

A large group of us stood at the bus stop right opposite a large statue of a Cross on the edge of Wildenrath Village. Only recently a public bus service from Monchen Galdbach had been put on this route and this was the last bus of the day. It was our last opportunity to be taken to Wassenberg. We knew we would have to walk all the way back to Camp after the party.

There was a lot of banter going on between us on the bus and we were all in high spirits and in party mood by the time we arrived at Zur Hotel Post.

Momma came bustling into the restaurant as fifteen of us filed in through the front door. She immediately threw her arms around my neck and kissed me in usual fashion whilst beaming at the rest of the group and ushering us all to sit down at the tables. We didn't have a chance to choose a drink because she poured a large glass of white wine for everybody, The wine was accompanied by a little plate on which sat a piece of brown bread which looked like a cork place mat and a chunk of orange looking cheese.

"Eat!" Momma ordered and everybody complied with her request.

Pete, never short of some witty remark, asked me if this was all we were going to have. I shrugged and didn't give a reply.

There was no sign of Puppi or Reiner but there was a delicious smell of cooking in the air. Momma sat with us with the usual glass of cognac in one hand and a cigarette in the other. She laughed with us but kept disappearing into the kitchen. A relative of Momma's and her husband were in to man the bar so it looked like Momma had freed herself up for the party.

In no time at all Puppi and Reiner came in all smiles and gave me a lovely silver framed photograph of myself which they had taken at one of my earlier visits. Puppi said "All is ready, please come this way."

She linked my arm with hers and led me down the length of the restaurant. At the bottom the restaurant went off into an L shape and there, hitherto hidden from view, were three or four tables linked together and shrouded in very white tablecloths. There were three large vases of flowers and the cutlery and cruets glistened. Twenty two chairs were positioned around the tables, ten either side and one at the head and one at the foot.

Fifteen of us positioned ourselves around the table and sipped at the wine and waited. Whilst we waited three German chaps came and joined us. Momma had invited them because I had befriended them during my stay at Wildenrath. Momma came in bearing two plates of steaming soup followed by Puppi and Reiner doing the same. When we had all been served they sat at the table and ate with us.

A delicious meal of lamb cutlets, potatoes and vegetables followed, all served by Reiner's mother and two other ladies that I had never seen before. Additional dishes of vegetables appeared as if by magic. It was very welcome because of the time we had all spent in the fresh air on the parade ground earlier in the day. We had not had any tea in preparation for what was to come. Our appetites were more than just a little keen.

We had almost finished the first course when Rolf arrived. I was delighted to see him because he was one of the first German fellows I had met a couple of years previously when I became a regular at Zur Hotel Post. He came in grinning and threw a wrapped gift in my lap.

"For your birthday" Rolf explained. "I trust you will have many such happy days."

The gift was a beautiful Pelikan fountain pen which writes just as beautiful now as it did the day Rolf gave it to me. It is something I have treasured for decades. Momma had invited Rolf to the party but he was a newspaper photographer and had to travel away on an assignment. He had managed to rush the job in order to get back in time for my party.

When Rolf sat at the table every chair was occupied. Momma could not have arranged the seating better. I had previously hinted that there would be seventeen of us but two had to drop out because they were put on duty at short notice.

The desserts were marvellous and there was such a variety. We ate well and some time later Matt expressed how we all felt when he rubbed his stomach and declared "I'm stuffed!" We all felt the same.

I had never seen Momma so energetic or so happy as that night. She smoked endlessly and had several glasses of her "penicillin" which she never ceased to explain was for "Momma's heart!" She went to the cellar and brought up three or four bottles of spirits. Reiner followed her with another armful and so the night was taken up with drinking, laughter, and loads of fun.

Pete and Matt never ceased to entertain us throughout the evening with their ever ready wit.

At well after midnight and an exhausting day we knew we were ready for bed. Momma made a speech and thanked everybody for making the night so special.

She also had two further surprises in store. First she had pre-arranged transport for getting us all back to Camp.

Rolf agreed to take his car and one of my other German friends offered to take his also. They decided to take us in two journeys but this was not necessary. The guy serving behind Momma's bar agreed to take his car and whilst we were arranging who went with whom, one of the pub customers, quite unknown to me, offered to take the overflow.

I tried to make a little speech to thank Momma and the family for a wonderful unforgettable twenty first birthday party. Everybody cheered and Momma beamed. Whilst we waited for the German friend to return with his car, Momma did the most unexpected thing.

She took a small square box from her apron pocket and said "This is for my best boy." I opened the box to reveal a beautiful gold signet ring. Pointing to a small stone in the corner of the ring she explained "That is a brilliant" which I think was her way of saying "That is a diamond."

I tried to say thank you for the gift and for all she and Puppi and Reiner and all the friends had done that night but it was cut short because I got too emotional. No tangible gift can ever compare with the gift of real love and friendship. I knew there and then that I was part of Momma's family for life.

The Guard Commander at Widenrath Camp looked a bit surprised when a convoy of cars turned up at the main gate and we all spewed out of the vehicles.

"Had a good night lads?" he asked.

"Fantastic" I replied as we all started fishing for our Passes. Satisfied he lifted the barrier and let us all through without asking if any of us were under twenty one.

If he had done so I would have been able to tell the truth for the first time ever.

We still had a mile to walk from the main gate to Hut 51 and we sang most of the way. Pete and Matt needed a bit of support which we gave between us.

We were all in agreement that we should do something in the near future for Momma, Puppi and Reiner and all who had been so good to us that night.

In retrospect I can see that we did come up with a lot of daft suggestions but the drinking and the early morning cold air wasn't doing much for straight thinking.

It was only later, when I was tucked up in my bed that I remembered I only had seven more weeks of military service left to do.

I decided that I would book Zur Hotel Post for a large meal and a gathering of my mates from the hut. I had the money that my parents had sent me for my birthday. I would think of some gifts I could give to those who had been so good to us. I would have to think of something very special for Momma.

Thoughts starting churning over in my mind.

Finally through sheer exhaustion I fell asleep. That day was truly unforgettable.

CHAPTER 34

Today much is said about computers and spread sheets. We, the Brylcreem boys, could never have envisaged such things in the nineteen fifties. The nearest thing to a spread sheet that Joey had on the wall above his bed was his demob chart. It was very impressive and took up most of the wall.

Not surprisingly most of the lads kept a demobilisation programme in some form or another. It was usually a large card ruled into small squares with a descending number in each square. It was very similar to an advent calendar but instead of counting down the days to Christmas it simply counted the days left to serve in the Forces.

I kept my demob chart on the top shelf of my locker. It was ruled out on the back of a piece of wallpaper. I remembered how I felt when I went from one thousand to nine hundred and ninety nine days left to serve. It was encouraging to see four digits reduced to three.

My crinkled wallpaper chart now clearly indicated that I was well down into double figures with only a few weeks left to serve. I knew in my heart that my reaction to the chart had changed considerably.

At the beginning it was good to cross off each day served. If you forgot it for a week there was a state of elation when you crossed off seven days at one go. Now that my time to leave the RAF was drawing near I felt a bit sad and apprehensive at the crossing off of each day. They were passing so quickly and there was so much I still wanted to do. Demob day seemed to be coming with speed.

I knew I would soon be missing all the little dramas that we made out of most things. The shock horror when one of the lads brought a caterpillar into the mess hall and pretended to find it in the bath of lettuce.

Finding someone had put breadcrumbs in between your sheets. Getting up late and rushing to go on parade only to find one boot missing, or, during the night the boots had mysteriously been tied together with masses of knots that could not be un-knotted.

The horror of waking up to find that someone has tied both of your feet to the bottom of the bed with a piece of rope. None of us were any good at escapology. Houdini I am not! Occasionally one would awake to find that you, complete with bed, had been re situated within the billet. One could never guarantee that you would wake up the same as you went to sleep. It was always good for a laugh to watch some guy's predicament but somehow it was never the same when it happened to you.

Robin was always complaining that Service life was more childish than being a youngster at a boarding school. I never knew about that but I did think some of our antics were extremely juvenile.

There are children. Then the elderly are often accused of going back into second childhood. I guess there has to be something childlike in between.

The seasons were very important. Since all the billet accommodation was dotted about in a large wooded area it was like living continually in the countryside. Spring brought a splash of colour with masses of primroses, bluebells and daffodils. During each summer the dense woodland ferns spread and the trees provided a large canopy from the sun and the rain. The smell of trees, ferns and flowers was almost intoxicating.

Autumn trees were aglow with all the coloured leaves and as they fell provided a thick carpet to walk on. But to my mind the winter was most breath taking.

We had a lot of very cold weather and snow between December and March each year. Some days it was impossible to open the windows for icicles that were thick and three feet long that hung down from the drain pipes.

Walking through the trees to the office and to the airmen's mess was very hazardous at this time of the year. It was very slippery underfoot and very often the snow was up to your knees.

Thick green pipes supported on concrete pillars ran in all directions through the trees. These carried the water for the billets and the central heating. Where ever the pipes went across paths the bridges had been put into place to avoid climbing over or underneath them.

The bridges were made of sloping railway sleepers with a small platform over the pipes. Wooden lathes had been nailed to the sleepers to assist climbing them but when they were covered in snow and ice they were dangerous.

Most days I would bring three or four mugs of steaming tea and toast back to the billets for lads who couldn't be bothered, or were too lazy, to go for meals. We often did this for each other. It was no easy feat to negotiate the railway sleeper bridges to get over the pipes when they were covered in ice. Carrying full mugs of tea was a hazard and I often slipped and ended up scalding my hands or losing the tea altogether.

I knew how much I would miss all these things when I left Wildenrath and all the occupants of Block 51 for the last time.

During the last few weeks of my stay in Germany we had some sad farewells as some of the lads finished serving their time and left for home. Almost every week a group of us would escort a comrade to Dalheim railway station and wave him off as he boarded a train for Ostend in Belgium to pick up the troop ship for return to England. I was particularly sad at Pip's departure as we had a lot in common and were great pals. He stuck his thumb up as he leaned out of the carriage window and said "Cheers mates" as the old heavy engine drew the carriages out of the station. Then with a cheeky grin he yelled "At least I am off to proper cups of tea back home. No bromide!" The sad departures were interspersed with a round of demob parties at various pubs in the villages around Wildenrath. I was still preparing for mine at Zur Hotel Post at Wassenberg.

We thought all our birthdays had come at once when Colin decided to buy a little car that he saw was for sale near the Camp. We all encouraged him to buy it as finally we saw some easing of our transport problems.

We were not disappointed and gathered in a group to admire it as it was parked outside Block 51.

We all helped Colin to clean and polish his car within and without. Almost daily some of us would be slopping water over it and frantically wiping windows and hub caps. The car brought new opportunities for travel and we were anxious to do our bit for the cause. In return Colin appreciated our help and the fact that between us we covered his petrol costs whenever he took us out.

I travelled more in the last three months of my service than in all the three years that I had been in Germany. After an initial day out in Monchen Gladbach Colin got bolder and agreed to take four of us to Dusseldorf. It was unfortunate for Colin that it was always the same little group that wanted to go and frequent arguments flared up because of it. There were times when Colin got huffy and refused to take anyone but we knew he would relent as soon as he needed some petrol money.

In retrospect it was funny how we all tried to become Colin's best friend. It was even funnier when we resorted to pull the shortest straw from a tumbler or draw the highest numbers out of a beret to determine who would be travelling.

I was not very successful at being a winner for a ride but I was lucky when Colin drove four of us to Koln (Cologne) where we had one of the most fantastic days of our lives.

We set out early in the morning of a day which turned out to be warm and dry, Not too hot but ideal for the beginning of summer.

Colin parked quite close to Cologne Cathedral and we wandered around the streets nearby. The shops were the best we had encountered in Germany and there were so many. Our main aim was to buy some hit music records, souvenirs and look for somewhere cheap to eat and a few bars for a few beers.

Our first stop to eat was at a vending van where we bought German sausages and chips smothered with mayonnaise. There was a lot of cardboard and rubbish paper near the van and the biggest rat I have ever seen ran across my foot. I screamed, jumped and dropped the chips.

Minutes later we saw a couple of what looked like teenage lads urinating against the wall support of one of the huge bridges across the River Rhine. The river is very wide at this point and the same bridge accommodates both road and railway for crossing.

Although our first visit to the city was not impressive with the rat and the unscheduled male toilet, it just got better and better.

The Cathedral is amazing and the twin towers beautifully carved. We climbed one of the towers and I made a fool of myself.

Tiny shallow stone steps have to be climbed, going round in circles, for the greatest part of going up one of the towers. There is not a lot of space as the stairway is narrow and you have to climb in single file. Suddenly you come out on to a wide wooden floor area where the bells are and an iron staircase that leads up to the next level of stone steps for ascending the rest of the tower.

I stepped on to the first step of the iron staircase and was foolish in that I looked down through the sheer drop of the tower to the ground beneath. I froze. I gripped the iron rail and started to perspire and shake. My legs would not move and a queue started to form behind me.

A couple of the lads had gone up before me and only Colin and I remained at the foot of the staircase. He hissed in my ear. "Get a move on Ken" but my mouth was dry and I could not answer and remained rigid gripping the stair rail.

A group of Swiss students came up behind us and realised that I was overcome by fear. A couple went up a few steps before me and reached out to take my hands whilst another two or three came behind me and propelled me forward.

Once clear of the staircase I was alright going on around the stone circled tower until we reached the summit. The view over Cologne and the winding sight of the River Rhine was breath-taking and we stayed up there for some time.

Coming down from the tower was far easier and not so challenging for the legs. I did not look down the iron staircase and heaved a big sigh of relief once we were back on the ground. I have been wary about not having a head for heights ever since.

The dark blot on those remaining weeks was when a couple of the lads from another block were killed in an accident. It was not clear what exactly had happened but it was rumoured that they were near some empty gas containers that exploded when they came into contact with some hot embers from an outside fire. The families came over for the funeral and we all paraded and it was all very heart-breaking and had a profound effect on us all.

The month of June arrived and my last couple of weeks for remaining at 402 Air Stores Park.

The Commanding Officer interviewed me prior to release and reminded me of the Station Commander's offer to extend my regular engagement with the Royal Air Force. I declined.

There was a crisis in the Suez Canal area crossing the Isthmus of Suez and linking the Mediterranean with the Red Sea. It was likely that a war was possible for that area and we were on standby to move there to give air assistance. The future in the RAF did not look very secure and I began to yearn for my independence.

Ian, a twenty year old, fresh in from England moved into our block to take over from Pip and to become my replacement.

It didn't take long for me to teach Ian all he needed to know. Once he got the hang of operating the unpredictable numbering machine all was well.

Matt asked our office Flight Lieutenant Pallett if a new machine could be obtained as it was generally felt I should be presented with the old one as a memento. The request was refused.

Explaining to Ian the workings of the job did not take long. However, advising him about looking after his interests in the block and beyond took some considerable time. He was well and truly warned not to leave his pop bottles on the window sill and to be on the constant alert for practical jokes.

All my official duties were now complete. The last couple of days were spent in returning various items of kit to their respective stores and getting my clearance chit signed to confirm that all library books had been returned, bills paid, and washed clothing put for disposal. My kit bag and a couple of suit cases were packed with the last of my belongings.

A couple of nights before my departure from Wildenrath I spent the evening with Mick, Shaun and Ian. First a snack at the N.A.A.F.I. and then the four of us queued up outside the Astra cinema to see a film. I cannot remember what the film was called but I know it starred Virginia McKenna because I must have been one of her most dedicated fans at the time.

It is strange but that night has always been indelible upon my mind. We ribbed each other and the jokes came thick and fast. With Ian being beside me all day at the office as he learnt my job, and, in the next bed beside me in the billet, we had learnt a lot about each other and became good friends. I had the knack of making him laugh continuously.

The cinema queue shuffled forward slowly once the doors opened. We had come to the late performance and the sky was growing quite dark and there was just one bright star shining above one of the tall fir trees opposite the cinema.

"See that star at the top of that tree?" Ian solemnly pronounced. "I reckon that is a reflection of you. You are a star. One day you will be the star at the top of your tree!" I laughed and mumbled something about being on a Christmas tree but the look on Ian's serious face and the way he said it meant so very much at the time. As in most things in life I always leave the best to last.

I had one more day and night left at Wildenrath and there was no doubt in my mind what I was going to do with that time. It was put aside for one last trip to Hotel Zur Post and party with Momma Schmitz, Puppi and Reiner. The lads were going to join me and it would be the last opportunity of saying farewell to my German friends who frequented the bar.

It was as though I was preparing for the grand finale.

I wrapped up a bottle of whisky for Reiner when we got in from the cinema. It was a bit like taking coals to Newcastle but I was short of ideas on what else I could give him as a gift. I planned to buy two enormous bouquets of flowers one each for Momma and Puppi as I prepared to say my goodbyes.

I was adamant in my resolve that this would not be my last visit to Momma and her family and Zur Hotel Post even if I was going back home to England. I had made up my mind that I would come back for holidays whenever it was possible.

I stepped outside Block 51 to breathe in some fresh air before turning in. The smell of the ferns and the chirping of the crickets brought back memories of the ill-fated exercise last year at Zandvaart.

Two Canberra jets screamed their way skywards and I listened to someone singing out of tune as they polished a pair of boots whilst sitting on the steps to the hut. These sounds and smells would soon be a thing of the past, but, I knew the memories would last forever as I went over the plans for my very last day.

CHAPTER 35

I opened my locker and saw that it was completely empty. It was a force of habit. I had forgotten that this was my last complete day at 402 Air Stores Park and I had emptied the locker the previous day. Almost everything was packed in my kit bag and a couple of suitcases.

All that remained in my small bedside locker was my wallet and my toilet bag. The waste paper basket was full of old discarded letters, sweet wrappers and the crinkled remains of the rolled wallpaper containing my demob chart. All the days were crossed off at last.

One last day left at Wildenrath and tomorrow back to England! I felt quite nostalgic as I wandered through the trees from Block 51 to the office for the very last time. I chose to walk it alone rather than go with a group of the lads. It was not a working day for me so I could wander in at will.

My thoughts turned to the hundreds of times we had walked those tracks. We usually went in pairs or a group but I wandered alone with my nostalgic thoughts.

I smiled when I thought of the times we trudged through the snow. The tall pine trees always looked very picturesque when covered in snow. Then someone would run and kick the trunk of the tree. The impact would cause an avalanche of snow to fall off the branches just as you got underneath and you ended up looking like snowman.

I felt a bit sad when I realised there would be no more carrying food and mugs of tea over the bridges that spanned the water pipes.

I did enjoy the stroll with my thoughts and recalled the many times when we had to run for all we were worth not to be late, and, evoke the wrath of Flight Lieutenant Pallett.

I smiled when I thought of the snowball fights or running to jump, not always successfully, the large puddles during the rainy seasons.

Not so happy thoughts of seeing snakes which I cannot stand, or, enduring the constant mosquito bites.

Taffy was on guard duty on the gate to the unit. He greeted me with an ear to ear grin.

"Last day then mate? You lucky sod."

"Yes, I can't wait" I lied. I showed him my Pass. A formality for the last time. The morning went very quickly.

I went on my last tour of the group of sheds simply to say my farewells to the stores lads. It seemed strange to be doing the rounds empty handed when usually I was humping around piles of vouchers.

My last tour of duty was to visit the few offices that remained in 402 Air Stores Park headquarters.

The Adjutant and Flight Lieutenant Pallet wished me well and both were very complimentary about my work. Even Flight Sergeant Moon our office manager had a lot of nice things to say and said he would never forget how I got his section a lot of credit through my sterling work on the last Exercise in Holland. I thought words come easy but promotion, extra pay and special privileges were not so forthcoming.

The Squadron Leader Commanding Officer was extremely nice. I smiled as I remembered how he had helped me through his window when I had gone through it to retrieve my pop bottles. He warmly shook my hand and said it had been a privilege to know me.

"I want to thank you again for all the effort you put into the Exercise" he continued and then handed me my RAF Service Book. He opened the book at the last page and as he stuck a finger on it he said "I mean every word I have written here."

I looked at where he was pointing and read .. Conduct: Exemplary.

Ability as aircrew or as a tradesman: Good. Personal Qualities: Good.

Commanding Officers Comments: This airman is extremely suitable for employment in the stores organisation of a large company. He is of smart appearance and has performed creditably in his RAF Service. He was officially commended by his Air Officer Commanding for meritorious service."

I thanked the Commanding Officer for everything he had done for me and left.

I looked back at the office block that had been the centre point of my life for the last two and a half years and grinned as I walked through the gate for the last time. When I got back to the billet I found Thumper sitting on the steps. Every time we met up I had a conscience about the time we stripped him and scrubbed him in the shower because he was so smelly. Today he was supposed to be resting because he had been on night duty.

"You took your time" he grumbled "I thought you would be glad to be out of that dump." That was his inference to our office block.

True to form Thumper was holding a bottle of cider and still didn't look too clean. "I just hung about to say cheerio" he said. "I'm going to miss you".

I sat beside him on the steps and we had a lovely chat.

Thumper always sought me out when he wanted help or advice. Months earlier I managed to get him out of a lot of trouble by covering for him for which he was eternally grateful and, at the time, said if he could ever do me a favour I only had to ask.

I used Thumper's promise to my own advantage. A know all Canadian Corporal said Thumper would never change and was very degrading with his remarks. "No-one will ever get him off the drink" he declared and bravely I said I thought I could. We decided to put a one pound bet on it that he could be persuaded to go through a whole week without one single drop of alcohol.

Immediately the wager was agreed I went off to find Thumper. I was up front and told him about our arrangement which he thought was hilarious.

"I know I can trust you, Thumper" I began hoping that I sounded more confident than I felt. "You said you would always help me out if I asked you a favour, well, I am now asking you for one. Don't touch a drop of liquor for a whole week and I promise I will give you the pound if you will let me win it."

That night Thumper solemnly announced to all in the billet that he was going on the wagon and everybody fell about laughing.

True to his word Thumper never touched a drop for a whole week. I think it nearly killed him but he was adamant that he was going to prove to me that he could do it. It was not easy for Thumper. He curled up on his bed most nights and slept or read. He went to the N.A.A.F.I. but stayed in the cups of tea side rather than the bar.

For three or four days some of the lads tried to break Thumper down by offering him cans of beer. Every time he refused and I kept up my daily encouragement.

I was delighted when he completed the whole week booze free. The Canadian duly but reluctantly handed over the one pound BAFF note and, true to my word, I passed it on to Thumper who immediately went off and bought some beer. Thumper recalled the incident as we laughed and chatted on the steps.

"Here's to you mate" he said as he stood up and threw the full bottle of cider at the wall of the billet. It smashed in pieces and the liquid ran down the wall.

I looked in amazement. "You wouldn't understand" he said shaking his head and quite out of character embraced me in a big hug.

"Thanks a lot mate for everything." He stuck up a thumb and as he ambled off his parting shot was "See you!"

One by one and sometimes in a group the lads came in from work. It seemed like an eternity whilst they chatted, showered and groomed. Fresh faces and Brylcreemed hair saw that we lived up to our slogan "The Brylcreem Boys."

Colin drove four of us to Zur Hotel Post in Wassenberg in his little car and returned to Camp to pick up another four. By various means about twenty of us ended up at Momma's for my last night party.

It was a great night to remember. The format of the evening was very similar to my twenty-first birthday except that this time we had a cold buffet and lots of chips and lots of drinks.

Happiness and laughter was the order of the night. Momma insisted on sitting on one lap after another and smoked and drank her "penicillins" relentlessly.

Puppi and Reiner sang along with some of the pub regulars. We didn't know the language or the words so we made up our own. Then we sang for them some old favourites and they looked just as amused at us.

Nobody got very drunk but just a little bit. Most of us got merry and ate, drank, ate and drank some more and had a good time.

I thought I would have been sad considering this was going to be the last night with my very special friends at Zur Hotel Post and the lads from the billet. I didn't feel sad at all.

I knew that within the next few weeks we would have all split up at Hut 51 anyway. We had all served our time in the Service and all of us would be going home. Those who had signed on for longer engagements would be posted elsewhere.

The Hut 51 family would no longer exist as such. If I had decided to extend my Service I could have been posted anywhere and I would have to start making friendships all over again. On consideration I was just glad that I was going now. It was far better for them to be saying farewell to me as I leave rather than me saying the same to them, one by one, in the coming weeks. Some had already left and that was hard.

I looked around the group all singing or eating and drinking. We had had some fantastic moments and all of us would remember these happy times probably for the rest of our lives.

In the early hours of the following morning I noticed Momma Schmitz was getting very sleepy. The lateness of the hour and too many cigarettes and penicillins were having their toll. I decided it was time we returned to Wildenrath.

Colin went to collect his car and I went out to it to collect the two bouquets for Momma and Puppi and the bottle of whisky for Reiner from the boot.

The ladies were delighted with the flowers and Reiner's mother went off to produce two large vases to put them in. Reiner kissed his bottle of whisky and said "All the best for going to England."

Momma went behind the bar and fished out a beautifully wrapped gift. "Open it" she ordered. "I hope you will like it. Reiner said you would."

I tore off the wrapping and discovered a beautiful box containing Russischled Leder Pre Shave balm and a lovely ornament with a picture of the Wassenberg rose garden on it. I still have both gifts to this day.

There were lots of hugs and kisses but no tears as I promised Momma and her family that I would return often.

Momma came out to the car and kissed me once more. Then one last word of command from her. "Wait!" Colin kept the car engine running as Momma disappeared back inside Zur Hotel Post. Moments later she re-appeared with a bottle of wine and said "Not to be drunk until you get back to England. Then you drink it and think of Momma." The following morning I said my last goodbyes to the rest of the lads in the billet and humped two cases and my kitbag the long way to the main gate of the Camp. A minibus transported me and a couple of other lads from other units at Wildenrath to Dalheim Station where we boarded a train bound for the Hook of Holland.

I was glad that there was no-one to see me off at the station.

I felt my excitement rising as I realised I was going to RAF Innsworth in Gloucestershire for a couple of days for debriefing and final medical and documentation before leaving the Service. Then I would be back home again with my family for good.

The train seemed to take for ages to cross the Netherlands until we arrived at the Hook of Holland. The last North Sea Crossing on the troopship Vienna to Harwich made me feel decidedly seasick as the sea was very rough. After travelling from Harwich to Gloucester via London I felt exhausted.

Other airmen and non-commissioned officers were waiting for RAF transport when I arrived at Gloucester Railway Station. I joined the queue with all the others bound for the Service Discharge Centre at Royal Air Force Innsworth.

I handed in most of my kit at Innsworth but was told I had to retain certain items of uniform as I had been transferred to Category 2 of Class E Reserve Forces. This meant I would not be entitled to any Reserve Pay and not required to attend for any training during the period of my Reserve Service. However, I would remain subject to recall to the Service in time of national emergency.

Finally until I was discharged from Class E Reserve I could not enter or enlist in any other branch of H.M. Forces or the Services of any other country or depart from the United Kingdom without permission from The

RAF Record Office. With these final instructions I was paid my last wages complete with accrued credits for not damaging government property.

I looked at the thirty nine pounds in my hand knowing I had never been so rich in all my life.

As the gates of Innsworth closed behind me I headed for Gloucester Station a free man. My Service was done and I was going home.

I saw a beggar sitting on the pavement by the station and I responded to his request for sixpence. Later on I reflected that I could have been a bit more generous. I was going to a home with a pocket full of money.

My Mum and Dad and my sister Audrey were thrilled to have me back home.

It was good to be back in my own room without a lot of noise in the background. The choice of food and lie ins in the mornings were a bonus but I knew this new found way of life could not last forever. It was time to seek some form of employment.

I went along to the Labour Exchange but there did not seem to be much on offer. A little grey haired chap behind the counter looked me up and down and said "The only thing we have which might be suitable is a clerical post at the Army Depot at Didcot."

"OK I'll give them a try" I volunteered but the little man behind the counter shook his head and refused to give me the green card of introduction which was necessary in those days.

"I cannot give you a green card for the Depot" he explained "they are only recruiting female staff at this time. Females are paid less than males for the same job. It is some government rule."

It took ten minutes of pressure and pleading before I could persuade the official to give me the green card. "You are wasting your time" was his final shot "they will not take you on."

That same afternoon I presented myself at the main gate of the Army Depot at Didcot. It seemed strange to see soldiers in khaki uniforms roaming about and in true military fashion I was ushered into the new recruitments office.

I was interviewed by a little lady in her fifties dressed from head to toe in black. She fiddled with her three rows of pearls as she looked first at the green card and then at me and then back at the card.

She went to great length to explain that I was the wrong sex for the job. Rules were rules. The vacancies were for administration workers in connection with army stores since this was an army store depot, but alas, was for female staff only. She understood that it was almost identical to the work I had been involved with in the Royal Air Force and that I would be ideal for the job.

I gave her a big smile and showed her my RAF Service Book where the Squadron Leader had actually written that I would be "extremely suitable for employment in the stores organisation of a large company." I began to wonder if that officer had had a premonition. My interviewer now suitably impressed took my Service Book and said she would have a word with a colleague. She disappeared for some time and then returned with a very tall upright pin striped suited civil servant. He beamed at me.

"Your credentials are very impressive." He smiled again. "It is quite obvious that you would be ideal for the type of work we do alongside the Army. We also have a commitment to encourage young men who have just completed national or longer Service to get back into normal civilian life. We are prepared to take you on. Miss Grimwade do the necessary documentation!" Miss Grimwade appeared more excited than I was and signed and stamped the green card to the effect that I was to commence work at the Army Depot in ten days' time.

The little man at the Labour Exchange was dumb-founded when I returned with the green card all signed and the job was settled.

"Well done!" he exclaimed. "I am very pleased for you. So it is off with the RAF and on with the Army then. What do you make of that?"

I gave him a cheeky grin and a nod and a wink.

"I didn't cause any aeroplanes to crash", I said, "now I've got to see if I can keep the tanks a rolling. I do not have a head for heights and going above the clouds is hardly my scene. I think I will stand more chance with a tank and keeping my feet well and truly on the ground."

I remembered when Mum and I went off to Oxford for my first day in the RAF, the lady at the bus stop said, "The RAF is not all a bed of roses." I wonder what she would say if she knew I was now going to work with the Army."

Only time can tell but that's another story.

Lightning Source UK Ltd.
Milton Keynes UK
UKOW04f1228190214

226757UK00001B/2/P